W9-AWN-798

Public Property and Private Power

Studies in Legal History

Published by The University of North Carolina Press
in association with the American Society for Legal History

Editor: G. Edward White

Editorial Advisory Board

John D. Cushing	George L. Haskins
Lawrence M. Friedman	J. Willard Hurst
Charles M. Gray	S. F. C. Milsom
Thomas A. Green	Joseph H. Smith
Oscar Handlin	L. Kinvin Wroth

——————— HENDRIK HARTOG ———————

Public Property and Private Power

The Corporation of the City of New York

in American Law, 1730–1870

The University of North Carolina Press

Chapel Hill and London

© 1983 The University of North Carolina Press
All rights reserved
Manufactured in the United States of America

Library of Congress Cataloging in Publication Data

Hartog, Hendrik, 1948–
Public property and private power.

(Studies in legal history)
Includes index.
1. Municipal corporations—New York (N.Y.)—History.
2. Local government—New York (N.Y.)—State supervision
—History. I. Title. II. Series.
KFX2015.H37 1983   342.747′1029   82-24724
ISBN 0-8078-1562-4   347.4710229

To my mother and father

Corporations having been established at
different periods, and with different views, the particular
constitution of each depends on the provisions of the charter
by which it was erected, or on the prescriptive usage which
time has imperceptibly introduced.

Stewart Kyd, *A Treatise on the Law of Corporations* (1793)

It is a remarkable characteristic of an
enlightened state of public opinion, though
resulting from the operation of obvious principles,
that a greater degree of power may be introduced into a
frame of government, which has its origin in the
people themselves; and that this power may be exercised
with less public excitement and discontent, than a
similar degree of power under a system, which has
its origin in an irresponsible source.

John Adams Dix, *Sketch of Resources of the
City of New York* (1827)

The notion of community self-government, as it
occurs in Western political thought, is not just a
nondescript, intermediate something that, relative to private
action, is regulation and, relative to central regulation,
is private action. Community self-determination is a
distinctive modality of choice, serving a
distinctive dimension of freedom.

Frank I. Michelman, "Localism and Political Freedom,"
in de Neufville, ed., *The Land Use Policy Debate in the
United States* (1981)

Contents

Contents

Tables and Figures

Acknowledgments

In the course of writing this book I have accumulated many debts. The librarians and archivists of the Municipal Archives and Records Center of the City of New York, the New-York Historical Society, the New York Public Library, the New York University School of Law Library, the Harvard Law Library, and the Indiana University School of Law (Bloomington) Library provided unfailing assistance. At various times I have received financial support from an Irving and Rose Crown Fellowship in the History of American Civilization, from a summer research award given by the Indiana University School of Law, from a Summer Faculty Fellowship granted by the Office of Research and Graduate Development at Indiana University, and from the American Bar Foundation's Legal History Fellowship Program. Sara Parisi typed the final draft of the manuscript. The New-York Historical Society graciously permitted me to reproduce maps from its collections. The American Society for Legal History and the William Nelson Cromwell Foundation generously provided subventions to support the book's publication.

Preliminary versions of the argument worked out here were given in papers at the 1977 annual meeting of the American Society for Legal History, a Columbia University Legal History Seminar in 1979, and the 1981 annual meeting of the Law and Society Association. The *Buffalo Law Review* published a sketch of the book's structure in 28 (1979): 91–109, and a draft of Chapters 1 through 5 appeared in the *Journal of Legal Studies* 10 (1981): 305–48.

John Reid introduced me to the fun of legal history when I was a student at New York University School of Law. Morton Horwitz impressed on me the significance and the seriousness of the subject. Conversations with Marvin Meyers played an important part in shaping my understanding of the relationships between political values and legal doctrine and practice. Perceptive readers will note the extent to which my periodization of New York's legal history has been influenced by David Hackett Fischer's reconstruction of the course of American social history. When the conception of this work was well along, Jerry Frug wrote me that he too was working on the history and political theory of the American municipal corporation. His encouragement has offered me hope that some lawyers will find this work of interest, and I have been stimulated by our differing perspectives.

Conversations with colleagues at Indiana University—including Arghyrios Fatouros, Stan Fickle, Lewis Perry, Bill Popkin, Harry Pratter, and Lee Teitlebaum—played a particularly important role in shaping my thinking on American legal history. Likewise, Michael Grossberg read my work and talked with me as we both learned how to be historians. Carolyn Sue Brenner, Jeffrey Given, Willard Hurst, William Nelson, Kent Newmyer, Aviam Soifer, Jon Teaford, and Sue Willey all read and commented usefully and critically on parts of the manuscript in different stages of its development. Finally, Morton Keller has served as a mentor throughout my training as a legal historian. I am grateful for his acute criticism and his ruthless editing but even more for the moral example of a historian he embodies.

To Nancy Hartog I owe much more than I can publicly say. Through much of the time that I have worked on this project, that would in fact have been all I could have written about her contribution, and I have teased Nancy that her acknowledgment would be of the form: "To Nancy, who has done little for the book but who has reminded me that there are more important things than this book." But when I most needed help Nancy cheerfully, if sleepily, read rough chapters at late hours of the night, which she then subjected to cruel and merciless criticism. And, throughout, Nancy has done more than her fair share of the childcare and housework. On the other hand, Lucas Hartog, Elisabeth Hartog, and Jacob Hartog did little to earn the right to see their names in print. Still, lawyers know that rights are often not earned. And in any case, my children have reminded me regularly that there are more important things than this book.

Introduction

I first became interested in the history of local government law ten years ago when I spent a summer and a fall working for New York City. At the time (near the end of John Lindsay's second term as mayor and during my third year of law school), city government was engaged in a campaign to improve municipal productivity by decentralizing some decision-making authority to local neighborhood administrators. I was one of several law students given internships in local district service offices, where we were expected to exercise our theoretical and intellectual gifts to devise new and better ways of delivering more sanitation or more health or more welfare to our districts without increasing the cost to the city.[1]

Needless to say, we failed abysmally. I spent several months working on a lead paint poisoning project, which I hoped would use the combined resources of several municipal agencies to eliminate peeling leaded paint from residences in the neighborhood. My plan was a model of rational ingenuity. On paper, at least, I had reorganized existing municipal services more efficiently and humanely, using the "private" management techniques that we had been told offered the best hope for improving municipal productivity. But I soon learned that my plan was politically inept and possibly illegal. Not only would the unions balk at any attempt to integrate distinct agency work forces, but to do so I was told was beyond the powers granted by the legislature to the city to deal with the blight of lead paint poisoning. The city's powers of ingenuity (let alone mine) were limited by the authority delegated to it by the state legislature. And in any case, so the litany went, I should have recognized the obvious differences between public and private enterprise.

This book represents my attempt to trace the history of the ambivalent and complex legal attitudes toward American city government revealed

1. The story of the productivity program is told in Charles R. Morris, *The Cost of Good Intentions: New York City and the Liberal Experiment, 1960–1975* (New York, 1980), 159–70.

not just in my trivial experience working for New York City but in the general practice of local government law and administration. In particular, it focuses on two central but curious features of the "discourse" of local government law: the identification of city power (or powerlessness) with state power and the insistent contrast between public municipal corporations and private business corporations.

For the past 150 years American lawyers and judges have used the term "municipal corporation" to characterize the legal existence of a city. In doing so they have pictured urban government in ways that might surprise those not fully acculturated into legal ways of thinking. American courts do not usually regard a municipal corporation as the embodiment of a local political community. To the contrary, a municipal corporation is said to be a public corporation created by a state legislature solely for the purpose of providing subordinate administration. In legal theory, cities, towns, counties, and villages exist only because they serve as useful agencies of state power. No local government has any natural or inherent rights or constitutional authority. A municipal corporation is whatever the state legislature says it is, and it does whatever the state legislature and the state courts say it can do. As John Dillon insisted in the famous "Rule" proclaimed in his treatise of 1872 (which remained for many years the definitive legal source in all matters local governmental), unless municipal authority was expressly granted, necessarily implied, or crucial to the accomplishment of a legislatively defined goal, its legitimacy would not be recognized by an American court. "Any fair, reasonable (substantial) doubt concerning the existence of power is resolved by the courts against the municipal corporation, and the power is denied."[2]

This judicial conceptualization of cities as powerless entities rests on important and recurrent themes in American political thought: the distinctively public as opposed to private quality of legitimate government, the uniformity of lawmaking authority within a jurisdiction, and the supremacy of the state as a source of power and authority. Much of American local government law elaborates on basic assumptions of American republicanism.

Yet in its denial of local diversity and customary autonomy, the law of municipal corporation also typifies a peculiarly positivistic[3] and reduction-

2. John F. Dillon, *A Treatise on the Law of Municipal Corporations* (New York, 1872), 101–2.

3. The term "positivism" is used in Anglo-American jurisprudence to characterize the contention that law is an analytically distinct sphere of human activity. Lawyers usually contrast legal positivism with natural law as contending schools of legal philosophy. As such, legal positivism has been closely identified with the claims that a law is the command of a political sovereign (as opposed to the expression of consensual moral values) and that a law need not be morally right to be legitimate (as contrasted with the view that legitimacy de-

istic strain in American public law. American judges have insisted that the character of local government law be rooted in the command of the sovereign. They have tirelessly deduced answers to almost all local matters from the principle of legislative sovereignty. They have founded their law of municipal corporations on the implicit claim that public and private spheres necessarily stand in a dichotomous relationship with one another.[4]

Legal commentators have often regarded the formal separation of public from private spheres as the distinctive hallmark of American local government law. It may seem difficult to define precisely or simply what distinguishes public from private entities. Cities provide police, but so, in effect, do private security services. It may not be immediately apparent why a college chartered by the state for the education of Indian youth is a private entity, yet a town chartered by the state for the self-government of a local community is a public entity. But to Dillon and other local government lawyers, the separation of public from private could never be "too much emphasized."[5]

In what we might call the classic version of municipal corporation law that flourished from the late 1850s to the near present, a municipal corporation is what it is because it is not a private corporation, . . . and vice versa. A municipal corporation is a purely public, political institution, created by the legislature "without the consent of the inhabitants." It is called into being "at the pleasure of the state."[6] The assumption that local governments act legitimately only to the extent that they decisively separate themselves from "private" spheres such as the marketplace and insofar as they demonstrate their independence from private sources of power and wealth lies deep within judicial perceptions of the political and legal nature of community life. In mainstream American legal thought, private wealth usually corrupts public authority, and the boundaries of local authority are properly defined by the power of the state.[7]

Local government lawyers typically trace these values to the United

---

pends on morality). Leading legal positivists include Thomas Hobbes, Jeremy Bentham, John Austin, and the Oliver Wendell Holmes, Jr., of "The Path of the Law." For the past century its critics have regularly demonstrated the inadequacy of legal positivism as a theory of the nature of law but have been unable to dislodge it from its position as the unstated premise of most legal practice.

4. See Gerald Frug, "The City as a Legal Concept," *Harvard Law Review* 93 (1980): 1057–1154. In *The Transformation of American Law, 1780–1860* (Cambridge, Mass., 1977), Morton Horwitz has argued that public law, unlike private law, remained formalistic from the early nineteenth century on (255–56). In the later chapters of this book I argue against that position, at least as applied to the law of municipal corporations.

5. Dillon, *Treatise on Municipal Corporations*, 70–76 and passim.

6. Ibid., 71; Charles W. Tooke, "Municipal Corporations," *Encyclopedia of the Social Sciences* (New York, 1933), 11:86–93.

7. See Frank Michelman and Terrence Sandalow, *Government in Urban Areas* (St. Paul,

States Supreme Court's 1819 decision in the *Dartmouth College* case.[8] They read the case as holding that municipal corporations are public entities, unlike charities and businesses, and therefore subject to the unrestrained power of the state.[9] The voters of an American city never "own" their municipal corporation, except derivatively as members of a state polity. In contrast to the members or stockholders of a private corporation, they hold no rights that demand recognition by the state. When the state plays with the specific structures, services, or practices of local government, it is not interfering with the workings of an autonomous entity, for a local public entity is (in theory) nothing more than an administrative subdivision of the state. Publicness is of a piece with a city's legal powerlessness.

New York City played a significant role—both as symbol and as litigant—in the formation of this judicial discourse. As a corporation with a royal charter and with a huge "private" estate, New York City entered the nineteenth century as the most private of public entities. It quickly became the dominant city in the new nation. It was, and remained, different from other American localities. Yet judges and treatise writers took particular pride in demonstrating that within their doctrinal domain New York City would be treated no differently than any other municipality. As New York City decisively separated itself from the countryside of a still rural America to become the financial and commercial center of the nation, the law governing cities came to insist on equating metropolis with village. By the middle of the century state courts had determined that New York City lacked any rights that could be asserted against the state. As its population grew from the fewer than twenty-five thousand inhabitants of the postrevolutionary city to the nearly one million inhabitants of Civil War Manhattan, New York City's legal status changed from one of autonomy and distinction to one of general powerlessness before the authority of the state.

Even its distinctiveness as a government body reinforced the judicial perception of its dependence as a legal entity. New York City was one of a small number of local governments which in the last years of the eighteenth century committed themselves to what Jon Teaford has called "municipal revolution."[10] Nineteenth-century cities may not have provided all of the public services we have grown accustomed to today, but, compared to their colonial predecessors, they changed Americans' expectations of ur-

---

1970), 155–97; Frug, "The City as a Legal Concept"; *People* v. *Morris*, 13 Wend. 325 (N.Y. Sup. Ct., 1835); *Hunter* v. *City of Pittsburg*, 207 U.S. 161 (1907).

   8. *Trustees of Dartmouth College* v. *Woodward*, 17 U.S. (4 Wheat.) 517, 638 (1819).
   9. But see chapter 12 for the more ambiguous contemporary meaning of the case.
   10. Jon Teaford, *The Municipal Revolution in America* (Chicago, 1975).

ban government. Streets were paved, swamps drained, wells dug, aqueducts constructed, and police forces hired, as city governments responded to and shaped unprecedented urban growth. More dubiously, perhaps, railroads were subsidized, franchises granted, and politically connected land speculators protected in their holdings. But all this new activity found its legitimacy only in direct and explicit legislative authorizations. The New York legislature devoted more attention to the city than to other local governments in the state, but paradoxically, the effect of legislative solicitude was to supersede the chartered rights and liberties that had once defined an autonomous corporate entity.

Disputes that tested the legal status of the corporation of the city of New York thus became "trouble cases" (to use Karl Llewellyn's phrase): the hard or aberrant situations that compel judges to explain the assumptions underlying their rulemaking.[11] Because New York City had been royally chartered, because the city was big, wealthy, and active, its presence as a litigant led judges to argue openly about the boundary between public and private action, the opposition between property and government, and the limits of discretionary action by municipal officials. General definitions of the powers and attributes of municipal corporations had to be tested by the judicial insistence that they be applied to New York City.

Cases involving New York City were leading decisions in many areas of municipal corporation doctrine. The opinions of New York State's appellate judges in determining the city's liability for the acts of its agents established the terms of legal discussion throughout the United States. The destruction of the city's rights as a landholder came to symbolize the national victory of a uniform image of public local government. The New York Court of Appeals' 1857 decision confirming the legislature's reorganization of municipal services—without consulting city officials and in express disregard of the city charter—became the paradigmatic event in the formation of a judicial law of municipal corporations oblivious to claims of local autonomy.[12]

New York City's judicial history revealed the political assumptions that underlay municipal corporation law. When I began my research I expected the history I would write to do more, however. I hoped to demonstrate the ways in which a particular form of judicial thinking about local administration and public power had been pressed on one recalcitrant and for-

11. Karl N. Llewellyn and E. Addison Hoebel, *The Cheyenne Way* (Norman, Okla., 1941), 27–29.

12. See cases cited in chapter 14; Jeremiah Smith, *Cases on Selected Topics in the Law of Municipal Corporation* (Cambridge, Mass., 1898); James Bryce, *The American Commonwealth*, 2 vols. (London, 1888), 2:281–90, and 3:173–76; Thomas M. Cooley, *A Treatise on the Constitutional Limitations* (Boston, 1868), 189–255.

merly autonomous local government. Implicitly I think I intended to show how legalistic thinking imposed from above had defeated my lead paint proposal.

In any case, when I began work on this book, I chose New York City as my subject less because I wanted to write the "legal" history of the city than because I wanted to understand the effect that American municipal corporation law had on American urban development. Like other legal historians, I was fascinated by the relationship between judicial doctrine and institutional behavior. And as a legally trained historian I suspect I harbored a more or less unconscious belief that legal doctrine could, should, and did make a difference in the "real" world.[13] Thus I first began studying the legal history of New York with the clear expectation that it would reveal how the law of municipal corporations came to change the governing assumptions of city government.

New York City seemed an ideal subject for such a project. Its institutional history appeared to exemplify the changes in judicial doctrine that I thought would be my primary concern. An autonomous British borough in the eighteenth century, possessing much real estate as well as its government, it had become the object of the overt interventions by courts and the state legislature by the middle of the nineteenth century, lacking in rights that could be asserted against the state. As already noted, judicial opinions declared that New York City was an agency of the state, a municipal corporation like other municipal corporations, indistinguishable legally from other local governments, subject to central norms.

Yet as my research proceeded I became more and more dissatisfied with the picture of legal change implicit in my early expectations. However interesting New York City's judicial history might be in drawing out the political assumptions of local government law, the legal history of how New York City itself became a municipal corporation was more interesting still. That history, I eventually realized, could not be explained by the external insistence of judges, legislators, and treatise writers that it not be anything else. In the crucial period of New York City's political transformation from a propertied corporation to a public instrumentality of state power, those external pressures had not existed. New York City became a public entity during the quarter century that followed the American Revolution. Its metamorphosis was not accomplished through the assertion of the power of the central state over subordinate local units. To the contrary, it resulted from the willingness of the city's leaders—both Federalists and Jeffersonians—to commit their government to the exercise of state-

13. See John Griffiths, "Is Law Important," *New York University Law Review* 54 (1979): 339–74.

derived powers. The law of municipal corporations cannot explain New York City's institutional transformation, because that transformation occurred well before the creation of that law.

As late as the early 1830s there was no legal category of "municipal corporations," no municipal corporation law. Only in the 1840s did the state judiciary become an active intervenor in local affairs. Yet half a century earlier the corporation of the city of New York was already taking steps to make itself into what only later would be regarded as a municipal corporation. By the early nineteenth century city government in practice looked systematically to the state legislature for enabling authority for contemplated local action. By then municipal powers were always justified by reference to central norms and institutions.

The modern legal concept of a city has recently been described as rooted in a political vision of properly powerless local governments.[14] But the origins of that concept, at least in New York City, belie the characterization. It was not the powerlessness of city officials within the state that needs delineation; rather, it was their power, their ability to mold New York City's government into an entity that accorded with a transformed and revolutionary political culture. New York City was not dragged kicking and screaming into the confines of a uniform legal ideology. It got there on its own.

I had begun my research by posing the wrong question about the legal history of the city. I had assumed that the problem to be solved was to explain how the law (as a structure of centralized norms) had imposed itself on the preexisting structure of the corporation of the city of New York. I had supposed that the judicial law of municipal corporations had been created to make public and dependent entities out of "private" governments like the eighteenth-century chartered city of New York. The basic historical issues, I thought, were when and how it had done so.

I eventually discovered, however, that the rules of municipal corporation law were formulated as ways of regulating the conduct of entities (like New York City) that judges already knew to be public. Their case law reflected a realization that the reconceptualization of the city as an agency of public, state-derived power had not produced an adequate commitment to the public good. Their doctrine responded to an already transformed institutional structure.

The real problem revealed by my research was to understand how and why New York City had changed legally during the quarter century after the Revolution in spite of the absence of significant legal intervention. As I had expected, New York City's legal modernization was intertwined with

14. Frug, "The City as a Legal Concept."

the emergence of a positivistic belief in the singular legitimacy of centralized state authority. I had incorrectly assumed, however, that such a
legalistic commitment could only have been produced by the formal imposition of centralized legal norms. And it was only after many months of
trying to make sense of recalcitrant material that I relearned the obvious
lesson that formal structures of authority and dependence may be interesting and important as ideological statements but rarely arise without support and legitimation from the general culture.[15]

The chapters that follow describe that changing content of what might
be called New York City's governmental culture in a period stretching
from the early eighteenth century through the first decades of the nineteenth century. They emphasize detailed pictures of institutional practices
as a way of understanding New York City's relationship with other structures of political authority, the implicit goals of municipal government,
and the techniques of action on which the city relied.[16]

These chapters demonstrate that New York City changed from a government insistent on governing through its personal, private estate, to one
dedicated to using a public bureaucracy to provide public goods for public
consumption. And they tell a story that might be characterized in alternative narrow or grandiose terms. The narrow version asks the reader to consider how it came to be considered inappropriate for a government to use
its private property as a continuing tool of governance. Many governments, notably New York City and the federal government, still spend
much time managing their corporate estates. For nearly two hundred
years, however, it has been a given that absent special circumstances or
uses for which public ownership might be appropriate (like parks), the
proper destination of publicly owned land is into private hands.[17] There
have always been competing visions of the efficiency and legitimacy of
public landholding.[18] In the wake of New York City's 1975 fiscal crisis, for
example, the eminent urbanist Robert Wood suggested that planners seri-

---

15. Peter Berger and Thomas Luckmann, *The Social Construction of Reality* (New York,
1966); Lucien Febvre, *Le problème de l'incroyance au XVIème siècle* (Paris, 1943).

16. I should emphasize that this book does not provide a complete governmental history
of the city in any period of its growth. A large part of that history is found in Sidney
Pomerantz's fine monograph, *New York: An American City, 1783–1803*, 2d ed. (Port Washington, N.Y., 1965), as well as in other institutional histories. Here I concentrate on the implicit legal theory that informed that history, on the unstated or partially stated legal assumptions that shaped the formulation of policy in the changing city.

17. See James Willard Hurst, *Law and Social Process in United States History* (Ann Arbor,
1960), 79; Robert C. Ellickson and A. Dan Tarlock, *Land Use Controls* (Boston, 1981),
990–1002.

18. See, of course, Henry George, *Progress and Poverty* (New York, 1880); John W. Reps,

ously "consider that the city take over ownership of city land. If, in urban renewal, we had leased land instead of selling it to private developers, most of the cities, including New York, would be better off."[19] Yet even in 1975 Wood felt compelled to preface his suggestion with the acknowledgment that it was "probably more theoretical or egghead" than asking the federal government to make massive infusions of money to save urban amenities. This book tells the story of how government use of private property became a utopian fantasy.

The grandiose version would treat New York City's legal history as nothing less than the emergence of the particular attitude to urban power usually labeled "liberalism." In the early republic New York City's leaders learned to describe municipal power in ways that contrasted it with private choices and private wealth, learned to justify the services the city provided either by the "fact" that private citizens had better things to do with their time or by the public necessity of providing a public structure within which the private market economy would flourish, learned that municipal activities were best financed through general tax levies. Postrevolutionary New York's liberalism was, of course, substantively distinct from the "cosmopolitan liberalism" often identified with New York City's public policy from the 1930s to the 1970s.[20] Unlike modern urban liberals, early nineteenth-century New Yorkers did not consider the amelioration of economic hardship a central responsibility of municipal government. Instead, they focused on the transformation of the physical environment. But it seems to me that they would have understood the forms of justification put forward by their twentieth-century counterparts. They too had learned to found the exercise of power on the "needs" of citizens for public municipal services. They too would have distinguished those objective, external "needs" from the "wants" that could best be satisfied (if wants are ever satisfied) by private choice and the private market. The positioning of the line between freedom and necessity, public power and private autonomy, and individuality and community has changed over the past two hundred years (although not so much as some may think). The perceived need to draw it has remained a constant.[21]

Whichever way it is characterized, the story told in the pages that follow

"Public Land, Urban Development Policy and the American Planning Tradition" in Marion Clawson, ed., *Modernizing Urban Land Policy* (Baltimore, 1973), 15–48.

19. *New York Times*, 30 July 1975, under the byline of Israel Shenker; reprinted in Roger E. Alcaly and David Mermelstein, *The Fiscal Crisis of American Cities* (New York, 1977), 6.

20. See Bernard C. Gifford, "New York City and Cosmopolitan Liberalism," *Political Science Quarterly* 93 (1978): 559–84.

21. See Frug, "The City as a Legal Concept," 1074–80.

is at least partially one of separation and loss. It describes our separation from a legal world in which property rights legitimized community self-determination and a city corporation might possess its government as well as its real estate. The values that animated the prerevolutionary corporation of the city of New York for the most part are lost to us, are ones to which we do not give even our philosophical loyalty.[22] We can reconstruct their features; we can even, perhaps, come to appreciate their internal coherence and their attractiveness to eighteenth-century Americans. We cannot make those values our own.

The story is also one of human creativity and ingenuity. The makers of the modern urban legal order shared with others of their generation a radical new belief that public power existed to be used to improve the material lives of Americans.[23] Hampered by a republican political culture that distrusted local autonomy and instrumental public action, New York City's postrevolutionary political leaders concocted a justification for local public action founded on formal subservience within a state polity. That justification, today identified with the law of municipal corporations, allowed city leaders to expand their responsibilities and the services they provided without doing violence to republican norms of public conduct. If the result was a formal reduction in local autonomy, that was a small price to pay, a cost willingly assumed, in their active pursuit of the public good.

We may wish to discard and disown the consequences of their actions. We might conclude that the image of the city they projected rested on too restrictive a view of community. We should not, however, discount their sincerity, their energy, or the significance of their animating vision. And we should not disregard their success in remaking an American city into the embodiment of their political values.

22. I think that the heroic quality of Frank Michelman's recent attempt to infuse those values with modern content as a way of offering constitutional protection to normally unprotected groups provides ironic confirmation of this argument ("Political Markets and Community Self-Determination: Competing Judicial Models of Local Government Legitimacy," *Indiana Law Journal* 53 [1977]: 145–206, 148; "Property as a Constitutional Right," *Washington and Lee Law Review* 38 [1981]: 1097–1114).

23. James Willard Hurst calls this belief the constitutional ideal. See his "Legal Elements in United States History," in Donald Fleming and Bernard Bailyn, eds., *Law in American History* (Boston, 1971), 3–94; Joyce Appleby, "What Is Still American in the Political Philosophy of Thomas Jefferson," *William and Mary Quarterly*, 3d ser., 39 (1982):287–309; Daniel Boorstin, *The Lost World of Thomas Jefferson* (Boston, 1948).

PART I

The Properties of the Corporation

CHAPTER 1

Reading the Charter

Eighteenth-century New York was a corporation; or, to borrow contemporary usage, the mayor, aldermen, and commonalty of the city of New York were a corporation.[1] In speaking of New York City as a corporation I am not using the term metaphorically. Notions of corporate personality have had a long and useful life at the hands of anthropologists, social historians, and other students of communities.[2] I am not, however, posing questions about the integration of social life in the provincial city. *Gemeinschaft* and *Gesellschaft* are only bit players in this story. It may be that New York City moved from the former to the latter during our time period. It is more likely that New York City was already too cosmopolitan, too complex, and too contradictory to justify being characterized as an organic community.[3] The focus of these chapters is less on the sociological texture of group life than on the evolution and transformation of legal categories. How was a particular identity imposed on an institution by a changing legal culture? And what were the relevant features of that legal culture?

As a corporation, one might suppose that New York City has always been the same. In 1731 and in 1981 New York City could be described as "an artificial person or legal entity created by or under the authority of the laws of a state or nation, . . . a body politic . . . regarded as having a per-

1. Throughout I shall indiscriminately use "the corporation," "the city," or "New York City," as referents for "the mayor, aldermen, and commonalty of the city of New York." Note that I am thereby equating the city with the corporation. I demonstrate in Chapter 3 that this equation is plausible, at least for the eighteenth century.

2. See Gary B. Nash, *The Urban Crucible: Social Change, Political Consciousness, and the Origins of the American Revolution* (Cambridge, Mass., 1979); Michael Zuckerman, *Peaceable Kingdoms* (New York, 1970); Sally F. Moore, *Law as Process* (London, 1978); M. G. Smith, *Corporations and Society* (London, 1975).

3. See Michael Kammen, *Colonial New York* (New York, 1975); Patricia U. Bonomi, *A Factious People* (New York, 1971); Milton Klein, *The Politics of Diversity* (New York, 1974); Thomas Archdeacon, *New York City, 1664–1710: Conquest and Change* (Ithaca, 1975).

sonality and existence distinct from that of its several members."[4] Yet the constancy of that definition should not mislead us. As a legal entity, New York City underwent radical changes. The law dictionary definition hides the depth of the conceptual transformation. Today, as in the nineteenth century, we regard New York City primarily as a member of a general category of agencies of public welfare; an eighteenth-century judge, by contrast, could have looked only to the chartered foundations of a propertied corporation. A judge searching for authority to justify action by the institution would have had to turn to the charters that created the city as a corporation. There was no general category of public institutions. There were only the particular powers granted to the singular institution of the city of New York by the various charters culminating in the Montgomerie Charter of 1730.

Though New Amsterdam on Manhattan Island began as a military encampment, the Dutch government had granted a charter to the citizens of the city by 1657. Eight years later, Richard Nicoll, the first English governor of New York, confirmed their right to civil government, granting a charter of incorporation under the administration of a mayor, alderman, and sheriff. And in 1686, Governor Thomas Dongan, the agent of the Duke of York, gave the mayor, alderman, and commonalty of the city of New York a more complete charter for municipal government. This charter is usually seen as the beginning of the modern governmental history of New York City. Twenty-two years later, Edward, Lord Cornbury added a ferry franchise to the grants previously made in the Dongan Charter. And in 1730, following a decade of petitions, Governor John Montgomerie granted a charter under royal seal that ratified, confirmed, and enlarged both the Dongan and Cornbury charters. Chancellor James Kent, writing in the 1830s, still viewed the Montgomerie Charter as the foundation for the government of the city. Even in the twentieth century, the Montgomerie Charter could be seen as a residual source of authority, as a part of the "organic" law of New York City.[5]

To modern eyes, the Montgomerie Charter is an awkward, prolix, and repetitious document. The language is archaic, the structure mystifying. It begins by reciting the city's previous charters of 1686 (the Dongan Charter) and 1708 (the Cornbury ferry grant). It concludes by announcing that

4. *Black's Law Dictionary*, 4th ed., rev. (St. Paul, 1968), 409.
5. See James Kent, *The Charter of the City of New York, with notes thereon. Also a Treatise on the Powers and Duties of the Mayor, Aldermen, and Assistant Aldermen, and the Journal of the City Convention* (New York, 1836), 108; Jerrold Seymann, ed., *Colonial Charters, Patents, and Grants to the Communities Comprising the City of New York* (New York, 1939); New York Charter Commission, *Report to the Legislature with a Draft of a Charter for the City of New York* (New York, 1923), 55.

the city will be free from any liability for the use or misuse of powers or properties not granted by these charters.[6] Throughout, it contains a seemingly disorganized series of grants from the crown to the corporation, each introduced with the following formula: "And further we of our Especial grace certain knowledge and meer motion have given granted ratifyed and confirmed and by these presents Do for us our Heirs and Successors give grant, ratify and confirm unto the Said Mayor Alderman and Commonalty of the City of New York and to their successors forever."

The need in the 1720s for a new charter arose because of the "diverse Questions Doubts Opinions Ambiguities Controversies and Debates" concerning the validity of the previous two charters, neither of which had been under royal seal.[7] The purpose of the Montgomerie Charter therefore was both to confirm what had been previously granted or acquired by the city and to provide new powers and rights. "Considering that the Strength and Encrease of our good Subjects in that our frontier province of New York does in a greater measure depend upon the welfare and property of our said City wherein the Trade and Navigation thereof are chiefly and principally carried on," the charter was drafted "to give Encouragement to the said City Inhabitants and Citizens and to remove utterly abolish and wholly take away all and all manner of Causes Occasions and matters whereupon Such Questions Doubts Opinions Ambiguities Controversies or Debates . . . may or can arise."[8]

What it granted can be divided into three categories. There were, first, the incidents of corporate existence. The mayor, aldermen, and commonalty were made "by force of these presents" one body corporate and politic, with perpetual succession, the capacity to get, receive, and possess all forms of property, to give, grant, let, or assign the same, and to sue and to be sued in courts of law "in as full and ample manner and form as any of our other Liege Subjects of our Said Province." New York City was recreated as a singular individual, a person like other persons capable of holding property both within and without the city limits.[9]

More specifically, that corporate person took on a tangible and particular shape. It was given a head in the creation of a structure of elective and appointive officers; it was given a body in the identification of the commonalty—the freeman and freeholders of the city—with the interests

---

6. For more on the significance of this release from liability see Chapter 2.

7. *The Colonial Laws of New York from the Year 1664 to the Revolution*, 5 vols. (Albany, 1894), 2:596–97. Copies of the Montgomerie Charter are in Kent, *Charter;* Seymann, *Colonial Charters;* and many other works published in the eighteenth and nineteenth centuries, as well as in the colonial laws. References throughout will be to the statutory version.

8. *Colonial Laws*, 2:596–97.

9. Ibid., 581, 587, 597.

of the corporation. No free citizen of the city need ever serve on any jury, fill any office, or discharge any public duty outside of the city. His only local responsibilities were to the corporation. Only the corporation could claim his allegiance.[10]

Second, and to city leaders most important, the Montgomerie Charter confirmed and extended the corporate estate of the city. This pattern followed that set by the earlier charters received by the city. External threats to title apparently supplied the usual impetus for petitions for a new charter. In 1708, for example, the attempt by Cornelius Sebring of Brooklyn to establish a competing ferry across the East River in derogation of claimed rights of the city prompted a petition to Governor Cornbury for a monopoly of ferry traffic to and from Long Island. In 1730 the threat was Cornelius Van Horne's application to Governor Montgomerie for a grant of a waterlot out beyond low-water mark, the limit of the rights granted to the city in the Dongan Charter.[11] As in 1708, city leaders got their wish. The Montgomerie Charter gave the city absolute title to all the land under water around the southern part of Manhattan up to four hundred feet beyond low-water mark. The Montgomerie Charter confirmed more than that, however. The "waste and common land" of Manhattan Island, which at the time included most of the island north of what is now Canal Street, the land under water surrounding the island as far as low-water mark (plus the aforementioned extra four hundred feet around the southern end of the island), the ferry monopoly, and the waterfront of Brooklyn, were all made part of the personal estate of the corporation of the city of New York.

In addition, the Montgomerie Charter granted to the city what might be seen as a hodgepodge of public governmental powers. A Common Council made up of four or more aldermen and four or more assistant aldermen plus the mayor and recorder was given the power to pass such ordinances and bylaws "which to them or the greater part of them Shall Seem to be good useful or necessary for the good rule and government of the body corporate." Specifically, that body was to pass regulations "for the further publick good common profit trade and better government and rule of the Said City and for the better preserving governing disposing letting and Setting of the land Tenements possessions and hereditaments goods and Chattels" of the corporation. The Common Council was to pass on the election of all officers of the corporation (except for the mayor and recorder, who were appointed by the governor). It also had authority to lay

10. Ibid., 602–11, 615–16.

11. *Minutes of the Common Council of the City of New York, 1675–1776*, 8 vols. (New York, 1905), 2:341–45 (1708) (ferry); 3:221–22, 278 (1720) (petition of Cornelius Van Horne). I have used "new style" dating; the year begins on 1 January.

out and open streets, to run and regulate the markets of the city, to regulate and license individuals in a variety of trades, and to appoint inspectors
for various goods. The mayor of the city was made the clerk of the market
and the water bailiff for the harbor, in both cases with the authority to
collect all fees and rents without any need to account to the agents of the
crown. The charter granted to the corporation general authority to erect
and fill houses of correction (Bridewells), almshouses, and jails. It also created two courts, both manned by officers of the corporation sitting as justices of the peace: one a court of general sessions of the peace to hear criminal offenses, the other a court of common pleas or mayor's court for civil
actions. Each court was created with the authority to act "as fully and
freely and intirely and in as ample manner and form as Justices of the
peace of us our Heirs and Successors anywhere within that part of our
Kingdom of great Britain called England."[12]

A reading of the Montgomerie Charter suggests a picture of a "mixed
corporation"—a corporate body with a combination of public and private
powers.[13] Nineteenth-century treatise writers such as James Kent and
Murray Hoffman certainly understood it as such. The central problem
Hoffman's treatise on the estate of the city of New York confronted was
how to decide which powers granted by the charter were subject to legislative interference and which were not. His answer was simple: a grant of
property was beyond the reach of the legislature, whereas a grant of political power could never be viewed as a "vested right" against the state.[14]
Similarly, Kent elaborately delineated the differences between grants of
derivative political power, such as a city's control of the streets, and its
different and more complete authority over property rights, such as the
ferry franchise to Brooklyn. In Kent's reading of the charter, the streets
were "a grant of public nature without any private interest or property or
revenue connected with it. . . . The Legislature interferes with the power
in their discretion, and I think there can be no question as to the right of
the Legislature to do so, for the power is not exclusive in the Corporation,
nor irrevocable, nor in the nature of the grant of private right." By contrast, the ferry franchise was a grant of private right: "The grant of political power is exclusively a matter of public and general concern, but the
ferriage grant was for the benefit of the grantees, and the rents, issues, and
profits were given exclusively to the inhabitants of the city. The inhabi-

12. *Colonial Laws* 2:610–23.
13. For the concept of a "mixed corporation" see Louis Hartz, *Economic Policy and Democratic Thought* (Cambridge, Mass., 1948).
14. Murray Hoffman, *Treatise upon the Estate and Rights of the Corporation of the City of
New York, as Proprietors*, 2d rev. ed., 2 vols. (New York, 1862), 1:44–45.

tants in their aggregate corporate capacity, have as vested an interest in
the entire grant of the old ferry, and of the right to establish others, as
they have individually in any government grant of lands, tenements, and
hereditaments."[15]

Such a reading of the charter makes sense of much of it. Following these
nineteenth-century treatise writers, we can categorize the elements of the
charter in familiar ways. Yet in light of the document itself such a reading is
nonsense. There was nothing in the charter to divide the "public" from
the "private" rights of the corporation.[16] Nowhere did the charter say,
"These things are subject to legislative intervention, but those things are
not." Nowhere were delegations of governmental authority distinguished
from grants of property. Indeed, the term "delegation" was never used.
All the powers earlier characterized as governmental or public—
following Kent and Hoffman—came to the corporation as private property. Thus to give the corporation regulatory authority over the streets, the
crown had to "give grant ratify and Confirm unto the Said Mayor Alderman and Commonalty of the City of New York and their Successors forever: that the Common Council of the city shall have such powers as were
thereby made necessary." The licensing power of the city was characterized in the charter as a grant of monopoly allowing it to grant licenses to
such persons as should be thought fit, along with the accompanying right
to demand such payments as should be agreed upon between licensor and
licensee (up to a specified limit), "without Any Account thereof to be rendered made or done to us our Heirs or Successors or any other person
whatsoever." Both the regulatory powers of the Common Council and the
right to hold courts were also drafted as grants—not delegations—from
the sovereign. Toward the end of the document, the drafters made a general confirmation of all of the property rights previously granted to the corporation with a covenant of quiet enjoyment. That confirmation encompassed not just the real estate of the corporation, including the ferries,
ferriage, dockage, cranage, wharfage, and other profits to be gained from
the newly granted waterlots, the market houses, and the other public
buildings of the city; it also included, among the properties to which the
corporation now had title, the "Jurisdictions Court powers Offices Au-

15. Kent, *Charter*, 141–43. See similarly, Frank J. Goodnow, *Municipal Problems* (London, 1897), 2.

16. This is not to deny that the drafters of the charter did distinguish between the powers
granted to the city over the streets and those granted over the ferry. At the end of the charter,
the city's right to hold the ferry franchise in fee simple absolute is singled out for confirmation, along with other properties of the city, but no specific mention is made of the control of
the streets (*Colonial Laws*, 2:631–32).

thorities fines Amerciaments perquisites fees" also granted in the charter. All of what seemed to be governmental attributes of the charter in fact were confirmed as the private property of the corporation.[17]

One might say that the charter provided a continuum of governmental powers running from the almost purely governmental to the purely private. At one extreme was the grant of a court structure and the bestowal of general regulatory authority on the Common Council; at the other was the real estate confirmed by the charter. In between one might usefully arrange the various powers granted to the city: market tolls and licensing fee structures tending toward the "property" side of the continuum, street regulation closer to the "governmental" end. This construct has the virtue of forcing the reader to look at the charter not as a collection of antithetical public and private rights but rather as a document creating (or, more precisely, confirming the existence of) a complex institution. The opposition between property and sovereignty often said to lie at the heart of nineteenth- and twentieth-century American law had no place in the Montgomerie Charter of 1730 and can only limit our understanding of the corporation of the city of New York.

But the charter itself—the creation of a corporate entity—basically was a conveyance from the crown to the mayor, alderman, and commonalty of the city of New York.[18] According to Sir William Blackstone, a charter was a franchise, an incorporeal hereditament, a property right over and above the specific properties granted in the document.[19] The Montgomerie Charter was structured like a deed with "premises" justifying and explaining the transaction, identifying the grantor and grantee, stating the consideration, and setting down the operative words of the transaction, followed by a long "habendum," which detailed the nature and extent of the various grants, covenants of title, and the various restrictions on the grants, followed by an execution clause containing the date, the signature of Governor Montgomerie as witness, and the royal seal.

17. Ibid., 615, 619, 631–35.

18. See generally Recorder Treby's argument in "Proceedings between the KING and the CITY OF LONDON, on an information in nature of a QUO WARRANTO . . ." 8 *Howell's State Trials* 1039 (1681–83), 1099–1147. Insofar as such conveyances characterized all incorporations, it is mistaken to argue as the Handlins did that all prerevolutionary corporations were public institutions, direct and derivative agencies of the state (Oscar Handlin and Mary F. Handlin, "The Origins of Business Corporations," *Journal of Economic History* 5 [1945]: 1–25). But neither were corporations private entities, that is, nongovernmental repositories of private wealth and power.

19. William Blackstone, *Commentaries on the Laws of England*, 4 vols. (London, 1765–69), 2:chap. 3; Matthew Hale, "De Portibus Maris," in Francis Hargrave, ed., *A Collection of Tracts Relative to the Law of England, from Manuscripts* (London, 1787), 1:54.

The very concern with formality that justified the need for a new charter in 1730 suggests that it was viewed as a property transaction rather than a delegation of governmental powers. In petitions to royal officials in the late 1720s, city officials argued that earlier charters had been an inadequate source of title in attempting to convey the property of the sovereign without the seal of the sovereign. Lacking the proper documents or muniments of title, the officers of the corporation could not be certain of their ability to assert their possession of the government of the city of New York and its properties. The Montgomerie Charter was drafted to remedy that situation.

CHAPTER 2

The Creation of Autonomy

What sort of entity did the charter "create"? What was the personality of the corporation?

The corporation resembled no modern governmental entity. More to the point, it resembled few governments in eighteenth-century North America. In the province of New York only Albany also governed by virtue of a charter. No more than seventeen communities in all of colonial America ever received corporate charters. Indeed, the earlier Dongan Charter of 1686 had been granted to provide concrete affirmation of the special status of New York City. According to the Duke of York's instructions, Governor Dongan was to draft a charter that would grant the city "immunities and privileges beyond what other parts of my territory doe enjoy."[1] The charter was meant to lay "the basis of a plan of government for a great city."[2]

The city's charter created an institution in which property and governmental rights were blurred and mixed. The charter was a grant of property, but it was a grant of property for government. The three chapters that follow this one examine the significance of property rights in the practice of government in eighteenth-century New York City. This chapter, however, outlines the significance in political thought of such a propertied incorporation.

The point is not that the corporation of the city of New York, as constituted, was an eighteenth-century novelty. If anything, it looks like an archaic throwback. "The struggle of ownership and rulership to free themselves from each other" is one of the great themes of medieval English legal history. One might have thought that that struggle had been

1. Marcus Benjamin, "Thomas Dongan and the Granting of the New York Charter, 1682–86," in James Grant Wilson, ed., *Memorial History of the City of New York* (New York, 1892), 411.

2. James Kent, *The Charter of the City of New York, with notes thereon. Also a Treatise on the Powers and Duties of the Mayor, Aldermen, and Assistant Aldermen, and the Journal of the City Convention* (New York, 1836), 118.

concluded. Yet New York City was expected to govern in terms reminiscent of Frederic W. Maitland's description of medieval Cambridge: "The 'belongs'. . . of private law begins to blend with the 'belongs' of public law; ownership blends with lordship, rulership, sovereignty in the vague medieval dominium."[3]

Even as a corporation among other corporations, New York City was a distinctive legal entity. Like many historical statements, this seems paradoxical until one realizes that it is actually tautological. For, in the eighteenth century what else could a corporation be but a singular institution? Corporations were chartered with particular rights, properties, privileges, and immunities to serve particular purposes. As Thomas Hobbes noted, a "charter" was distinguished from a law by the fact that a law might "bind all the subjects of a commonwealth . . . a liberty or charter is only to one man or some part of the people." In fact, said Hobbes, a charter was not law, but rather an "exemption" from law.[4]

There was no general categorization of different corporate entities. The well-known confusion of Blackstone's discussion of corporations was an accurate reflection of the corporate landscape of eighteenth-century England. To Blackstone, "lay corporations" included the king, towns and cities, manufacturing and commercial concerns like the "trading companies of London," churchwardens, the college of physicians and company of

3. Frederic W. Maitland, *Township and Borough* (Cambridge, 1897), 31, 11. By contrast, notions of rulership and ownership were kept apart in other government structures in colonial North America. The townships of New England are only the most obvious examples of local governments established without attendant property rights, as derivative agencies of local administration (see Michael Zuckerman, *Peaceable Kingdoms* [New York, 1970], who does not make the argument that propertylessness should be equated with powerlessness). When the Dutch recaptured New York in 1683, Governor Anthony Colves gave a "charter" to the English towns of Long Island that was nothing but a set of orders on the conduct of elections and social control, without any of the elements of a property grant (Edmund B. O'Callaghan, *The Documentary History of the State of New York*, 4 vols. [Albany, 1849], 1:655–58). Counties and towns in the eighteenth-century English province of New York also were defined almost entirely by their administrative and regulatory concerns (see Patricia U. Bonomi, "Local Government in Colonial New York: A Basis for Republicanism," in Jacob Judd and Irwin Polishook, eds., *Aspects of Early New York Society and Politics* [Tarrytown, 1974], 29–50). Conversely, grants of property might be made to communities—to "town proprietors" and others—but usually without any attendant political powers. In 1708, for example, the freeholders of Eastchester, in what is now the Bronx, received a "Patent" confirming their right to hold the lands they had previously manured and improved, with free commonage over a larger area. They were given permission to elect a deputy constable and to arbitrate disputes among themselves. But all other governmental matters were to be settled by the sessions court in Westchester (Jerrold Seymann, ed., *Colonial Charters, Patents, and Grants to the Communities Comprising the City of New York* [New York, 1959], 353–55).

4. Thomas Hobbes, *Leviathan* (London, 1651), pt. 2, chap. 26.

surgeons in London, the Royal Society, the society of antiquaries, and the colleges of Oxford and Cambridge.[5] Each of these, as well as a great variety of others, was defined not by its membership in a general category but by its particular property rights and privileges, by the specific terms of its charter.

Thus New York was not a member of a general category of municipal corporations, sharing its status with Albany and Philadelphia.[6] It was a particular institution defined by what had been granted to it in its charter. That New York City received "all the waste and common land of Manhattan Island" and that Albany had been granted the monopoly of the fur trade and the right to buy land from the Indians served less to join them in a common category of propertied corporate communities than to distinguish them by the specific natures of their respective grants.[7]

It was not the abstract legal category of corporations that gave New York City its legal identity. Nor was it the political act of incorporation. Rather, it was property that created the public and political character of boroughs like New York City. Just as we say that an object is described by its properties, so in the eighteenth century a person—whether an institution or a human being—was described by his or her or its properties.[8]

In the seventeenth and eighteenth centuries property was defined not simply as material possessions but as all the attributes of personality that created individuality. It would not have seemed strange, therefore, for the officers of the city of New York to claim that they possessed their charter. Life, liberty, religion, "conjugall affection," as well as wealth were all supposed to be held as property rights. Hobbes (and here he seems to have been characteristic of his age) considered property to be a "subjective con-

5. William Blackstone, *Commentaries on the Laws of England*, 4 vols. (London, 1765–69), 1:469.

6. See Judith Diamondstone, "Philadelphia's Municipal Corporation 1700–1776," *Pennsylvania Magazine of History and Biography* 90 (1966): 183–201.

7. Compare the Dongan Charter of Albany, *The Colonial Laws of New York from the Year 1664 to the Revolution*, 5 vols. (Albany, 1894) 1:195–216, with the Dongan Charter of New York City incorporated into the Montgomerie Charter, *Colonial Laws*, 2:575–90.

8. Indeed, it was their landholdings that had first driven medieval towns to seek charters from the crown in the fourteenth century. See Colin Platt, *The English Medieval Town* (London, 1976), 129, 142.

Thomas Madox devoted much space in *Firma Burgi*, his great eighteenth-century legal treatise, to a demonstration that incorporation could not define or determine the relationships between boroughs and the crown. "There were several advantages which a Corporate-Town had above a Town not-corporated." But those advantages related to the internal governance and commerce of cities, not to their partial autonomy within the eighteenth-century polity. Local autonomy, insofar as it existed, was a reflection of the property rights held by a community (*Firma Burgi* [London, 1726], 3ff, 295–96).

cept depending on the ordering of individual intelligences."[9] Property rights and civil or individual rights could not be placed in opposition to one another. They were of a piece and conceptually identical. It was the quality, the permanence, and the security of an individual's property rights that gave him political significance.[10]

Property, then, was a guarantee of independence. Without it there was no protection from "the political dependence upon others which constitutes corruption."[11] The autonomy that property made possible was not simply a form of resistance to interference or intervention. It was closely tied to the very possibility of an individualized personality, to a classical notion of citizenship. Property made it possible for a person to shape an identity rather than to be shaped by external forces.

This notion contained an implicit tension. Property was seen as control and as a way to resist change imposed by external authority. Yet property also implied change and instrumental action, the shaping of an individual future. Change in and of itself was no virtue. It was closely identified with instability and corruption and with the disorder of the English civil wars. Those negative attributes of change were often identified with the crown and with central authority. And thus the problem for local governments, as for all persons who wished to retain their autonomy, was to establish a basis for freedom from centralized control, both to protect themselves from externally imposed "innovation"[12] and to help shape their individual futures.

Not all forms of property served equally well to guarantee individual autonomy. Real property, by its permanence and its creation of a spatial analogue for personal autonomy, had a preferred position.[13] But all property that was not transitory or easily alienable, that was in some measure permanently identifiable with the identity of an individual, might protect au-

9. Frank M. Coleman, *Hobbes and America: Exploring the Constitutional Foundations* (Toronto, 1977), 82–83.

10. See generally, J.G.A. Pocock, *Politics, Language and Time* (New York, 1973), 80–103; C. B. McPherson, *The Political Theory of Possessive Individualism* (Oxford, 1962); Gordon Wood, *The Creation of the American Republic* (Chapel Hill, 1969), 214–22.

11. Pocock, *Politics, Language, and Time*, 92.

12. Consider the words of Recorder Treby, defending the City of London against the *quo warranto* action by the crown in 1682: "All innovations (as this must certainly be a very great one) are dangerous" (8 *Howell's State Trials* 1039 [1681–83], 1143).

13. Pocock, *Politics, Language, and Time*, 91; see also the Common Council's wish list in its 1720 petition for a new charter in which real property grants—the extension of the lands and limits of the city to four hundred feet beyond low-water mark, the ferry franchise, and all the docks, slips, wharves, cranage, and wharfage—were given priority over everything else desired from the crown (*Minutes of the Common Council of the City of New York, 1675–1776*, 8 vols. [New York, 1905], 4:6–7; hereafter *MCC*).

tonomy. When the Dongan Charter of 1686 spoke of New York City as "an Antient City" that had "antiently been a body Politick and Corporate," and when it confirmed all of the "Liberties privileges franchises rights Royalties free Customs Jurisdictions and Immunities which they . . . antiently had held,"[14] the effect was to assert the corporation's preexisting claim to properties for which there was no formal grant or charter, to assert title by prescription. But prescriptive title was not simply an archaic equivalent for adverse possession. A prescriptive right—an anciently held right—was a virtuous, a politically significant right. It was a form of property that could be interposed against change and corruption. It was property that articulated the personality of the holder.[15]

The history of New York City between the British conquest and the granting of the Montgomerie Charter was marked by a continuing tension between the desires of the members of the corporation for new and greater grants from provincial and royal authorities and their inclination to assert forms of preexisting or prescriptive title. Consider two episodes in the history of New York City's claim on the ferry franchise. In September 1683, before the Dongan Charter, the mayor and aldermen submitted to Governor Dongan a petition in which they asked for confirmation of a variety of "privileges" of the corporation, including the franchise in ferries to Long Island. The governor responded with some exasperation at the unending stream of demands made on him by the corporation ("that he much wondered [that] having lately granted almost every particular of a large and considerable petition Lately preferred by [the] preceeding Mayor [and] aldermen he should so suddenly Receive another petition from [the] present Magistrates"), and he denied many of the city's requests. In particular he restricted the city's rights over ferries "in any other place but what is already," seemingly a denial of the city's right to a franchise in the ferry traffic to Long Island. A committee was immediately appointed by the Common Council to entreat the governor to remove such restrictions. And in March of the following year the restrictions imposed in the governor's letter were removed. They were, wrote Dongan, intended merely as "directions not as Tenure."[16] Tenure—the property right in the ferry franchise—was held by the corporation as a preexisting right, beyond the reach of central authority.

14. *Colonial Laws*, 2:575, 577.

15. On the political significance of customary and prescriptive forms of tenure, see E. P. Thompson, "The Grid of Inheritance: A Comment," in Jack Goody, Joan Thirsk, and E. P. Thompson, eds., *Family and Inheritance: Rural Society in Western Europe, 1200–1800* (Cambridge, 1976), 328–60. For the later history of title by prescription, see Morton Horwitz, *The Transformation of American Law, 1780–1860* (Cambridge, Mass., 1977), 43–47.

16. *MCC*, 1:111, 121, 127 (1683–84).

In January 1708, Cornelius Sebring of Kings County (Brooklyn) petitioned Governor Cornbury for a grant of the right to run a ferry from his
farm on Long Island to the city in competition with the corporation. The
petition was underwritten by forty individuals who believed "that such a
ferry would be of a considerable advantage to the City & County if the
Prises for Transportaçon be not Excessive."[17]

The challenge was taken very seriously by the corporation, which immediately remonstrated to the governor. "The inhabitants of the city and
corporation" had "peaceably and quietly Possess'd and Enjoy'd" the various rights and properties granted to them by both the English and the
Dutch for more than seventy years, "to the great increase of her Majestys
Revenue and the Sensible Growth and Advancement of her Majestys said
City and Province." Among those various properties, the ferry between
the city and Long Island had a preeminent place. The corporation had
spent much money in erecting several public buildings that rendered service "commodious" to all persons involved in the loading and unloading of
wheat and other provisions. No one had ever complained about the service. The profits had always been applied to the government of the city
"and is the only considerable Income left to support the public buildings
Bridges Goals Landing places fire and Candle for their Watches, Sallaryes
of their officers Bellmen &c, and to defray the other publick and necessary
Charges of the Said City." But the competing ferry proposed by Sebring
"for his own private Lucre and gain" would "make Considerable Improvements to Ruine and destroy the present ferry the Chief Income and
Support of this Corporation." Therefore, because "you [Cornbury] will
Ever prefer the publick welfare of so Loyal and Considerable a People as
this Corporation," Sebring's petition should be rejected.[18]

The argument made by the corporation—successfully—was that its
rights in the ferry were not simply those of a private owner but rather were
of a piece with its existence as a flourishing and useful government institution. Governance and ownership were intertwined in the conception of the
ferry franchise. The city had been shaped by its seventy years of possession of an exclusive franchise, and the "improvements" that might result
from competition would ruin and destroy this element of its personality.

The Common Council then petitioned Cornbury for an enlargement and
an absolute confirmation of the grant to the corporation. By securing both
"all the Vacant and unappropriated Ground on Nassaw Island [Long Is-
land] from High water to Low water marke fronting unto this City" and an
exclusive franchise in the ferry, the city hoped to prevent competition

17. Ibid., 2:341–45 (1708).
18. O'Callaghan, *Documentary History*, 3:25–26; *MCC*, 2:341–44 (1708).

from future Cornelius Sebrings and "to hinder and prevent that priviledge and Liberty which divers persons now take of Transporting themselves and goods to and from the Island of Nassaw over the Said River without Coming to or Landing at the usual and accustomed place where the said ferry Boats are kept and Appointed to the great loss and damage of the petitioners."[19]

The result was the Cornbury Charter, which granted the city all the real property it requested (the exclusive franchise and the shoreline of Long Island) but refused to forbid residents from transporting themselves across the river. The ferry, according to the Cornbury Charter, was held by the city under "diverse antient Charters and grants by diverse former Governours and Commanders in chief of our said Province." But the profits thereof had declined because of the inability of the city to control and exclude competition.[20] Thus the enlargement of the grant by the 1708 charter was really only to make effectual and secure the preexisting ancient claim. But the right of residents of Long Island to transport themselves across the harbor was itself an ancient preexisting right, a prescriptive easement in the property of the corporation. It was, one might say, formative of the personality and the autonomy of the inhabitants of Long Island and therefore as inviolate as the title of the corporation.

The rights granted in the charters of the city of New York did not belong to an archetypal, archaic world of customary tenure and hazy group personality. To the contrary, those rights need to be located in an age of great legal change and conflict. Prescriptive, customary forms of tenure were under attack throughout the eighteenth century. As E. P. Thompson has written, "Small victories . . . in defence of customary practice, were won here and there. But the campaign itself was always lost."[21] The grants made in the charters to the corporation of the city of New York derived their authority less from the references to claims based on "antient" practices than from the fact that those charters transformed preexisting claims into rights held by the city in fee simple absolute. The grants in the Montgomerie Charter provided exclusive dominion.

For example, the waste and vacant land of Manhattan Island, first granted to the city in the Dongan Charter of 1686, became the "commons" of the city. But the grant of that vast "commons" extending over the greater portion of Manhattan Island gave no use-rights to the inhabitants of the city. The commons was considered part of the estate of the corporation, as a corporation. Unlike some contemporary boroughs in England,

19. *MCC*, 2:341–44 (1708).
20. *Colonial Laws*, 2:591.
21. Thompson, "The Grid of Inheritance," 348.

freemen held no "right of common"—no right to pasture their animals, gather firewood, and so forth—as a privilege of their freemanship.[22] The Common Council, acting for the corporation, managed its estate to the exclusion of any "common" rights; to the corporation the commons was simply a large piece of real estate absolutely owned. And through the first seventy-five years of the eighteenth century the Common Council leased plots, prosecuted trespassers, and tore down encroachments, all to the end of conserving the value of the property.[23]

The uses property served in determining the autonomy of the corporation rested, moreover, not on any timeless "essence" of corporateness but were fixed by the peculiar history of borough charters, franchises, and privileges in the last twenty years of the seventeenth century. In 1680, Charles II began a campaign to change the face of Parliament by forcing boroughs to return less whiggish representatives. The strategy he adopted was to threaten an action *quo warranto*—to compel the boroughs to come to court to defend themselves against charges of misuse of their franchises—if they would not agree to terms with the crown. The lynchpin of this strategy, according to later "whig" historians, was the famous *quo warranto* action actually brought against the city of London, a seat of opposition sentiment. London would be compelled to return its charter to the crown and thereby to give up all its chartered properties. The case would "reduce the City of London to the status of a small village, . . . place its government entirely in its [the crown's] own hands and . . . strip it of all rights and privileges."[24]

In the short run, the strategy worked. Judgment was given for the crown (although the city never actually gave up its charter), and most other boroughs quickly capitulated and returned their charters to the crown. By 1688, however, a desperate James II was forced to issue "A Proclamation for restoring Corporations to their Ancient Charters, Liberties, Rights and Franchises."[25] And after the Glorious Revolution of 1688, the arguments of Recorder Sir George Treby and Sir Henry Pollexfen for the London Corporation during the trial became enshrined as constitutional gospel.

The Glorious Revolution "sanctified" the privileges of English bor-

22. See examples collected by Maitland in *Township and Borough*, 197.
23. *MCC*, 1:403 (1696); 2:97–98, 113, 127, 129 (1700), 258–59 (1704); 3:229–30, 240–41, 245 (1720).
24. Jennifer Levin, *The Charter Controversy in the City of London, 1660–1688, and Its Consequences* (London, 1969), 2; see also Michael Landon, *The Triumph of the Lawyers* (University, Ala., 1970).
25. 8 *Howell's State Trials* 1039, 1277–78.

oughs, making them into unquestioned "vested rights."[26] In England this meant that borough officers might become increasingly corrupt in their use of corporate property and might separate corporate wealth from any perceivable public purpose; yet they would remain beyond any central control.[27] Parliament responded by shifting much of the governmental responsibilities—the public services—of local government to statutory commissions and other derivative agencies, making boroughs as irrelevant as possible to the necessary processes of local government. But full intervention into borough life had to await the future formulation of a conception of corporate personality that was not dependent on property rights, had to await the separation of the protected "connection between corporateness and privilege."[28]

At the same time that the crown was "waging war" upon the chartered rights of England's boroughs, Governor Dongan, James's agent, was granting a "liberal" charter to New York City. Chancellor Kent, writing nearly 150 years later, thought this "quite singular."[29] But in view of James's express desire to create a strong government for New York City, only a grant of property rights through a charter would serve his purposes. No other form of power for local governance would have been plausible. The City of London Case did not involve an argument over the legitimacy of creating an autonomous corporate personality through property rights; on that issue there would have been consensus. The substantive legal question that divided the two sides was the nature of corporate existence underlying or absent grants by the crown. Was there a "real" corporate person, or was corporate personality a creation of royal franchises?[30]

26. Maitland, "Trust and Corporation," in *Selected Essays* (Cambridge, 1936), 141–222, 217, and *Collected Papers*, 3 vols. (Cambridge, 1911), 3:321–404.

27. A cause of much distress to the Municipal Corporation Commissioners of the 1830s; see Maitland, *Township and Borough*, 12–13.

28. Maitland, "Trust and Corporation," 217.

29. Kent, *Charter*, 108. Kent's explanation for this "singular" occurrence was twofold: the influence of Governor Montgomerie, "a man of integrity and moderation," and the partiality of King James "for a province of which, as Duke of York, he was the proprietary."

30. To Recorder Treby, the fact that Magna Charta had confirmed the liberties and privileges of London but not the "being" of the corporation, demonstrated that that "being" was beyond confirmation. Unlike other cities, London had existed "time out of mind" and was beyond the reach of an action in the nature of a *quo warranto* (8 *Howell's State Trials* 1039, 1144). On the other side Soliciter Finch argued, "Where all the franchises of a corporation are forfeited, what is the corporation? Truly, it is nothing, it is but a name" (ibid., 1090). On this substantive issue, the results of the case were ambiguous. According to one modern account, the charter controversy ended in a partial victory for a "concession theory" of corporate existence, the basis of which was the claim that "all privileges and property belonged to the King, and that only he can concede the right to them" (Levin, *Charter Controversy*, 77;

To New York City, this issue was moot. New York City had an identifiable beginning. No one claimed that its property was anything but a "concession" from the crown. Still, its charter was property and therefore definitive of its personality. Thus autonomy could be defined (and limited) by a charter with unquestionable authority as a determinant and a boundary.

In any case, the language used in the Montgomerie Charter of 1730 remained as a direct legacy of the charter controversies of the 1680s. The last five pages of the document declared that the crown would never sue New York City in an action *quo warranto*. The properties granted by the charter were held in fee simple absolute, beyond the reach of attacks for misuse; the city was free to use them as it pleased. Nor would the city's claim to other properties, however acquired and however used by the corporation, trigger action by central authorities. The charter assured the city of the same autonomy enjoyed by an eighteenth-century English borough—an institution whose properties were sacrosanct. "By these presents," by the various grants of property contained in the charter, the charter drafters proposed to constitute New York City as "a free City of itself."[31] Unlike London, the city of New York could never have claimed perpetual existence as a basis of legitimacy, for it had an identifiable point of origin. But it no longer needed to assert the "antient" quality of its privileges. In the wake of the Glorious Revolution, rights granted by the crown in a formal charter would be sufficient to make New York "a free city of itself."

This is not to say that there were not important theoretical and practical limitations on the autonomy of the corporation. The charter cannot be read as a complete grant of governmental power. In a variety of ways, the city of New York remained dependent on the provincial government. Two limitations in particular should be mentioned: the governor retained the right to appoint the mayor and the recorder, and the provincial legislature was the only body capable of ordering direct taxation. In the first case one must presume that retention of the power of appointment by the governor was intended as a limitation on the autonomy of the city, as a way of retaining external control; indeed, the petition by the Common Council to Montgomerie for a new charter in 1730 specifically asked for the power to elect a mayor.

The second limitation presents a more ambiguous picture. On the one

---

8 *Howell's State Trials*, 1039, 1102, 1159. See also Maitland, "Trust and Corporation"; and "Moral Personality and Legal Personality," *Selected Essays*, 223–39, and *Collected Papers*, 3:304–20; Otto Von Gierke, *Natural Law and the Theory of Society, 1500 to 1800*, ed. Earnest Barker [Cambridge, 1934]; Sidney Webb and Beatrice Webb, *The Manor and the Borough*, 12 vols. [1908; reprint, London, 1963], 1:267, 272).

31. *Colonial Laws*, 2:635–39, 597.

hand, it is hard to imagine a more direct denial of local autonomy than for a central authority to retain absolute control of taxation. On the other hand, until the 1760s, direct taxation was only rarely used by the corporation as a revenue source.[32] On four occasions between 1731 and 1750 the need for revenue was so great that city officials had to seek authorization from the legislature to lay a tax.[33] Rents and other corporate revenues were usually sufficient for the purpose of municipal governance, and we might guess that the existence of a "freely disposable income" from the properties granted it gave the corporation concrete affirmation of its autonomous status within the province.[34]

Still, in many respects the city remained the "political child of the province."[35] Authorization to repair streets or build new ones came from the provincial legislature, as did a variety of police regulations; ferriage rates and other rate structures were usually set outside the city. The Mayor's Court, which might have retained a separate style of decision making, had become simply a court of common pleas for the city by the 1730s. Its decisions and practices were largely indistinguishable from those of other county courts elsewhere in the province.[36]

It is not at all clear if city officials regarded these two limitations as restrictions on their freedom. It appears that most of the provincial legislation that affected city practice was passed at the instigation of the representatives from the city. There is, moreover, a growing recognition among historians of colonial New York that from the time that English control of the province was secured New York City dominated the political life of the province.[37] Still, it is undoubtedly true that the government of the city was closely integrated with the general governance of the province. The autonomy granted by the charter was always partial and incomplete.

The very political theory that joined property with political autonomy also placed limits on that connection. Property gave a corporation the right to control its own affairs free from systematic external interference. But that autonomy was always derivative and dependent. Property rights did not justify disobedience. To the contrary, John Locke had written "that

32. George William Edwards, *New York as an Eighteenth Century Municipality: Part II, 1731–1776* (New York, 1917), 197–99.

33. *Colonial Laws*, 2:1061–63; 3:158–62, 542, 619–20.

34. Maitland, *Township and Borough*, 24–25.

35. Jacob Judd, "New York: Municipality and Province," in Judd and Polishook, eds., *Aspects of Early New York Society and Politics*, 2.

36. Herbert A. Johnson, "The Advent of Common Law in Colonial New York," in George A. Bilias, ed., *Law and Authority in Colonial America* (New York, 1965), 83; see generally Richard Morris, ed., *Selected Cases of the Mayor's Court of New York City* (New York, 1935).

37. See Robert C. Ritchie, *The Duke's Province* (Chapel Hill, 1977).

every man that has any possessions or enjoyment of any part of the dominions of any government does thereby give his tacit consent and is as far forth obliged to obedience to the laws of that government, during such enjoyment, as anyone under it."[38] New York City may have been a "free city of itself," but it was "of itself" only in relation to those areas of governance defined by its property rights. Even there, its dominion could never be severed from the intermittent interference of central authority.

On the other hand, the eighteenth-century chartered city of New York was not a municipal corporation, at least not as we would understand the term today. In his classic discussion of New York City as an eighteenth-century municipality, George William Edwards had written: "But we must remember that as an eighteenth-century municipality it was merely an agent of the provincial government, devised, as Goodnow aptly says, 'for the discharge of those functions interesting the state government which demanded local treatment.' It is therefore always necessary to be mindful of this dependent position of a municipal corporation as we view its relations to the provincial government."[39]

He was mistaken. Occasional intervention by the province did not define the nature of the corporation. Property did. The property rights of the eighteenth-century city were not tangential to the nature of the institution. As defined and described in the Montgomerie Charter, they are what constituted its corporate personality. Today we may believe it possible to distinguish governmental from nongovernmental institutions according to the use and ownership of property. In the eighteenth century, such a task was complicated by the peculiar presence of propertied "governmental" corporations, like the mayor, aldermen, and commonalty of the city of New York.

38. John Locke, *The Second Treatise on Government* (London, 1690), §119.
39. Edwards, *New York*, 34.

CHAPTER 3

The Business of City Government

In 1730 the estate of the corporation of the city of New York included all of the "waste and common" lands of Manhattan Island, the land lying under water surrounding the settled city up to four hundred feet beyond low-water mark, much of the shoreline of what is now Brooklyn, and the ferry franchise between the city and Long Island. All of this property, and more, the city owned in fee simple without restrictions on use or fiduciary obligations to any public beneficiary. The absolute right of every legal owner of property to hold it against all others—the Englishman's right celebrated by Blackstone in the *Commentaries*—was not limited to private persons. Municipal corporations throughout Great Britain "had as sacred and undoubted a right to retain the property legally vested in them as the Lord of a Manor or the purchaser of a freehold."[1]

Earlier students of the institutional history of eighteenth-century New York have regarded the property acquired under the city's charters as important only for the revenue it provided for the administration of city affairs. In so doing, they underestimated the important role that corporate property played in creating distinctive forms of municipal governance. The need for new revenue surely is one explanation of the Common Council's decision to apply for new grants in a new charter in the 1720s.[2] The income from the corporate property assumed a significant place in municipal finances throughout the prerevolutionary period: making taxes little needed until the 1750s, keeping the tax rate low thereafter, and giving the

1. Sidney Webb and Beatrice Webb, *The Manor and the Borough*, 2 vols. (1908; reprint, London, 1963), 2:733–34. See Douglas Hay, "Property, Authority, and the Criminal Law," in Hay, et al., *Albion's Fatal Tree* (New York, 1975), 17–64.

2. During the decade before the reception of the Montgomerie Charter the revenue of the city declined from a high of 731 pounds in 1722 to an average well below 300 pounds. See David T. Valentine, "Financial History of the City of New York, from the Earliest Period," in *Manual of the Corporation of the City of New-York* (New York, 1859), 506. It was a perception that only a new charter could provide new revenue for the corporation that seems to have spurred the Common Council to apply to the governor of the province.

city ready collateral whenever it needed to borrow funds.[3] But the existence of freely disposable income scarcely exhausts the uses of property in the life of the corporation. The estate of the city also provided a means for planning, growth, and innovation unavailable to unchartered and unpropertied local governments. The relative autonomy created by the Montgomerie Charter and its predecessors was not meant simply as protection from external interference. It also liberated the city from the commitment to a status quo that characterized most local governments in provincial America.[4] The property rights of the Montgomerie Charter were granted in pursuit of the goal of creating a major seaport in New York City. In protecting the corporation of the city of New York from the harm of externally imposed change, the charter also encouraged internally instituted innovation.

In arguing that the corporate estate of the city was a significant tool of local governance, I would separate the institutional history of eighteenth-century New York City from two major interpretations of the history of the American city. One interpretation, closely identified with the writings of Sam Bass Warner, asserts that the history of the American city has always been shaped by a culture of privatism. American cities were the products neither of community planning nor of public initiative but of the individual decisions of individualistic Americans: "The physical forms of American cities, their lots, houses, factories, and streets have been the outcome of a real estate market of profit-seeking builders, land speculators, and large investors."[5] Government always has been inadequate; indeed, it usually has been irrelevant to the main processes of growth and change. Even before the Revolution, Warner argues, the domain of public action was limited and separated from the economic life of the American city.

3. The most complete and reliable account of the finances of the eighteenth-century city is George William Edwards, *New York as an Eighteenth Century Municipality: Part II, 1731–1776* (New York, 1917), 190–205. Edwards (191) offers a table of the returns from the revenue properties and franchises of the corporation. Slightly different figures for 1740 appear in Valentine, *Manual*, 507.

Although Edwards was at pains to argue the case for the growing dependence of the city on tax powers that could be delegated only by the provincial legislature, even he conceded that "for many years the returns from the revenue-bearing properties and franchises of the corporation were barely sufficient to meet expenses." See also Edward D. Durand, *The Finances of New York City* (New York, 1898), 7–40; George E. Black, *Municipal Ownership of Land on Manhattan Island* (New York, 1891); and Sidney Pomerantz, *New York: An American City* (Port Washington; N.Y., 1965).

4. See Chapter 6.

5. Sam B. Warner, *The Private City: Philadelphia in Three Periods of Its Growth* (Philadelphia, 1968), 4.

By contrast, another interpretation, most recently restated by Jon Teaford, views the early American city as a reflection of the regulatory traditions and practices of the medieval English borough. The chartered corporation was introduced into the colonies as a way of controlling and fostering commercial life. Until the Revolution, American city government—with the exception of the unchartered "town" of Boston—had no proper sphere beyond the regulation of economic activity.[6]

These two interpretations offer dramatically different perspectives on America's urban past.[7] They converge, however, in their general picture of mid-eighteenth-century urban governance. According to Teaford, the spread of libertarianism during the middle years of the eighteenth century weakened the regulatory control of municipal corporations and necessitated a partial withdrawal by urban authorities from their traditional fields of primary authority. In a few cases their attention shifted to newer areas of health and safety regulation and public works. But in other cases municipal corporations "reacted to change with lethargy and indifference."[8] The middle of the eighteenth century should, therefore, be regarded as a transitional period, when urban government was separated from an increasingly private market economy but had not yet fixed on a modern conception of its role in urban life.

Warner undoubtedly would agree with that characterization of eighteenth-century practice, although he sees the absence of a proper public role as a more or less permanent feature of American cities. The Philadelphia of revolutionary America that is his model of a "private city" had "a regime of little government. Both in form and function the town's government advertised the lack of concern for public management of the community. The municipal corporation of Philadelphia, copied from the forms of an old English borough, counted for little. . . . By modern standards the town was hardly governed at all."[9] Teaford and Warner agree that the

6. Jon Teaford, *The Municipal Revolution in America* (Chicago, 1965). One finds here strong echoes of the perspective of the institutional studies of urban government that flourished in the early twentieth century. See, for example, Robert F. Seybold, *The Colonial Citizen of New York City: A Comparative Study of Certain Aspects of Citizenship Practice in Fourteenth Century England and Colonial New York City* (Madison, 1918).

7. According to Teaford, the postrevolutionary era witnessed the triumph of a "public welfare" theory of urban governance, which entirely eclipsed the earlier commercial focus of the premodern chartered corporation. Warner, more pessimistic, argues that there is a depressing continuity in a culture of privatism in American urban history. A moment's reflection suggests that both positions might be—and probably are—equally true as perspectives on our urban past.

8. Teaford, *Municipal Revolution*, 56.

9. Warner, *Private City*, 10.

chartered corporate governments of early modern America were fast becoming—or had already become—anachronisms irrelevant to the communities they were presumably intended to serve.

Philadelphia provides the model of eighteenth-century corporate government for both historians. Teaford, for whom the shape of municipal activity is largely defined by rulemaking, found Philadelphia's failure revealed in the fact that between 1740 and 1776 the corporation of that city passed only one new ordinance. Municipal authorities cared only about the management of their corporate property. The "closed" corporation became increasingly inbred and distanced from the concerns of Philadelphia's inhabitants. Warner implies that a negative judgment ought to be balanced against the manifest ability of most city dwellers to get along nicely with very little government.[10] Both of their accounts, as well as other studies of prerevolutionary Philadelphia, make it clear that in those few instances when government activity was needed, Philadelphians looked not to the corporation but to statutory authorities established by the provincial legislature to take charge of the vital affairs of the community. Or they looked to voluntary associations such as fire companies and libraries. The corporation survived, but "decade by decade it lived through a metamorphosis into a kind of chamber of commerce for the great merchants of Philadelphia."[11]

Warner and Teaford may have correctly identified features of Philadelphia's corporate life that typified eighteenth-century American municipal behavior. In several respects, however, the government of New York City was very different from that of Philadelphia. New York's corporation remained inextricably identified with the city it was chartered to govern. Whereas the "closed" corporation of Philadelphia effectively excluded most residents of the city from participation in its affairs, the Montgomerie Charter made the corporation of the city of New York into a classically "open" organization. Anyone might be admitted as a freeman, a politically active member of the corporation.[12] In 1731 the cost of becoming a freeman of the city was set at three pounds for merchants or shopkeepers and twenty shillings for craftsmen, but the Common Council could and did

10. Teaford, *Municipal Revolution*, 56–59.

11. Judith M. Diamondstone, "The Government of Eighteenth-Century Philadelphia," in Bruce Daniels, ed., *Town and Country* (Middleton, Conn., 1978), 238–63, 249; Diamondstone, "Philadelphia's Municipal Corporation, 1701–1776," *Pennsylvania Magazine of History and Biography* 90 (1966): 183–201.

12. Milton M. Klein, "Democracy and Politics in Colonial New York," in *The Politics of Diversity* (Port Washington, N.Y., 1974), 20–25; Beverly McAnear, "The Place of the Freeman in Old New York," *New York History* 21 (1940): 418–30; Edward F. Countryman, *A People in Revolution* (Baltimore, 1981), 55–67, 72–98.

grant the privilege gratis to residents who could not pay.[13] The result was that in New York City "the commonalty" of the corporation became in effect the entire populace of the city, or at least the white male populace, whereas in Philadelphia "the commonalty" of the corporation was a distinct community, a particular identifiable elite, within the larger city.

Throughout the eighteenth century, moreover, the corporation of New York remained the government of all aspects of city life subject to public control. There were no statutory authorities; most voluntary associations were under corporation sponsorship. When public action was necessary, it occurred under the auspices of the corporation, or it did not occur at all. Well into the nineteenth century, New Yorkers could speak of "our Corporation" when they referred to the government of their city.[14] The separation of government from corporation that characterized eighteenth-century Philadelphia occurred much later in New York City.

The issue is not the marginal differences between Philadelphia and New York City but how to characterize corporate government in eighteenth-century America. Was New York City "a regime of little government" like Warner's Philadelphia, or was it a regime whose government can only be understood if we put aside our conventional expectations about the nature of a public sphere?

Teaford has used what he calls a "content analysis" of ordinances to argue that there was a moderate decline in the emphasis on commercial regulation in cities throughout provincial America. By his calculations, 54 percent of New York City's ordinances dealt with trade or commerce in 1707, but 47.6 percent did so in 1773.[15] But all forms of legislative activity—and eighteenth-century ordinances in particular—have weaknesses when used to define the concerns of a government institution.[16] Tea-

13. *Minutes of the Common Council of the City of New York, 1675–1776*, 8 vols. (New York, 1905), 4:96–97 (1731), for the equivalent rates for 1702 and 1751, see ibid., 2:198–99, and 5:326; hereafter *MCC*.

14. See Charles Rosenberg, *The Cholera Years* (Chicago, 1962), 17. This is not to deny that eighteenth-century New Yorkers could distinguish their individual interests from that of the corporation whenever the two diverged. Nor should this statement be taken as denying the class conflict that underlay the rhetoric of "our" corporation. See Countryman, *A People in Revolution*, and Gary B. Nash, *The Urban Crucible: Social Change, Political Consciousness, and the Origins of the American Revolution* (Cambridge, Mass., 1979).

15. Teaford, *Municipal Revolution*, 18–52.

16. Teaford's expectation that an analysis of the subject matter of ordinances would reveal the nature of a corporation is, I think, flawed as a research strategy. First, legislative activity is inherently ambiguous. Is legislation passed because legislators feel the need to act in a particular area or is legislation passed as a substitute for action, as a form of symbolic politics? The fact that Philadelphia passed almost no new ordinances between 1740 and 1776 might as easily be evidence for the effectiveness of its regulatory structure as for Teaford's presump-

ford's statistics understate the disinterest of the midcentury Common Council of New York City in commercial regulation. If one looks at the minutes of the council—the record of its ordinary activity—it becomes apparent that trade regulation consumed a minuscule proportion of its work time. Of some 97 entries in 1737, no more than 9 can in any way be characterized as dealing with the regulation of trade and commerce; and in 4 of those entries it is unclear whether the measures ordered by the council were intended to achieve the goals of promotion or control of economic life in the city or were intended for some other governmental purpose.[17] Similarly, in 1767 only 11 of 157 entries had anything to do with commercial regulation[18] (see Table 3.1).

Indeed, we may wonder if the "medieval" notion of a city as a monopolistic, commercial community had any legal significance in the life of the corporation of the city of New York after the reception of the Montgomerie Charter. The members of the Common Council made no attempt to preserve city trade for city residents, much to the dismay of local retailers —particularly butchers and fresh produce vendors—who felt victimized by the "Country People" who rented stalls in the city markets and undersold the local competition.[19] Even the oath given to newly admitted freemen soon came to reflect a more open vision of the political community. In 1707 the Common Council authorized a version that closely paralleled a

---

tion of a quiescent government. There is, moreover, no way to learn anything from Teaford's narrative about enforcement patterns. Is legislation passed because it is expected to validate ideological presuppositions of what a municipal corporation ought to be doing? It might be, in fact, that the bylaws of the corporations Teaford has studied reveal the survival of an archaic ideology of a commercial community long after the actual practice of local government in those communities had changed in dramatic ways. Second, reliance on ordinances creates the false impression that the proper business of a government is necessarily some form of regulation. For Teaford the history of the municipal corporation in America is one of the choice between trade regulation and health and safety regulation. But it is equally possible that government might be concerned with different questions or, more precisely, might be pursuing governmental ends through nonregulatory techniques. Teaford's methodology forces him to consider that which is nonregulatory in the affairs of an eighteenth-century corporation as almost necessarily nongovernmental.

17. *MCC*, 4:361–410 (1737). In entries that were ambiguous I allocated half values between categories in Table 3.1.

18. Ibid., 7:51–105 (1767).

19. See Petition of Israel Harsfield, Timothy Harsfield, Richard Green and other Butchers, Petition File, 1735, Municipal Archives and Record Center, New York; hereafter MARC. The solution offered by the Common Council was to give resident butchers a discount rent for their market stalls. One reason why the city stopped trying to exclude nonresidents from its economic life was that a growing number of residents depended on the trade of the nonresidents. Whenever restrictions against country people were too stringent, there would be complaints that the regulation depressed business. See Petition for Francis Koffler, an innkeeper who farmed the ferry, Petition File, 1766.

TABLE 3.1. *Entries into the Minutes of the Common Council by Subject Matter, 1737 and 1767*

	1737	1767
Total entries in year*	97	157
Property (management, supervision enforcement of corporate estate)	13[†]	25.5[†]
Trade or commercial regulations	7	9.5[†]
Public (noncommercial) regulations	8[†]	8[†]
Appointments, licenses		
commercial	3	4[†]
noncommercial	4	2
Payment of accounts, salaries, and other bills of the corporation	37	88
Taxes and audits of the fiscal affairs of the corporation	4	7.5
Certification of elections and swearing in of officers (also the appointment of the mayor, high sheriff, and coroner by the provincial governor)	19	9
Other business	4	4

Source: *Minutes of the Common Council of the City of New York, 1675–1776*, 8 vols. (New York, 1905).

*The beginning of 1737 is taken as January 1, 1736/7. The total number of entries does not equal the disaggregated sums because in each of the years analyzed there were one or two entries in which two distinct orders were made by the Common Council.

[†]Counts in these categories include "half-entries" in cases where the intent of the Common Council was ambiguous. Examples include orders to clean slips (public regulation/commercial regulation), leasing of the market house (property management/commercial regulation), or repair of the ferry.

fourteenth-century London oath.[20] Among other things, it ordered the new freeman to warn the mayor whenever he heard of "Forreigners" (or nonresidents) buying or selling within the city boundaries, forbade him from suing any other freeman of the city in a court outside of the city, and prescribed the terms under which he would take and care for appren-

20. Seybold, *Colonial Citizen*, 20–23.

tices.[21] In 1731, after the reception of the new charter, the council drew up an oath eliminating all references to the commercial life of the city and to the particular significance of city boundaries in establishing a commercial community.[22] The city as a government was separated from older perceptions of a city as an economic unit. And this latter version remained the "oath" of the city throughout the prerevolutionary period.

There remained a rhetorical identification of the corporation with the commercial life of the city. Petitions to the Common Council usually justified requests for varieties of commercial franchises by referring to the commitment to commercial growth that united the members of the corporation.[23] As Teaford suggests, there are some indications of a new rhetorical concern for public health and safety regulation in the records of the period.[24] Still, the desire for regulation—whether for public health or commerce—should not be exaggerated. Questions of "public," noncommercial regulation were raised no more frequently before the Common Council than were questions of commercial regulation. In both 1737 and in 1767 the minutes of the council record only nine entries even arguably concerned with health and safety.

It is clear that by 1730 the corporation of the city of New York could not be defined as the embodiment of a commercial community. Neither was it a public welfare agency on the order of a nineteenth-century municipal corporation. What, then, was its proper business? How may its concerns be described?

From the perspective of the citizens of the city who petitioned the corporation the answer was unmistakable. The proper business of the corporation was the management, care, and disposal of the real estate it owned. Approximately 60 percent of the petitions consulted in my research concerned the property rights of the corporation. Between 1765 and 1767 the

21. New York Historical Society, *Collections* 18 (1885):460–61.

22. *MCC*, 4:121 (1731). On the failure of earlier attempts to enforce trade restrictions, see Klein, "Democracy and Politics in Colonial New York," 21.

23. For example, a petition by individuals living near Burling's Slip asked the council to exclude "sea vessels" from the slip in order to leave room for smaller trading boats. The petitioners argued: "That as the rising Grandeur and the Riches of this City must entirely depend upon the Successful Traffic of its Inhabitants. Your Petitioners humbly conceive it to be the true Interest of the Public that every Individual in whatsoever Branch of Trade and Business should meet with due Encouragement in his Labour" (Petition of Sundry Persons dwelling and residing and being owners of the Houses and Lots of Ground near and adjacent to Burling's Slip, Petition File, 1766; see also Petition of the Inhabitants of Crown Street, Petition File, 1767). Other petitions justified the request for a particular privilege or exemption noting that commercial "advantage to this City" would be the inevitable result (Petition of Cornelius Van Vorst, Petition File, 1765).

24. Petition of Joseph Simson, Petition File, 1755.

figure rose to nearly 75 percent.[25] Petitioners requested abatement of their
rents to the corporation,[26] a new lease,[27] the right to farm the ferry.[28] The
Reformed Protestant Dutch Church asked for a lot in the commons because its present cemetery was full.[29] Merchants and others on occasion
sought permission to clean or improve or repair or "encroach" on some
piece of city property, usually a pier or a slip.[30]

Most of all, petitions to the Common Council revolved around requests
to the corporation for grants of waterlots, that is, grants of the land under
water surrounding the settled part of the city up to four hundred feet beyond low-water mark. Petitioners "inclined to make considerable improvements"[31] to those waterlots asked for grants on terms detailed in the
next chapter. But petitions for waterlots were frequently followed by
counterpetitions that attempted to dissuade the council from making a
particular grant to a particular individual or set of individuals. Counterpetitions might argue that the corporation was violating its own customary
procedures for making grants, "that the Custom and Practice of this Corporation with Respect to granting their Water Lotts, so far as the Peti-

25. These percentages are based on a reading of all petitions in the Municipal Archives
files for the years 1735–37, 1745–47, 1755–57, and 1765–67.

26. Petition of Francis Koffler, Petition File, 1766.

27. Petition of John Kelly (slaughterhouse), Petition File, 1736; Petition of Jacobus Rick-
man (room in commons for brick kiln), Petition File, 1747; Petition of Isaac Delameter
(small house), Petition File, 1756; Petition of Nicholas Bayard (slaughterhouse), Petition
File, 1767.

28. Petition of Cornelius Van Vorst, Petition File, 1766.

29. Petition of the Minister *et al* of the Reformed Protestant Dutch Church, Petition File,
1766; see also Petition of the Minister *et al* of the English Presbyterian Church, ibid.

30. Petition of William Cornell, lessee of ferry, Petition File, 1737; Petition of sundry individuals living near Clark's Slip, ibid.; Petition that the encroachment made by Robert
Munro on the slip may be permitted to continue, as it is more convenient, Petition File,
1766.

31. See Petition of Jacob Brewerton, Petition File, 1765. See also Petition of Elizabeth
Richards and others, who presented on 22 May 1761 "that their houses front that part of the
East River Commonly called Hunter's Bay which has become a great Nuisance by the Settlement therein of all kinds of Garbage, Filth and Dirt . . . and that the water between the East
and West Piers is become so shallow as to render the same useless and greatly detrimental to
the Health of the Petitioners . . . and therefore conceived that the filling up the same Water
lots would greatly add to the Ornament of the City as well as the conveniency of the Harbor,
prayed that the said Mayor Aldermen and Commonalty would be favourably pleased to grant
to them the said water lots so far into the said East River as the Present Wharfs on the East
and West sides extend under such reasonable rents etc. as should be thought fit and reasonable." Elizabeth Richards was one of several active women merchants who sought and secured waterlots during this period. See the Corporation Grant to Elizabeth Sharpas, spinster,
23 August 1739, Grant Book B, MARC; see also Jean P. Jordan, "Women Merchants in Colonial New York," *New York History* 58 (1977):412–39.

tioners are Acquainted therewith, has ever been to give the Preference to those, who held the Lotts fronting the River."[32] Or the counterpetition might set out a claim of title in theory superior to that of the original petitioner(s).[33] The point is not that these petitions should determine our sense of the nature of the eighteenth-century corporation. Rather, they demonstrate what part of the business of the corporation provoked the interest—more precisely, the self-interest—of its citizens.[34] It was the property of the corporation, not its economic regulatory powers or its public welfare regulatory powers, that claimed the attention of eighteenth-century New Yorkers.

In keeping with that congruity of interest that characterized the relations between New York City residents and their corporation, the minutes of the Common Council also reflect a continuing preoccupation with the management of the corporate estate. In both 1737 and 1767, property decisions were much the most important substantive area of council concern. If we ignore or set aside the routine, nondiscretionary business of the corporation (such as entries in the minutes for warrants to the mayor to pay the accounts and the salaries owed by the corporation, for raising taxes and auditing accounts, and for certification of elections and the swearing in of officers), it is evident just how important the corporate estate was in the work of the corporation. In 1737, fully one-third of all the discretionary entries in the minutes dealt with property owned by the corporation; in 1767 nearly half of these entries were so concerned. Neither trade regulation nor public (noncommercial) regulation or other action constituted more than one-fifth of the discretionary business of the council. If the minutes of the Common Council are to be believed, the concerns of a property owner best defined the business of the corporation of the city of New York.

This description of the corporation at first glance seems very similar to Teaford's picture of Philadelphia in the years before the American Revolution. His Philadelphia was a city government that "neglected both the traditional tasks of trade regulation and the newer duties of safety and public works" in order to concentrate its efforts on managing corporate properties. In so doing, according to Teaford, the corporation of Philadelphia ig-

32. Petition of Owners of lots in Montgomery and Out Ward, Petition File, 1765. There were limits to the protests the council would entertain. Mr. Brownjohn protested against the corporation appropriating a waterlot fronting his lot for the use of a slip, to which the council responded, "This Board conceiving the same to be an insolent and impertinent paper did thereupon unanimously resolve and ORDER that the same be thrown under the table and the same is thrown under the table accordingly" (*MCC*, 7:27 [1766]).

33. See the various petitions protesting the waterlots proposed to be distributed in "rotten row" in 1766, Petition File, 1766.

34. See also the controversy over waterlots conducted in the *Independent Reflector* in 1753 (Milton Klein, ed., *The Independent Reflector* [Cambridge, Mass., 1959], 118–27, 151–56).

nored its governmental responsibilities.[35] Likewise, the corporation of the city of New York appears to have devoted an inordinate amount of time to its corporate—private—property. But in New York the "obsession" with corporate property did not lead to a separation of the concerns of the community from those of the corporation. A paradox? Why did New Yorkers regard as their legitimate government an institution whose attention was firmly fixed on its own private property interests?

One could argue that New Yorkers of the time wanted a lethargic and neglectful government or, alternatively, that we—and not the corporation of the city of New York—have neglected its true governmental functions. Both perspectives may be true. It may be that New Yorkers preferred at least a version of Warner's "private city." But without losing sight of the commitment of city leaders to private economic growth, another perspective demands our attention here, a perspective that views the management of a corporate estate as a mode of public planning and governance. Such a vision insists that we put aside later assumptions as to the irreconcilability of property concerns with government action and as to what constitutes the proper business of a public institution. The corporation of the city of New York spent most of its time managing its property; yet it remained the government of the city. What we need to understand is how property offered the city of New York a legitimated structure of action within the constraints of Anglo-American political and legal theory.[36]

35. Teaford, *Municipal Revolution*, 56.

36. In demonstrating that there were public purposes that shaped the management of New York's corporate estate all that might be shown is its distinctiveness and isolation within the world of eighteenth-century local government. That may be the case, although in the absence of studies of the use (or disuse) of corporate property in other cities of colonial America, I wonder. It is possible that New York's Dutch heritage separates its history from the rest of provincial America. There was, after all, a strong tradition in Holland of public, municipal investment. See Jan de Vries, "Barges and Capitalism: Passenger Transportation in the Dutch Economy, 1632–1839," *A.A.B. Bijdragen* 21 (1978): 33–398. But some historians of English local government also stress the importance of corporate property in the life of eighteenth-century English corporations. François Vigier, *Change and Apathy* (Cambridge, Mass., 1970), offers a case study of a relatively "activist" use of property in Liverpool. The other, more common image of corporate lethargy and quiescence can be found in Robert W. Greaves, *The Corporation of Leicester, 1689–1836* (Leicester, 1970), and Malcolm I. Thomis, *Politics and Society in Nottingham, 1785–1835* (London, 1969).

CHAPTER 4

Planning by Granting

In the forty-five years between the reception of the Montgomerie Charter and the beginning of the American Revolution, disposing of the waterlots of lower New York City was unquestionably the major property-related concern of the officers of the corporation.[1] Indeed, insofar as property management properly characterized the government of the prerevolutionary city, a waterlot grant should be regarded as an appropriate symbol of that government. The waterlots were the only new property granted to the city under the 1730 charter, and it appears that their absence was the main reason why the members of the Common Council decided to seek a new charter in the 1720s. The first time the "need" for a new charter is mentioned in the minutes of the council was in 1722, after Gerritt Van Horne petitioned the governor of the province for a grant of "all the land that may be Gained out of the East River [between Maiden Lane Slip and the end of Wall Street] . . . to extend into the Said River two hundred foot with Liberty to Erect Buildings, Cranes, Stairs, etc. And to Receive the Profits and Wharfage thereof." The Common Council remonstrated to the governor as to "the great prejudice the Granting thereof may be to the Publick in General and this Corporation in Particular," and then decided that it had better itself petition for a new charter that would include a grant of all the land that might be gained out of the harbor, plus "Such other Privileges Franchises and Immunities as are Usually Granted to Cities and Towns Corporate in England."[2] In every petition thereafter the waterlots headed the wish list of the corporation.[3] And as soon as the new charter was secured and confirmed, the council set about the difficult business of granting away the lands under water and the right to develop the waterfront of the growing city.[4]

1. See for example, *Minutes of the Common Council of the City of New York, 1675–1776*, 8 vols. (New York, 1905), 4:25–211, for the years 1731 to 1734; hereafter *MCC*.
2. Ibid., 3:271–78 (1722). The origins of this conflict began in 1719–20 (3:221 [1720]).
3. Ibid., 4:5–8, 19–22 (1730).
4. The centrality of waterlots in the plans of the corporation is underscored by the fact

Still, a waterlot grant might seem to be a peculiar focus for a discussion of planning and governance in an eighteenth-century corporation. The process of disposing of the most valuable property owned by the corpora-tion at nominal quitrents perhaps ought rather to be regarded as the an-tithesis of active governmental planning. The disposal of the waterfronts of New York City bears a suspicious resemblance to the disposal of the public domain by the federal government during the nineteenth century, which students of American history still learn delivered up the develop-ment of the West to private speculator control. And historians of New York City usually judge the waterlot grants made by the eighteenth-century corporation in similarly harsh terms, when they regard them at all. John W. Reps, the leading historian of American city planning, sees eighteenth-century New York City as a prime example of an unplanned city.[5] George W. Edwards concluded that the city acted "with utter dis-regard for the future" in allowing its rich riparian rights to fall into the hands of private individuals.[6] Another historian speculates: "Perhaps the government simply anticipated New York's growth by abandoning in ad-vance any influence over it."[7]

Historians tend to consider these grants as typifying the corruption of the corporation—an earlier version of the shame of the city.[8] Based on a 1753 "exposé" in William Livingston's *Independent Reflector*, waterlot grants are seen as nothing but a series of "shady land deal[s] by which some local businessmen, in collusion with the City Council, planned to get valuable shoreline property for a song."[9] A letter with commentary in that paper revealed a series of transactions by which council members were to receive grants to waterlots at low prices without public bidding. The as-serted justification was that because the council members owned lots fronting waterlots they therefore owned the preemptive right to purchase those waterlots whenever the city decided to convey them. As Livingston

that Van Horne was bribed to withdraw his petition to the governor with a promise that when a new charter was obtained he would get a four-hundred-foot lot instead of the two-hundred-foot lot he had petitioned for (ibid., 25 [1730]). The promise was fulfilled in 1734 (211 [1734]). See also Corporation Grant to Cornelius Van Horne, 26 July 1734, Grant Book B, Municipal Archives and Records Center, New York; hereafter MARC. It appears that Van Horne was the only grantee throughout the prerevolutionary period to receive a lot that ex-tended more than two hundred feet into the river.

5. John W. Reps, *The Making of Urban America* (Princeton, 1965), 150–54.
6. George William Edwards, *New York as an Eighteenth Century Municipality: Part II, 1731–1776* (New York, 1917), 150.
7. Josef W. Konwitz, *Cities and the Sea: Port City Planning in Early Modern Europe* (Bal-timore, 1978), 65.
8. Edwards, *New York*, 150–51; Milton Klein, Introduction, in Klein, ed., *The Indepen-dent Reflector* (Cambridge, Mass., 1959), 30; Carl Bridenbaugh, *Cities in Revolt*, rev. ed. (New York, 1970), 39.
9. Klein, Introduction, 30.

noted, it was "incredible" that a majority of the council "should join in so iniquitous a Concession." After all, "Does Contiguity of Land infer a Right?" The making of waterlot grants was nothing but an institutionalized abuse of power, a way for corrupt council members to "lavish, in manifest Violation of their Trust, the Property of the City, to enrich and gratify a few Individuals."[10] To label it a form of city planning would be to rob language of meaning.

Yet one may wonder. Those historians who have allowed the *Independent Reflector* to shape their vision of the waterlot grants appear not to have read the grants themselves. Neither have they considered the significance of a later issue of that journal, in which a correspondent argued that the situation revealed in the earlier issue was no exceptional abuse of power: "But further, Sir, excepting a few Instances, it has invariably been the Practice of the Corporation, to grant the Water Lots to particular Petitioners, upon Terms agreed on between them, and not at Vendue [public auction]. In these Grants, the Preference has generally been given to the Proprietors of the Upland, contiguous to the Water Lots." Livingston responded that although he would concede that perhaps the petitioners were not acting improperly in relying on a "common Practice," still they had "no more Colour for pretending, that the Contiguity of their Lands, entitles them to what belongs to the City, than to the lands of any adjoining Neighbors." The expectations created by a common practice did "indeed place the Conduct of the Petitioners in a more favourable Light; but render that of the Corporation . . . the more inexcusable and unjust. Have former Corporations made a Practice of giving the Lands of the City, it should be an Inducement to their Successors, to obliterate the Remembrance of those Transgressions, by a more inviolable Attachment to their Duty."[11]

From the twin perspectives of Whig political theory and a "Blackstonian" theory of property rights founded on the absolute power of a possessor to exclude, Livingston was clearly correct in his general condemnation of the conduct of the corporation.[12] But neither of these views accurately reflected the legal world of eighteenth-century New York City.[13] Whether or not waterlot grant petitioners ought to have presumed that

10. Klein, ed., *Independent Reflector*, 124.

11. Ibid., 153, 155.

12. See Klein, Introduction, 1–50.

13. Nor should it be seen as a direct and accurate reflection of the legal world of eighteenth-century England. See E. P. Thompson, *Whigs and Hunters* (New York, 1976); E. P. Thompson, "The Grid of Inheritance: A Comment," in Jack Goody, Joan Thirsk, and E. P. Thompson, eds., *Family and Inheritance: Rural Society in Western Europe, 1200–1800* (Cambridge, 1976), 328–60; Daniel Boorstin, *The Mysterious Science of the Law* (Cambridge, Mass., 1941).

contiguity created a legitimate interest in the real estate of the city, those with land fronting waterlots certainly did make such a presumption. In their view, sale by public auction would have constituted a deprivation of their own property rights. Practically every successful petition for a water-lot grant was premised on the fact that the petitioner's land fronted on a waterlot.[14]

A long petition to the Common Council in 1765 put the case forcefully for the propriety of a practice of private sale. Those who owned land front-ing the East River, wrote the petitioners, have looked upon their right to purchase the contiguous waterlots as a practice of "long and almost invari-able usage and custom": "[They] have been so far enfluenced by the Con-sideration as to look upon it, like a Sort of unalienable Priviledge belong-ing to their Estates, and hence in their Transfers from one to another, the Price and Value of those Estates, has been by that means, proportionally increased." The petitioners did not mean to imply that the corporation was "bound never to depart from a rule of this Kind"; but they did insist that the council should "be tender of the Rights of Individuals" when the effect of deviating from the "rule" would be to "diminish the Value of every Estate that is now held, under this particular Circumstance."[15]

In effect the petitioners argued that they had a property interest in the water rights owned by the city, perhaps on the order of the right every property owner has to prevent the existence of a nuisance of his or her neighbor's property, or a right of first refusal. But we should be careful not to make this expectancy interest appear more precise than in fact it was. The corporation had the power to appropriate a waterlot to public uses—such as a public slip or dock—without offering any compensation to the contiguous owner.[16] Moreover, if the owner of the frontage was unable or unwilling to take the waterlot on the terms set by the corporation, the Common Council might transfer the right in the waterlot to another, per-haps at public sale.[17] Indeed, it appears that the owner of the frontage

14. Exceptions were when a grant of a waterlot was preceded by a grant of the contiguous land. See, for example, Release of Lot . . . to Anthony Rutgers, 24 July 1766 (of the land between high- and low-water mark), followed immediately by a corporation grant of the waterlot (Grant Book C, MARC).

15. Petition of Sundry Persons & Proprietors of Lotts of Ground situate in Montgomery and the Out Ward of the City of New York—fronting the East River, Petition File, 1765, MARC.

16. See *MCC*, 7:27 (1766). Two petitions from the file of 1766 revealed the fears of some individuals that if all the waterlots were granted away in Rotten Row (which was being devel-oped at that time) there would be no place left for any "public edifice"—for an exchange or a market; both petitions asked that the Common Council reserve space for the use of the public.

17. See ibid., 4:212 (1734), for the Common Council's action on the petition of Jacob

owned nothing personally; the interest was appurtenant to the land he or she held. Even the petitioners quoted in the previous paragraph conceded that their "priviledge" was inalienable.[18]

It is hard to say whether the process of making waterlot grants was corrupt or even to decide what it would have meant in the context of the general political culture of eighteenth-century New York to call the process corrupt.[19] We can assume that the waterlot grants were usually made to the rich and powerful of the city and that in many cases these were also members of the Common Council. Still, the obligations imposed through the terms of those grants were so severe as to make it unlikely that anyone but a relatively rich person would have had an interest in receiving a waterlot grant. More important, even a "corrupt" process may work, may succeed as a planning tool. The problem the granting process was designed to solve was how to expand and develop the port facilities of the city. To understand how waterlot grants functioned to effect goals of commercial expansion and growth, we shall have to put aside juridical questions of the guilt or innocence of corporate grantees and corporate officers and look to the grants themselves: what they conveyed away from the city and what they required of the grantees.[20]

During the prerevolutionary period waterlots were granted out at intermittent and irregular intervals. In 1772 the corporation made twenty-nine waterlot grants. In five other years, fifteen or more grants were made. But

Goelet and Abraham Van Wyck, the executors of Andre Teller. They had petitioned for and been granted a waterlot for the use of Teller's daughter. The grant included a covenant for "Docking Out the same within a Certain Limited time, which Neither the Said Child nor we the Executors are Capable of performing." And the "privilege" of the grant was transferred to Stephan Bayard.

18. In 1766, however, a petition was presented to the corporation by Josiah Smith and others that they had a right to waterlots on "Rotten Row" (where the Common Council was at that time making grants), even though the petitioners no longer owned land fronting the waterlots. They deposed that in conveying away their lands they had explicitly retained their rights to purchase the waterlots severed from the contiguous property (as a kind of easement in gross) (Petition File, 1766). Ultimately, the Common Council did not accept that claim, but evidently enough was thought of the argument to grant the petitioners a special hearing before the council (*MCC*, 7:37–38 [1766]).

19. See Stanley Katz, *Newcastle's New York* (Cambridge, Mass., 1968), and Edward F. Countryman, *A People in Revolution* (Baltimore, 1981), 80–82.

20. The following discussion of the provisions of the waterlot grants conveyed by the corporation is based on a reading of all copies of the grants held by the New York Historical Society (NYHS) (about fifty) and a more selective examination of grants from the official Grant Books (primarily from Books B and C) held in the Municipal Archives and Records Center (MARC). All grants of the corporation, including those found in the New York Historical Society, were recorded in full in the Grant Books of the corporation (A through F) and are arranged in chronological order.

most years the number of grants never exceeded three.[21] Usually grants were made to groups of neighboring landowners.[22] Either the city waited for such groups to come forward with a plan for the development of a particular part of the waterfront, or the corporation developed a plan and then solicited petitions for grants, or the process involved elements of both alternatives. Without more research into the real estate concerns and plans of the city's commercial elite, it is impossible to say where the original impetus for making the grants came from.[23] In any event, the process culminated in a grant that both memorialized the agreement between the corporation and the grantee and constituted the conveyance of the waterlot. The conveyance was recorded in a Grant Book of the corporation, and the grantee received title to the land lying under the water of his grant.

What was conveyed? Typically, a grantee received a lot that extended two hundred feet into the East River[24] from "low-water mark"[25] or (what was usually the same thing) the border of the grantee's own lands. The breadth of the waterlot was determined by the grantee's frontage and ranged from a low of 16 feet to a high of 116 feet.[26] Along with the title, grantees uniformly received the eventual right to charge rent for the use by merchants and shipowners of the docks, wharves, and piers that would be constructed on the lot. This potential rental value—the right to collect dockage, wharfage, pierage, slippage, cranage, and so forth—was the main incentive to apply for a grant. Every conveyance of the city's waterlots hinged on the transfer of the "profits and advantages" that were appurtenant to the lots.

Quitrents for these grants, payable annually on 25 March, could be as little as one peppercorn or as much as eight pounds, five shillings. In general the amount of quitrent was figured on an equal per foot of breadth rate for all grants made in a particular area at a particular time, which might

21. See Corporation of the City of New York, "Corporation Property, 1734–1837," MARC.

22. See the Location Index in Corporation of the City of New York, "Indexes to Water Grants, 1686–1904," MARC.

23. There is nothing in Virginia D. Harrington, *The New York Merchant on the Eve of the Revolution* (New York, 1935), on speculation in city lands. For a later period see Kenneth Wiggins Porter, *John Jacob Astor: Business Man*, 2 vols. (Cambridge, Mass., 1931), 2:910–52.

24. Until after the Revolution, relatively few grants were made along the Hudson because of the fear that ships moored along docks there might be damaged by ice floes.

25. In the wake of the Dongan Charter of 1686, the corporation granted away most of the lots between high- and low-water marks, which as a result had been filled in. "Low-water mark" thus often meant the end of a lot bordering on the river.

26. Corporation Grant to T. Jeffreys, 19 April 1735, Grant Book B, MARC; to S. Farmer, 24 July 1766, Ellison Family Papers, NYHS.

vary from four pence[27] to the high rate of three shillings per foot charged to a group of grantees who received title to grants by Coenties Slip between 1772 and 1775.[28] The quitrents did not constitute the major cost to the grantees, however; no one seems ever to have complained that his or her quitrent was too high, although grantees regularly complained to the Common Council about the burdensome nature of their grants. The actual cost to a purchaser of a waterlot was hidden in a long, complicated, and highly formalized series of provisions that made up the bulk of the grant document.

Along with their lots and their potential profits, grantees accepted a set of restrictive covenants that ran with the land and determined the precise ways in which the real estate would be developed. Satisfying the terms of these covenants was the major consideration paid by grantees. Almost uniformly the city required grantees to build two streets or wharves, one at either end of the length of their lots and each parallel to the river. These streets were to be constructed and paved by the grantees at their own expense, were to be dedicated and applied to the use of the public, and were to be maintained in perpetuity for the benefit of the public and the city by the grantee, his assigns, or heirs.

Additional responsibilities specific to a particular grant usually were added. When in 1758 the corporation granted to Oliver Delancey a large lot on the Hudson in trust for the children of Sir Peter Warren, the deed included covenants for the construction of a forty-foot-wide wharf or street on the inside boundary of the lot, a forty-foot wharf or street on the outside of the lot, a fifteen-foot wharf to run from Cortlandt Street to the river, which would front a slip dedicated to public use to be made and left by Delancey, and two posts that were to be put on the latter wharf twenty feet from one another as an aid for boats docking there. Moreover, it was stipulated that "all profits, fees, perquisites, and Emoluments arising or accruing from the wharf or street" running by the slip "shall be taken and received by the Mayor Aldermen and Commonalty" of the city. These covenants had to be satisfied within seven years or the corporation would repossess the waterlot. Until those terms were entirely satisfied, the children of Sir Peter Warren could not profit from the development of their lot.[29]

27. Corporation Grant to Oliver Delancey, 13 March 1758, Delancey Deeds, NYHS; to Henry Bogart, 15 May 1739, Grant Book B, MARC; to Elizabeth Sharpas, 23 August 1739, ibid.

28. Corporation Grant to Hendrick Remsen, 10 July 1772, NYC Deeds, Box 8, NYHS; to Peter Jay, 10 July 1772, ibid.; to James Van Cortlandt, Augustus Van Cortlandt, and Frederick Van Cortlandt, 3 February 1773, ibid; to Elizabeth Delancey, 29 April 1773, BV Delancey Deeds, 1731–84, NYHS; to Nicholas Gouvernor, 21 March 1775, Gouvernor Family Papers, NYHS.

29. Corporation Grant to Oliver Delancey, 13 March 1758.

Many grants included an obligation to construct a public space in addition to the streets at front and rear that were a part of almost every grant. Frequently the grantee agreed to construct and maintain a public slip, dredge it, and make sure that at all times it would be usable for deepwater ships. All boats were "to have free liberty to load and unload goods, wares, merchandizes" at the slip. And the corporation was to have "all profits, fees, perquisites, and emoluments" arising from the use of the piers or streets that were directly contiguous to the slip.[30] Other grants insisted on the construction of an extra dock, a bulkhead, or a third street.

At times the size and complexity of the "public works" required by the corporation were of such a scale as to necessitate joint enterprise by a group of merchants or neighbors. This was the case in 1772 and 1773, when a number of merchants applied for waterlots on the east side of Coenties Slip.[31] The city insisted that the grant be contingent on the construction of a large and costly "basin," which forced the merchants to develop a formula for distributing the costs of the project. "If Grants . . . should be obtained," wrote the applicants, "it would be necessary for them . . . to raise sundry large sums of Money in order to comply with the Terms upon which such Grants would probably be made and that as some of them . . . would derive a greater Advantage from the said Grants than others and of consequence ought to bear a greater proportion of the Expence," it was decided that the task of ascertaining "the several and respective Proportions of the whole Charge" should be given over to arbitrators. These decided that both the costs of construction and maintenance and the eventual profits (the wharfage) should be divided in proportion to the breadth of the respective lots, and their report became a contract binding the parties.[32]

How frequently grantees so redistributed the costs of construction among themselves is unclear. But the very existence of such an agreement demonstrates the inadequacy of a simple equation of waterlot grants with municipal corruption. Of course grantees applied for grants, anxiously worked out financing arrangements that would allow them to meet the terms imposed by the city, and usually abided by those terms for reasons that presumably had something to do with long-term economic advantage and gain. Grantees expected to benefit from their grants. And it may be that many of the recipients of grants got their waterlots because of influence within the Common Council. But to look only to the private *cui bono* with-

30. See, for example, Corporation Grant to Henry Van Borson, 23 July 1737, Grant Book B, MARC.

31. These were the same grants cited in n. 28.

32. Arbitrator's Report, bound with Corporation Grant to James Van Cortlandt, et al., 3 February 1773.

out at the same time considering the benefit to the city and its corporate entity is to lose sight of the calculated ways in which grants of property could function as instrumentalities of government action. The terms of the grants were shaped by the long-run interest of the city in a developed and expanded waterfront. It was up to the grantees to work out ways of meeting the terms set by the corporation.

The legal control the corporation exercised over waterlots was not limited to setting affirmative and executory duties. Grants often included restrictions on the timing of a development.[33] In some cases the city required construction of a project at a relatively distant point in the future, tying the actions of the waterlot holder to future urban growth. In the case of the "basin" grants of the 1770s, the corporation insisted that at the end of twenty years or as soon as the basin was filled in, the grantees would have to build a third street of forty-five feet in width "so far as the right of the Mayor Aldermen and Commonalty extends."[34] Thirty-three years earlier Henry Bogart had similarly covenanted

> that whenever hereafter it shall happen that three or more of the freeholders and Owners of the Lotts of Land and Waterlotts in the Neighborhood . . . shall Conclude and agree together to Erect and make wharfes and streets thereon and wharfes out and fill up the Same for better Improvement thereof into Hudsons River . . . that he the said Henry Bogart . . . at his . . . own proper Cost Charge and Expence shall wharfe out behind his said Ground and Lott . . . as far as the Neighborhood shall wharfe out and fill up behind their own Lotts.[35]

If the terms of the grant were fulfilled—that is, if the quitrent was paid every year, the covenanted streets, wharves, and other public facilities constructed within the period of time set out in the deed, and all "public" parts of the property properly maintained—the corporation guaranteed the good title of the grantee, that he or she should be able to have the "quiet enjoyment" of the property in perpetuity, and that "in consideration of [the grantee and his or her heirs and assigns] . . . maintaining and keeping in repair the streets and wharfs before mentioned [they] shall and lawfully may at all times and from time to time forever hereafter fully and freely have use enjoy take and hold to their own proper use and uses all manner of wharfage cranage benefits advantages and emoluments growing arising or accruing by or from the said wharf fronting the East River."[36]

33. Corporation Grant to Cornelius Van Horne, 26 July 1734.
34. Corporation Grant to Hendrick Remson.
35. Corporation Grant to Henry Bogart.
36. How much that covenant of quiet enjoyment might be worth in nineteenth-century America is revealed in Chapter 6.

But if the terms of the deed were not satisfied by the grantee, the document allowed the corporation a number of sanctions. Nonpayment of rent gave it the right to distrain the goods and possessions of the grantee. Ten days after the due date for payment of the quitrent, the agents of the city could enter onto the waterlot and "bear lead drive and carry away" all the movable property of the grantee until the rent had been paid. In some cases, if a grantee had not paid his rent or properly built wharves or streets within the time period set out in the deed, the corporation had the right to "Reenter" the property and "to have again, Retain, Repossess and Enjoy as their former Estate." This right of entry created a future interest in the waterlot that was retained by the corporation even as it conveyed title to the grantee. Ultimately the fee simple received by the grantee was made conditional on the satisfaction of the covenants; failure by the grantee in meeting the corporation's terms might result in a forfeiture to the corporation.[37]

But in most cases the corporation evidently saw no need to create a possibility of a forfeiture.[38] The fact that a grantee who had not fulfilled the terms of his or her grant could not collect wharfage, slippage, pierage, cranage, and other fees for the use by others of the facilities constructed on the lot was sanction enough. Only a satisfactory grantee could profit by his investment in a waterlot.

The waterlot grants made by the city allowed it to shape, control, and profit from the development of its waterfront without any obligation to fi-

37. The full "condition" was set out in the following standardized language: *"Provided always, and if it shall so happen that the Wharfe of twenty five foot, to be part of the street of forty foot aforesaid, shall not be laid Built, Erected and made, in manner aforesaid on or before the twenty fifth day of March, which will be in the Year of Our Lord One thousand, seven hundred and forty, and that the two Wharfes or Streets aforesaid of fifteen foot, and of forty foot, shall not be Built, Erected and made, and completely finished on or before the twenty fifth day of March, which will be in the year of our Lord one thousand, seven hundred and forty six; or that the said yearly Rent of thirty shillings and three pence shall be behind and unpaid in part or in all by the Space of ten days . . . over or after the said Days of payment thereof, before mentioned (being lawfully Demanded) that then and in such Case it shall and may be lawfull to and for the said Mayor Aldermen and Commonalty of the City of New York . . . into the said Granted Premises with the appurtenances and into every part thereof, in the name of the whole, wholy to Re-enter and the same to have again, Retain, Repossess and Enjoy as their former Estate; and the said Gerrardus Duyckinck . . . utterly to Expell put out and amove; this Indenture or anything herein contained to the Contrary . . . in any wise notwithstanding"* (Corporation Grant to Gerrardus Duyckinck, 26 July 1734, Grant Book B, MARC).

38. The corporation in 1734 began granting its waterlots with conditional rights of entry. But after 1735 most grants did not contain a right of entry provision. But sée Corporation Grant to Abraham Mesier, 4 July 1760; to Robert Leake, 1 August 1763; to Nicholas Roosevelt, 7 March 1765; and to Cornelius P. Low, 28 October 1765, all in Grant Book C, MARC.

nance that process. This was not, however, a hidden form of "municipal socialism." Planning through the disposal of waterlot grants by necessity would be an incremental process, dependent in every instance on private market forces. Only a merchant who expected to profit quickly and substantially from investment in a waterlot grant could be expected to seek or accept such a deed. Under such a system of control, the construction of waterfront facilities would not move ahead of demand.

In the eighteenth century, as in every period of New York's history before the rise of the skyscraper, the seaport dominated the shape of the city. Views of the city inevitably placed its harbor in the foreground, and travelers' accounts dwelt on New York's shipping facilities. Descriptions typically began with an account of the "multitude of Shipping with which it [the city] is thronged"[39] and continued with a comparison of the relative advantages and development of the ports of New York and Philadelphia. Doctor Alexander Hamilton "saw more shipping in the harbour" of New York, and Peter Kalm thought "New York probably carries on a more extensive commerce than any town in the English North American provinces," although "Boston and Philadelphia . . . come very close to it." Travelers agreed that the port was "a good one." Ships of any tonnage could lie in at the docks and wharves, and the facilities were sufficient to meet the demand. All boats could load and unload at dockside without the aid of lighters.[40] Moreover, travelers and boosters alike thought that its saltwater port gave New York a definite advantage over Philadelphia, which because of its location on a freshwater river that froze "During the Severity of Winter . . . is locked up from all marine Correspondence with the rest of the World, and thus, necessarily for several Months every Year, exposed to an almost total Stagnation of Trade." By contrast, "No Season prevents our [New York's] Ships from launching into the Ocean and pursuing their Traffick—The Depth of Winter scarce obstructs our Commerce, and during its greatest Severity, an equal unrestrained Activity runs thro' all Ranks, Orders and Employments."[41]

But as of 1770, and indeed throughout the eighteenth century, shipping

---

It appears that the right of entry may have become a bargaining tool used by the city and grantees in exchange for larger grants (see the Low grant), or lower quitrents.

39. Thomas Pownall, *A Topographical Description of the Dominions of the United States of America (being a Revised and Enlarged Edition of [a] Topographical Description of such Parts of North America as are Contained in the (Annexed) Map of the Middle British Colonies, & c. in North America)* (1784; reprint, Pittsburgh, 1949), 43. See in general the incomparable I. Phelps Stokes, *The Iconography of Manhattan Island*, 6 vols. (New York, 1915–28).

40. Carl Bridenbaugh, ed., *Gentlemen's Progress: The Itinerarium of Dr. Alexander Hamilton 1744* (Chapel Hill, 1948), 44; Adolph Benson, ed., *Peter Kalm's Travels in North America*, 2 vols. (New York, 1937), 1 : 124, 133; Bridenbaugh, *Cities in Revolt*, 39.

41. Klein, ed., *Independent Reflector*, 436; see also William Smith, Jr., *The History of the*

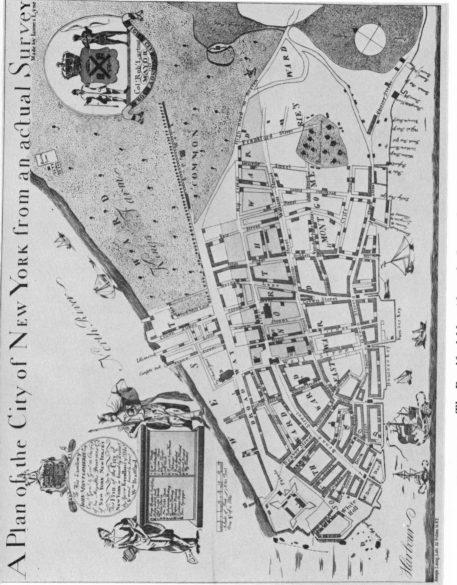

FIGURE 4.1. *The Bradford Map (from the Lynne Survey), 1728–1730*

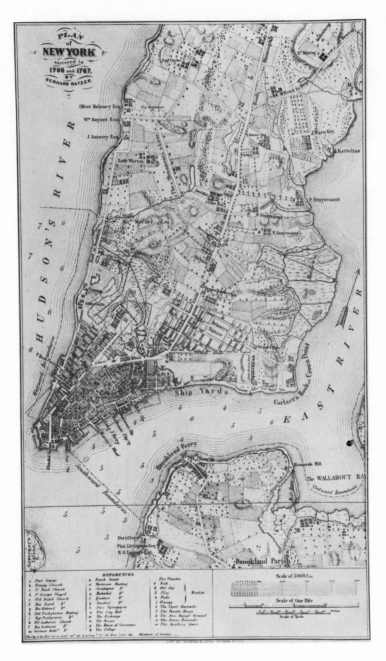

FIGURE 4.2. *The Ratzer Map, 1767*

FIGURE 4.3. *Plan of the City of New York, 1797*

tonnage arriving and clearing in New York City lagged behind that of the other two major colonial ports.[42] Carl Bridenbaugh and other historians have argued that New York's comparative failure resulted from the policies of its government. The mayor and Common Council "failed to provide their city with all the facilities it needed"; indeed, "no town was so poorly equipped to care for its shipping as New York."[43] They may be correct in their condemnation of the actions of the city, although their evidence is impressionistic and their judgment ultimately founded on the misperception that waterlot grants were unrestricted gifts of property. But the causal relationship between government land use planning and economic growth and change remains a most controversial and largely unexplored area of economic and historical research.[44] And it is beyond the scope of this study—not to mention the skills of its author—to say whether the technology of planning employed by the corporation of the city of New York constituted the most efficient choice available.

Clearly, the waterlot grants made by the corporation changed the face of the city. Over the last two-thirds of the eighteenth century, the harborside facilities of New York were transformed. Two full blocks were reclaimed out of the East River. The city once had ended at Pearl Street; by the end of the century, Front Street was the southeastern border of lower Manhattan. Much of this growth probably was the consequence of the large number of grants made in the last ten years before the Revolution. But by the mid-1760s the pace of growth and change was already extraordinary. Perhaps the city would have grown at the same or an even greater rate had some other form of planning or port development been in effect. It is a certainty, however, that waterlot grants were used, as they were designed, to provide New York City with the streets, wharves, and port facilities of a growing seaport.[45]

Province of New York, ed. Michael Kammen, 2 vols. (Cambridge, Mass., 1972) 1:201–2; Benson, ed., *Kalm*, 1:133; Pownall, *Topographical Description*, 45.

42. Robert Albion, *The Rise of New York Port* (New York, 1939), 5.

43. Bridenbaugh, *Cities in Revolt*, 30; Konwitz, *Cities and the Sea*, 65; Carl Bridenbaugh, *Cities in the Wilderness* (New York, 1955), 328.

44. The central text on the problem—and the closest to a demonstration of a solution—is James Willard Hurst, *Law and Economic Growth* (Cambridge, Mass., 1964).

45. Waterlot grants may also have created new health hazards for a town that had once prided itself on its healthful environment: "New York is scituated upon a point between two rivers. The one on the west side of town and other on the east. The shipping lye all on the east side & there all along the shoar from one end of the Town to the other there is a continuation of wharfs to which the ships lay their sides except at the ends of those streets which run nearly perpendicular to the river & terminate upon the river where the wharfs are discontinued & Gaps left called Slips into which the Periguas & small Vessels enter & unload & here

at the ends of these streets the Market places are built. These slips are likewise the common shores into which all the filth & nastiness of the town & streets is emptied so that in the summer time there is constantly a most offensive abominable smell in them. . . . All that part [of the City] where wharfs are is low ground About 9 or 10 years since the royal Battery was built at the entrance into the harbour near the confluence of the two rivers and as it extends a considerable way into the stream of the river it stopt the current all along the whole extent of the wharfs. Before this the stream in a great measure by the swiftness of the current along the sides of the wharf carried away a great part of the filth that was thrown off the wharfs & came from the slips which now settles & sometimes keeps floating in the eddy" (Cadwallader Colden to Dr. John Mitchell, 7 November 1745, writing in the wake of an attack of yellow fever on the city, Colden Papers, vol. 8, New York Historical Society, *Collections* 67 [1934], 329–30); see also Klein, ed., *Independent Reflector*, 434–35 (on the "putrid stench" of Rotten Row).

CHAPTER 5

The Political Theory of
a Waterlot Grant

If viewed as the conveyances of a private landowner, the corporation's waterlot grants appear to violate several fundamental tenets of the law regarding real covenants. They specified affirmative obligations on the estate of the grantee that not only radically limited the uses to which he or she might put the lot but actually directed its development. Sometimes the satisfaction of the covenants was ensured through a clause granting the corporation a right of entry whenever the grantee should fail to meet the terms set out in the deed. When they did so, the covenants were effectively transformed into conditions subsequent. But treatise writers from Sir Edward Coke on had emphasized that conditions subsequent were not to be favored in the law.[1] Even when, as was more often the case, only the right to take the profits from the waterlots was made conditional on the performance of the covenants, the latter format still merged or "confused" covenants with conditions in ways that property lawyers might have found unsettling.[2]

The waterlot grants are equally perplexing as the planning tools of a mu-

---

1. "If it be doubtful whether a clause in a deed be a condition, the courts will incline against the latter construction" James Kent, *Commentaries on American Law*, 4 vols. (New York, 1826–30), 4:127.

2. See the arguments of Hamilton and Troup in *Mayor v. Scott*, 1 Caines Rep. 543, 548 (1804), and the discussion in Chapter 8. Further questions that might be raised concerning the legality of the grants as property conveyances include: Did they violate the Statute Quia Emptores in creating a kind of estate not recognized by the common law? Were they actually a hidden fee simple determinable, with a possibility of reverter to occur whenever the terms of the grant were not satisfied? Consider that grantees who could not fulfill their covenanted obligations returned their lots to the corporation (presumably because the value of their lots became nil without the ability to reap the profits). Finally, it is not clear how alienable the lots really were. Nor is it evident that grantees who no longer felt that they could fulfill the terms of a grant were free to sell their lots to the highest bidder who could meet the city's terms.

nicipal government. The corporation of the city of New York had absolute ownership of the most important resource for the city's commercial development: the waterfront. The corporation could have planned the facilities for the port and then directly implemented that scheme. Instead, it granted away the property intermittently and then compelled its grantees to develop their grants according to municipal directives. The structure of action thereby created seems an open invitation to inefficiency and corruption. It is no wonder that historians of city planning have judged the actions of the corporation to be a wholesale surrender of its proper responsibility.

Nor can it be argued that the typical waterlot grant was the only disposition that members of the Common Council could have imagined making. The corporation could have simply granted the waterlots and thereby given up control over the development of the waterfront. Indeed, at an earlier time the city made relatively unrestricted grants of the waterlots that it received under the Dongan Charter of 1686 (from high- to low-water marks).[3] And throughout the prerevolutionary period, whenever corporation authorities chose for one reason or another to sell an occasional lot out of the commons, the grant memorializing the conveyance lacked the covenants or conditions that characterized the waterlot grants.[4] We must assume that waterlot grants were drafted in their particular form because the governing members of the corporation intended to control the development of the city's waterfront. But still, if control and authority were what the corporation of the city of New York was after, why did it choose this way of achieving it? Liverpool, for instance, offered the alternative model of a city government building a great and usable waterfront facility on its own.[5]

We do not and probably cannot know why city authorities chose in the

3. On 7 September 1692, the corporation made grants of lots between high- and low-water mark to William Morris, Hephanus Van Cortlandt, and Dirrick Van Den Bergh. Each agreed to pay one peppercorn per year quitrent and to construct and maintain one street thirty feet in breadth on the inside of the lot. Failure to perform the latter covenant on time would result in a fine of twenty shillings for every month's delay, but the profits were not made contingent on the completion of the project. In fact, the city covenanted that the grantees had an absolute right to the profits and that the corporation would make good any losses suffered by the grantees (Grant Book A). See also George Ashton Black, *Municipal Ownership of Land on Manhattan Island* (New York, 1891), 21, 27, who argues that after 1686 the lots between high- and low-water mark from Wall Street to Beekman's Slip were sold at public auction in fee simple absolute without the reservation of a quitrent.

4. See, for example, Release of the Corporation to William Walderon, 24 September 1731, New York City Deeds, Box 4, New York Historical Society; Counterpart of 33 year lease to Ann Aerison, 24 April 1771, Grant Book C, Municipal Archives and Record Center, New York; hereafter MARC.

5. Sidney Webb and Beatrice Webb, *The Manor and the Borough*, 2 vols. (1908; reprint,

early 1730s to adopt the policy they did. But it is possible to understand what made such a policy rational and plausible. The structure of action represented by the waterlot grants constituted a distinctively attractive form of public action in an eighteenth-century political culture in which all direct forms of public action were constitutionally suspect. Liverpool, the model for Sidney and Beatrice Webb of an activist municipal corporation, stood alone throughout the eighteenth century. Other English commercial cities, notably Bristol and London, found it impossible to follow Liverpool's example and develop their waterfronts directly.[6] By contrast, the use of land grants as planning tools had roots in an English planning tradition that stretched back to the new towns created by Edward I in the thirteenth century.[7] Waterlot grants that covenanted action by their recipients offered the city a way to initiate change without doing violence to some of the central tenets of eighteenth-century political culture.

To understand how that could be so, we should begin by briefly summarizing some relevant elements of an eighteenth-century theory of government.[8] What was government supposed to do? What was the purpose of public action? In the eighteenth-century context the best answer to those questions would have been that government ought to do little; its role was to make certain that others did as they ought to. Public action could not be separated from private action. Just as a "public" institution had "private" rights, so private individuals had public obligations. The primary function of government was to enforce the peace of the community: to maintain the order of society by insisting that private individuals fulfilled their public responsibilities.[9]

As a result, there was little that could be considered direct government action or service. Governments did not act so much as they ensured and sanctioned the actions of others. The characteristic forms of "public" ac-

---

London, 1963), 2:481–91; François Vigier, *Change and Apathy* (Cambridge, Mass., 1970), 40–43.

6. Webb and Webb, *The Manor and the Borough*, 460–61 for Bristol, 690 for London.

7. John W. Reps, *Tidewater Towns* (Williamsburg, 1972), 1–22.

8. This argument is spelled out in greater detail in Hendrik Hartog, "The Public Law of a County Court: Judicial Government in Eighteenth Century Massachusetts," *American Journal of Legal History* 20 (1976):282–329.

9. See Frederic W. Maitland, *Township and Borough* (Cambridge, 1897), 79: "It is long before the community outgrows the old, automatic, self-adjusting, scheme of 'common' rights and duties. Cambridge was very dirty; its streets were unpaved. In 1330 the masters of the University complained to the King in Parliament. What, let us ask, will be the answer to their petition? How ought the town to be paved? Should the municipal corporation let out the work to a contractor, or should it institute a 'public works department'? Nothing of the sort. The mayor and bailiffs should see that every man repairs the road over against his own tenement. That is the way in which the men of Cambridge should pave the town of Cambridge. That is the way in which they will pave it in the days of Henry VIII and of George III" (footnotes omitted). See also Vigier, *Change and Apathy*, 54–55.

tion were not street cleaners or road-building crews but ordinances oblig-
ing residents to clean the portions of streets abutting their houses or pre-
sentments against the selectmen of a town or a group of neighbors for
failing to maintain or repair a road or highway, or, in New York City's case,
a lease or grant of corporation property.

The problem of governance in New York City, as everywhere in provincial America, was to shift the burden of action to private individuals. The
ordinances of an eighteenth-century corporation are best read as a way of
organizing private action. For example, New York City's ordinance to
pave and clean the streets did not provide a corps of public employees to
perform that service. Mobilizing an army of public servants would never
have occurred to the members of the Common Council; indeed, such a
program would have accorded with their notion of corrupt government.
Rather, the ordinance was a list of what homeowners could or could not do
in the care of streets that fronted their property.[10]

Even when government action involved the city's own corporate estate,
the role of the city was usually supervisory and directive. If a slip had to be
cleaned, the landowners whose property abutted the slip would be ordered
to clean it at their cost. In 1737 a grand jury held the public pier near Fly
Market to be a nuisance because it was "so narrow that [it] often proves
Very dangerous as to Carts passing and Repassing both in Respect to
grown People as well as Children" and ordered the residents living near
the market to petition the Common Council for permission to enter onto
the corporation's property in order to widen the pier.[11] When in the same
year William Cornell, the lessee of the ferry, complained that the disrepair
of the markethouse at Clarke's Slip was cutting into his business by dis-
couraging "Country People" from coming to the city, he did not conclude
his petition as we might have expected by asking the corporation to maintain its property properly. Instead, he asked the Common Council to order
the neighbors of the markethouse to repair it (an order that was preempted
by a petition by those very neighbors who volunteered to enlarge and improve the markethouse).[12] No one, it seems, contemplated asking the corporation to take care of its own property.

At one level, the insistence that action be conducted by private individ-

10. New York City, *Laws, Orders, and Ordinances* (New York, 1731), c. 22; New York
City, *Laws, Statutes, Ordinances, and Constitutions* (New York, 1749), c. 14; New York City,
Laws, Statutes, Ordinances and Constitutions (New York, 1763), c. 14. By 1763 this ordinance
"for Paving and Cleaning the Streets, Lanes and Alleys, within the City of New York" had
become a general nuisance ordinance and included a variety of sections that had nothing to do
with the streets.

11. *Minutes of the Common Council of the City of New York, 1675–1776*, 8 vols. (New York,
1905), 4:403 (1737); hereafter *MCC*. The petition of the residents was, not surprisingly,
granted.

12. Petition File, 1737, MARC.

uals might be regarded as a substitute for a nonexistent public bureaucracy. Public action depended on the participation of the public.[13] But that insistence was deeply tied to the belief that government ought not to bear the costs of action. Perhaps the most striking manifestation of that belief from our perspective lay not in what we might consider local government at all but in the judicial presumption that criminal defendants should pay the costs of their trials even if they were judged not guilty.[14] We can see that view reflected as well in many elements of the practice of the New York Common Council during the early eighteenth century. Virtually every council order was premised on the conviction that whatever was to be done the corporation would not pay for it. Lessees of the corporation—whether of the ferry, the public docks, or land in the commons—held their leases subject to their willingness to assume all liability for repairs or improvements.[15] The oath taken by a freeman made his obligation to avoid imposing costs on the corporation second only to his responsibility to maintain its property.[16]

Indeed, one might argue that the estate granted to the corporation was less a way of generating revenue than a tool of governance that vitiated the need for revenue. It is true that the charters gave the city an income freed from the restrictions and the intervention of the provincial assembly and that the income from corporate property gave the city a partial and temporary substitute for tax revenues. But the waterlots and other parcels of corporate property also offered city authorities the opportunity to act without any costs to municipal administration. As we have seen, the corporation uniformly required waterlot grantees to build streets or wharves at the front and at the rear of their holdings. These covenants should be read as meaning exactly what they say. The city was not simply reserving a portion of the granted lands for public uses, nor was it merely assessing the costs of street construction. These covenants meant that the city would do nothing, the waterlot holders everything. It was the waterlot grantees who would build and finance the public streets along the waterfront of the city.

---

13. This argument is developed for Massachusetts by William Nelson, *The Americanization of the Common Law* (Cambridge, Mass., 1975), 13–35; and John P. Reid, *In a Defiant Stance: The Conditions of Law in Massachusetts Bay, the Irish Comparison, and the Coming of the American Revolution* (University Park, Pa., 1977).

14. Julius Goebel and T. Raymond Naughton, *Law Enforcement in Colonial New York* (New York, 1944), 731–48; Hartog, "Public Law of a County Court," 320, 326–27.

15. The responsibility of the lessee of the ferry for all repairs led to constant petitions asking for rent reductions to enable the lessee to meet the maintenance and repair costs of the docks from which the ferry left. Frequently the corporation granted those petitions, and in a sense the corporation did therefore "pay" for repairs. But the corporation was far less concerned with the size of its revenue than with the avoidance of all direct responsibility for action.

16. *MCC*, 4:121 (1731).

This was government by delegation, government committed to a policy of externalizing the costs of actions. New York City was also a government that lacked most of the powers of coercion and enforced obedience of the modern state. Neither the "watch," the constabulary, nor the sheriff and his deputies constituted what we would consider a police force. Compared to the monopoly on legitimate violence of the modern positivist state, government at every level in eighteenth-century America was relatively ineffectual. In this regard the government of New York City was indistinguishable from other local governments. Like them, it was dependent on the involvement and the participation of the local community. Public action became possible only to the extent that city government could enlist the support and the interest of its public.[17]

Dependence on direct public support meant that most local governments operated with a very limited range of objectives. Governments pursued consensus as the only legitimate basis for action; when consensus was unachievable, which was often, governments did nothing. Others have written of the committed and conscientious parochialism of local government in colonial New York, and some historians have concluded that all forms of government in eighteenth-century America sought to preserve a consensually determined status quo.[18] But different publics might come to differing conclusions as to the proper sphere of public action. And in New York the members of the Common Council could legitimately—within the accepted norms of their political culture—direct the activities of the city toward change, planning, and development.

New York was preeminently a commercial city. Shipowning was relatively widely dispersed throughout the population.[19] The fortunes of nearly everyone in the small city rested on the quality and quantity of its harbor facilities.[20] As a result, waterlot grants to particular individuals provided a

17. See, for example, Petition of the Vestrymen, Petition File, 1755, MARC, who asserted that the keeper of the almshouse did not perform the duties of his station and behaved in a surly and abusive manner to justices of the peace and vestrymen. If he were not fired immediately the vestrymen threatened that they would not attend to their monthly meetings "with that Alacrity and Chearfullness as they would Willingly do for the Publick Good."

18. See Patricia U. Bonomi, "Local Government in Colonial New York: A Base for Republicanism," in Jacob Judd and Irwin Polishook, eds., *Aspects of Early New York Society and Politics* (Tarrytown, 1974), 29–50; William Nelson, "The Eighteenth-Century Background of John Marshall's Constitutional Jurisprudence," *Michigan Law Review* 76 (1978): 893–960; Michael Zuckerman, *Peaceable Kingdoms* (New York, 1970); Sung Bok Kim, *Landlord and Tenant in Colonial New York* (Williamsburg, 1978).

19. Bruce M. Wilkenfeld, "The New York City Shipowning Community, 1715–64," *American Neptune* 37 (1977): 50–65.

20. The significance of shipping facilities to a city whose population never exceeded twenty-two thousand in the colonial period would be equivalent to the significance to a modern university town of the school's legislative appropriation or the level of student enrollment.

form of redistribution from the wealthy to the larger community of the city, which would bear none of the costs of development but would gain the benefits of an improved port. William Livingston thought that the corporation's waterlot grants meant that council members eventually would "experience the Resentment of an injur'd People, at a Time when they are most solicitous about the popular Esteem."[21] But he may have been wrong. The corporation may have used its corporate estate in ways that accurately reflected the desires of its constituency.

In any event, the property rights granted New York City through its charters allowed it to achieve governmental objectives that were beyond the reach of unpropertied local governments. Instead of sanctions against failures of performance, the city could offer leases, licenses, and grants to private individuals willing to implement various city-defined goals. New York City did not itself build streets, fill in swampland, or dig wells; the public works projects that characterized nineteenth-century urban government would have been incomprehensible to the city fathers of eighteenth-century New York. Yet it could act. Whereas a country court could only present a town or individual for failing to maintain a street or bridge, New York's property gave it a way of building streets and bridges; the property of the city allowed it to plan and initiate action without doing violence to the basic premises of eighteenth-century governance.

The waterlot grants of New York City thus typify the singular governmental authority of a propertied corporation. Their terms made possible a form of capital investment and development without reliance on the exactions of the tax gatherer or the exertions of a public bureaucracy. They suggest that even within a political culture opposed to publicly instituted change and innovation, a propertied corporation could control and direct the destiny of a community. In a world of governance in which instrumental public action was inherently suspect,[22] the waterlot grants of the city constituted a technology of public action that was prima facie legitimate and proper. It was not a standing army or a police force that gave effect to the decisions of the city government; it was the hallowed operation of English property law. The fact that the corporation held its property as a private landowner made it possible for the city to delegate to private individuals major responsibility for the construction of its commercial heart, without at the same time abandoning control over that process.

There are signs that after the middle of the eighteenth century, the po-

21. Milton Klein, ed., *The Independent Reflector* (Cambridge, Mass., 1959), 156.
22. See John P. Reid, "In Legitimate Stirps: The Concept of 'Arbitrary,' the Supremacy of Parliament and the Coming of the American Revolution," *Hofstra Law Review* 5 (1977): 459–99; Bernard Bailyn, *The Origins of American Politics* (New York, 1968).

litical assumptions of local governance began to change. More and more government activity was made directly chargeable to the New York City corporation. In 1755 the Common Council made it a standing rule that whenever repairs to public wharves were necessary, the aldermen and assistants of the ward in which the wharves were located should proceed immediately to contract out work and charge the costs to the corporation.[23] In 1767 a group of merchants petitioned the corporation about the sorry state of Beekman's Slip with the expectation that the Common Council would respond by appointing a committee with power to correct the situation directly, placing the whole cost on the corporation.[24] Indeed, the growing dependence of the city on the taxing powers of the provincial assembly—its increasing inability to finance its work out of corporate income—may be one indication of a growing willingness to internalize the costs of action.[25]

It may be that the theoretical underpinnings of local governance in colonial America were beginning to fall away. There is some evidence of what might be called a bureaucratization of public affairs, and there are clear indications of a new dependence on public authority.[26]

Yet the scope and the range of public activity did not grow; nothing suggests that there was a general reevaluation of the legitimacy of direct public action. The increased willingness of the corporation to assume the costs of maintaining corporate property may in fact stand for the rather different proposition that the members of the Common Council were increasingly aware of a problematic separation of the estate of the corporation from the general government of the city. Consciousness of that separation would grow after the Revolution, eventually becoming a central obsession of the American law of municipal corporation. But in the 1750s through 1770s the dichotomous relationship of public power and private wealth was at most only a subterranean theme in the institutional history of New York City. The city continued to govern through its corporate estate. Waterlot

23. I. Phelps Stokes, *The Iconography of Manhattan Island*, 6 vols. (New York, 1915–28), 1 : 197. On political change in New York City, see Edward F. Countryman, *A People in Revolution* (Baltimore, 1981), 55–67.

24. *MCC*, 7:77–79 (1767).

25. George William Edwards, *New York as an Eighteenth Century Municipality: Part II, 1731–1776* (New York, 1917), 35, 190–205. After 1750 criminal courts also increasingly made the costs of trial a government responsibility. See Goebel and Naughton, *Law Enforcement*, 731–48, Hartog, "Public Law of a County Court," 326–27.

26. See Kenneth Lockridge, "Social Change and the Meaning of the American Revolution," *Journal of Social History* 6 (1973):403; Douglas Jones, "The Strolling Poor: Transiency in 18th Century Massachusetts," *Journal of Social History* 8 (1975):18; Hartog, "Public Law of a County Court," 282–329; James Henretta, *The Evolution of American Society, 1700–1815* (New York, 1973), 119–57.

grants remained at the center of the governmental business of the corporation of the city of New York until the city was abandoned to the British in 1776.

The waterlot grants of New York City were one solution to the problem of how an eighteenth-century commercial city might expand and develop its commercial facilities. This practice may be a prototypical example of the "privatism" that we so deplore in modern life: the subsidization of private gains by public agencies and the definition of social goals in terms of private advantage. But from a less presentist perspective, waterlot grants offered the possibility of achieving positive governmental goals—paving the streets, developing the harbor—at a time when there was no theory of direct government action. How do you get something done if you do not know how, or rather, if you cannot conceive of doing it yourself? You get someone else to do it for you. In colonial America and Georgian England, most local governments could get only those things done that had always been done, or that had at least always been supposed to be done, because the only sanction available was punishment for not acting. One cannot after all punish someone for not doing what he or she was not obliged by law or tradition to do. On the other hand, a chartered city with a substantial estate could use its wealth to achieve goals, to induce change, even in the absence of a theory of direct government action. The promised reward of the waterlot (and its profits) gave the city the power to coerce grantees to do things that they were not obliged as citizens to do. And ultimately the singularity of the practice of government in New York City was defined by that possibility of action, by the ways in which the seemingly distinct public and private spheres were united in the achievement of positive governmental goals.

PART II

City Power in Republican America

CHAPTER 6

Burying the Past

In the summer of 1822 yellow fever swept through New York City for the last time in the city's history. As in similar episodes in 1795, 1798, 1803, and 1819, all who could afford to leave the city for safe locations did so, and the business of city government came to a standstill. But in the fall, after the disease had run its course, the Common Council met to consider what might be done to prevent the return of the fever.[1]

One public remedy proposed was an absolute prohibition on burials in the settled portion of lower Manhattan, south of Canal Street. Such a ban had been a subject of governmental debate since 1798, when a report of the New York Medical Society suggested that all interments in the "compact" part of the city be forbidden between May and November.[2] And the state legislature had given the city authority in 1803 to prohibit interments whenever the Common Council decided that it was "necessary."[3]

But until the fall of 1822 general proposals to close cemeteries had always been referred to committee, where they languished.[4] Except for a municipally owned Potter's Field reserved for paupers and strangers (located on what is now Washington Square in Greenwich Village), burial grounds and vaults were the private property of the churches of the city. Individual cemeteries might be regulated when public opinion demanded action,[5] but previous city administrations evidently saw little to be gained from challenging religious authority.

1. For a history of yellow fever in New York City and of the public health reforms that resulted from the recurrent epidemics of the early republic, see John Duffy, *A History of Public Health in New York City, 1625–1866* (New York, 1968), 97–270.

2. *Minutes of the Common Council of the City of New York, 1784–1831*, 21 vols. (New York, 1917–30), 2:494–96 (21 January 1799), hereafter *Min. CC*; Duffy, *History of Public Health*, 218.

3. *Laws of New York*, 26th sess. (Albany, 1803), c. 70, sec. 1; this section was incorporated directly into the *Revised Statutes*, 36th sess. (Albany, 1813), c. 86, sec. 267.

4. See *Min. CC*, 11:255 (1820).

5. In 1807, for example, the Common Council ordered the African Zion Methodist Epis-

In November 1822, however, Mayor Stephan Allen gave the prohibition of at least some interments a prominent place in his administrative program. "It appears to be the opinion of Medical Men," wrote Allen, "that the great numbers of the dead interred in the several cemeteries within the bounds of this City, is attended with injurious consequences to the health of the inhabitants." This time the Common Council heeded that "opinion." On 31 March 1823 it passed an ordinance prohibiting all burials in the private cemeteries of the city. Graves could not be dug, nor vaults opened, under penalty of a $250 fine for each violation of the ordinance.[6]

The public health was said to demand a radical interference with traditional urban customs. Contemporary medical opinion was united in the conviction that rotting corpses were a direct cause of contagion. A "pernicious exhalation or vapour, floating in the atmosphere, is the primary and essential cause" of yellow fever. "To produce this vapour there must be a concurrence of heat, moisture, and a quantity of decaying animal and vegetable matter." A ban on interments, moreover, was a prerequisite for safe city drinking water. Reported the Common Council's Committee on Laws (quoting a French physician):

> The vapours continually attracted from these sources of Corruption [graveyards] by the sun, infect the air, whilst the rain penetrating, washes in the graves the putrid remains of the bodies, and carries with it into the wells detached, infected particles, from which it could not be disengaged by filtration, in the short space it has to go.
>
> After this remark, (he continues) which I can only think of with pain, may not an individual say, before he drinks a glass of water, "I am about to feed upon a being like myself, to swallow particles from

---

copalian Church to close up its vault after the city inspector had reported that the vault—into which 150 bodies were committed every year—emitted an unendurable stench during the summer months. In exchange for compliance, the members of the church were granted a fifty-foot-square portion of Potter's Field to keep as their own burying ground (ibid., 4:522–25). White churches were not subjected to similar orders, although complaints against them are reported in the council's minutes. See ibid., 10:487 (1819), and 11:767 (1821). Churches did have to apply to the council for permission to open new vaults, if the vaults extended under the adjoining streets, and such permission might at times be rescinded (ibid., 5:595, 611 [1809]; *Min. CC*, 10:327 [1819]).

6. Ibid., 12:510, 560, 624, 723, 810, 811 (1822–23). This ordinance went beyond what Allen had recommended. He believed that the council ought to distinguish between graves and open vaults, whose use should be prohibited entirely, and the private family vaults of the rich, which might "be used by their owners as formerly." But a majority of the Common Council disagreed and passed a blanket prohibition, which Allen later described as shaped by a determination "that the [same] equality should exist in the case of the dead as with the living" ("Memoirs of Stephan Allen" [New York, 1927], 102, typescript, at New York Historical Society).

dead bodies, and perhaps those once dear to me, and whom I still regret."[7]

Behind this manifest rationale, however, lay more complex and diffuse justifications for action that revolved around the commitment of city leaders to the growth of their city. Somehow, and for reasons that went beyond health and smell, the presence and use of urban cemeteries hampered urban growth. Thus members of a council committee appointed to consider where to locate a new public burying ground

> did not think it necessary to add their testimony to the many others that are accumulating in favour of a measure so vitally important to the safety and health of the Citizens at large as the burial of the Dead at a suitable distance from the habitations of the living. They will only remark that this City is destined at no great distance of time to rival some of the Capitals of the Old World and whatever can be done to promote its commercial and local advantages ought to engage the attentions and exertions of every inhabitant as the dictate no less of interest than of Patriotism. And whatever measures shall tend to security and comfort of human life and render our situation a place of safe and agreeable resort for strangers and of habitation for our resident citizens must in the nature of things advance the solid and permanent interest of all.[8]

Urban cemeteries had become disagreeable places, for they breached that proper separation between the dead and the living. To moderns, Trinity Church and its cemetery by Wall Street may be a visual treat, a respite from the monolithic quality of twentieth-century lower Manhattan. If it had not been planned that way, it should have been. But in the 1820s city leaders saw an urban cemetery as a disruption of urban order: as a reminder of the atavistic anarchy of an earlier city and, perhaps, a depressant on local land values. It was in every way a fit object for regulation and even prohibition.[9]

7. *Min. CC*, 14:593, 596 (1825); see in general, ibid., 576–634.
8. Ibid., 13:116 (1823).
9. For renewed appreciations of that anarchic style of urban organization, see Jane Jacobs, *The Death and Life of Great American Cities* (New York, 1961), and Richard Sennett, *The Uses of Disorder* (New York, 1970). These should be compared with Joseph Story's famous consecration address at the opening of the Mount Auburn Cemetery, in Cambridge, Massachusetts. This speech might be viewed as the rallying cry of the "rural cemetery movement," of which New York's cemetery prohibition was, of course, a part: "Why, then, should we darken, with systematic caution, all the avenues of these repositories? Why should we deposit the remains of our friends in loathsome vaults, or beneath the gloomy crypts and cells of our churches; where the human foot is never heard, save when the sickly taper lights some new guest to his appointed apartment, and 'lets fall a supernumerary horror' on the passing

Not everyone agreed with these sentiments, of course. "Yesterday," editorialized the *New York Evening Post*, "the late violent and unjust ordinance of the Corporation, infringing upon the rights of individuals by taking from them their property against their consent, and without an equivalent, went into effect."[10] To the city's churches the passage of the bylaw must have come as disastrous news. More than a dozen congregations submitted remonstrances to the council within three weeks of its passage.[11] Much of the land on which cemeteries sat had been granted in deeds that restricted land use exclusively to the burial of the dead. The sale of vault and coffin space, moreover, had been an important source of church revenue. As far as churches were concerned, the city's action constituted a taking of property and an unjustified incursion by public authority into private, religious business.[12]

And so, as might be expected, after the council rejected their petitions for relief, the churches took their complaints to court. The validity of the ordinance was first tested in 1824 before Judge John T. Irving of the municipal court of common pleas. In 1826 and again in 1827, the New York Supreme Court twice considered the ordinance: first in an action for a breach of the covenant of quiet enjoyment brought by the Brick Presbyterian Church against the corporation, then in an appeal of Irving's previous decision.[13]

The churches' argument against the cemetery closings took three interconnected forms. First, the regulation was said to be an overt taking of vested property rights. Even a properly constructed piece of legislation, which the ordinance was not conceded to be, could "not possess the power of arbitrarily divesting an individual of any of his fundamental rights." In

---

procession? Why should we measure out a narrow portion of earth for our graveyards in the midst of our cities; and heap the dead upon each other, with a cold, calculating parsimony, disturbing their ashes, and wounding the sensibilities of the living? Why should we expose our burying-grounds to the broad glare of day, to the unfeeling gaze of the idler, to the noisy press of business, to the discordant shouts of merriment, or to the baleful visitations of the dissolute?" (William W. Story, ed. *The Miscellaneous Writings of Joseph Story* [Boston, 1852], 572).

10. *An Account of the Proceedings of the Corporation of the City of New York in regard to the existence of cemeteries in the City, as published in the New York Evening Post* (New York, 1823), 3.

11. *Min. CC*, 13:5, 25 (1823).

12. Churches were usually assessed at a lower rate than contiguous property owners when streets were improved or laid out on the theory that their holdings would not be benefited by improvements because the market value could not rise, no change in use under the terms of the grants being possible (ibid., 10:132–33 [1818]).

13. *Mayor of New York* v. *Slack*, 3 Wheeler's Criminal Cases 237 (1824); *Corporation of the Brick Presbyterian Church* v. *The Mayor of New York*, 5 Cowen's 538 (1826); *Coates et al* v. *The Mayor of New York*, 7 Cowen's 585 (1827).

more than one case cemetery property derived from land grants made by the corporation; in other instances cemeteries resulted from direct grants by the crown. Were not such grants the equivalents of the contractual obligations recently upheld by the United States Supreme Court in the *Dartmouth College* case? The ordinance, moreover, destroyed the only use to which much cemetery land could legally be put. Without the right to commit bodies into vaults and graves, the land became valueless. At minimum, argued the churches' lawyers, there ought to be compensation for the loss: "The fault is not on our side. That very public which now interferes with our right held out to us the assurance of protection, and bound us to the duty of using the places as cemeteries."[14]

Second, the city's urban cemeteries were said to be as old as the city. The churches' rights were not merely vested but "ancient." Burial in the graveyards of lower Manhattan was a practice legitimated and honored for nearly two centuries, a customary right of city residents. How could the Common Council now declare that practice a nuisance? What transformed a cemetery into a threat to the public health? An institution of such long-standing legitimacy should not be destroyed by a mere local bylaw.[15]

But most important, the ordinance was a particularly unjustifiable act by the corporation of the city of New York. A government that had granted land to be used solely as burial ground, had licensed sextons, and had lent its authority to the burial practices of lower Manhattan should be prevented from undoing its own commitments. How could it have the right to decide when a prohibition had become "necessary"? As the city government used that word, "necessary" became the equivalent of "expedient." What better formula for arbitrary, unrestrained government action?[16]

The ordinance thus appeared to raise three legal issues. Were the rights

14. *An Account in regard to cemeteries*, 3; *Coates et al* v. *The Mayor of New York*, 7 Cowen's 585, 589, 590 argument of G. Griffin (1827).

15. *An Account in regard to cemeteries*, 5, 10; *The Mayor of New York* v. *Slack*, 3 Wheeler's Criminal Cases 237, 246 (1824). The two arguments of vested right and antiquity of use were joined by some opponents of the measure in an attempt to turn aside the public health argument of the proponents: "Your memorialists, however, cannot but think that the provisions for the ordinance are a violation of the sacred rights of private property; many of them or of their ancestors, having at a considerable expense, sunk vaults for themselves, their families and friends, which, in future, if the present ordinance is continued in force, will become wholly useless and a lasting reproach to those by whom they have been interdicted. Your memorialists will further observe that the late ordinance will, by compelling the relations and friends of the dead, to attend, in many cases, their remains at a great distance, and often in inclement weather, subject great numbers of the citizens to much additional charge and expose them to fatigues, dampness and cold which may bring on disease of the most fatal kind and render even decent attention to the dead a source of danger and destruction to the living" (*An Account in regard to cemeteries*, 10).

16. *Coates et al* v. *The Mayor of New York*, 7 Cowen's 585, 588–89.

of churches and vault owners vested? Did those rights gain any additional authority by their antiquity? Was the Common Council by its prior conduct estopped from prohibiting interments?

To the answers given by the churches, the corporation countered with its own arguments. Against the vested rights of private property, it posed the rights of the public. Against the antiquity of legitimated use, it argued the necessity of change, the blessings of progress, and the enlightened state of modern opinion. Against the presumptive illegitimacy of action by this city government, it argued for the necessity of public action by a public institution unrestrained by the mistakes or customs of the past.[17]

And at every stage of the litigation, judges confirmed the validity of the ordinance. The measure was nothing, they said, but a routine and legitimate act of regulation. All such acts in their nature harm "vested" property rights of one kind or another. The fact that these rights had been exercised for more than a century was an unfortunate but legally irrelevant consideration. All that mattered was that regulation be legitimate in its own terms, without reference to the condition or the status of affected individuals. When an action became "necessary" was a judgment properly delegated to city government, and that judgment meant nothing more than that such an action was deemed "expedient" for the public good. The prior actions of the corporation did not limit its discretion or its authority to act. In fact, as a public agency the corporation had no authority to limit its legislatively derived public powers. So long as the ordinance was a proper exercise of the derivative power of the state, of what American judges would later learn to call "the police power," there need be no compensation for the losses suffered by the churches.

Underlying these conclusions was an awareness of the explosive and extraordinary growth of New York City in the new republic. Judge Irving of the court of common pleas conceded that there was "something sacred in those peaceful sepulchres in which the remains of our fathers and kindred repose, and where we have cherished the hope of one day being gathered with them; and I am aware that it is an ungracious task to mar those feelings which cling to the remembrance of those who were dear to us in life, and to apply the strict rules and principles of law to this hallowed species of property." But change was unavoidable and ought not to be hampered by antiquities and archaic practices. "Does the right to continue to use these cemeteries as places of interment consist in the long use which has been made of them for that purpose? If such were the case, then, however urgent might be the public necessity of any alteration, and which necessity might, in fact, have grown out of this very use, yet the antiquity of the use

17. Ibid. (arguments of M. Ulshoeffer and P. Jay), 593–601.

would prevent such interference, however salutary it might be, and however imperiously required by circumstances."[18]

The city's physical growth, in fact, constituted an independent reason why the legitimacy of the ordinance ought to be sustained. According to the New York Supreme Court, the increase of population had transformed a "common," bounded on one side by a vineyard, into an urban "nuisance," which might be enjoined at the pleasure of the corporation.[19] "Every right, from an absolute ownership in property, down to a mere easement, is purchased and holden subject to the restriction, that it shall be so exercised as not to injure others. Though at the time it be remote and inoffensive, the purchaser is bound to know, at his peril, that it may become otherwise by the residence of many people in its vicinity; and that it must yield to by-laws, or other regular remedies for the suppression of nuisances."[20]

These conclusions exemplify familiar themes in the writing of American legal history. The judges' opinions were explicitly "instrumentalist" in rhetoric; the forces of precedent and of past practice were subordinated to the perceived needs of a growing community. Conflicts between churches and government were regarded, at least in part, as conflicts between the unrestrained dynamics of urban and economic growth and the traditional vested rights of churches and vault owners. The judges implicitly characterized the churches as *rentiers*, as owners who wished only to sit on their holdings; the city, by contrast, stood revealed as an agency promoting progress and change. In validating the ordinance, the judges indicated their approval of the use of public action to nurture growth, even at the cost of destroying property rights.[21]

The rhetoric of these cases would be familiar to every student of

18. *Mayor of New York* v. *Slack*, 3 Wheeler's Criminal Cases 237, 245–47. Similarly, the Committee on Laws of the Common Council took the fact that the corporation at one time had made grants for graveyards in the area of the city then "considered as lying in a manner out of Town, or at a distance from the dense population of the city" as demonstrating only that future councils ought to look much further "beyond the heart of the City in the establishment of new ones [graveyards]." The very growth the city was experiencing "presents an important reason, not then existing, for passing the ordinance in question" (*Min. CC*, 13:601 [1824]).

19. *Corporation of the Brick Presbyterian Church* v. *The Mayor of New York*, 5 Cowen's 538, 542.

20. *Coates et al* v. *The Mayor of New York*, 7 Cowen's 585, 605.

21. Morton Horwitz, *The Transformation of American Law, 1780–1860* (Cambridge, Mass., 1977), 1–62; James Willard Hurst, *Law and the Conditions of Freedom in the Nineteenth Century* (Madison, 1956), 3–32; Harry Scheiber, "Property Law, Expropriation, and Resource Allocation by Government: The United States, 1789–1910," *Journal of Economic History* 33 (1973):232–51.

nineteenth-century legal history. Still, there remains something jarring and discordant about them. The problem is not that judges visualized the conflict as between active public authority and passive property owners. Several studies have demonstrated the ways that public agencies were used as entrepreneurs and as central economic actors in the life of the new republic.[22] The problem is that these cases are only tangentially about the conflict between public authority and private property owners.[23] To the judges of the New York courts, the issues these cases raised revolved around the nature of the corporation of the city of New York alone. In the end, it was not the vested rights of the churches that had to be disposed of; it was the ability of the city to act as a government in spite of its parallel status as a propertied corporation. Could the corporation of the city of New York act so as to deny and destroy its own private commitments and obligations? What was the proper relationship between a local government's "capacity for holding and transferring property and its capacity to legislate for the good of the place with whose government it is invested"?[24]

The opinion in *Brick Presbyterian Church* v. *The Mayor of New York* is the best-known of the trilogy of cemetery cases.[25] In 1766 the corporation had conveyed a lot to the trustees of the church. The trustees promised to pay an annual rent, to build a church and a cemetery, and never to use the premises for secular purposes. In return the corporation "covenanted that

22. Oscar Handlin and Mary F. Handlin, *Commonwealth*, rev. ed. (Cambridge, Mass., 1968); Louis Hartz, *Economic Policy and Democratic Thought* (Cambridge, Mass., 1948); George Rogers Taylor, *The Transportation Revolution, 1815–1860* (New York, 1951); Robert A. Lively, "The American System: A Review Article," *Business History Review* 29 (1955):81–96; Harry Scheiber, "Government and the Economy: Studies of the 'Commonwealth' Policy in Nineteenth-Century America," *Journal of Interdisciplinary History* 3 (1972): 135–51.

23. The cases have, however, been used as evidence for the proposition that government has the right to regulate the uses of private property under the police power. See James Kent, *Commentaries on American Law*, 4 vols. (New York, 1826–30), 2:274–76; Thomas M. Cooley, *A Treatise on the Constitutional Limitations* (Boston, 1868), 127, 206–7, 283, 595; Christopher Tiedemann, *A Treatise on the Limitations of Police Power in the United States* (St. Louis, 1886), 427, 583; Ernst Freund, *The Police Power* (Chicago, 1904), 565; Note, "Land Use Regulation and the Concept of Takings in Nineteenth Century America," *University of Chicago Law Review* 40 (1973):854–72; Scott M. Reznick, "Empiricism and the Principle of Conditions in the Evolution of the Police Power: A Model for Definitional Scrutiny," *Washington University Law Review* (1978):1–92; see likewise *Gozzler* v. *Corporation of Georgetown*, 19 U.S. (6 Wheat.) 593 (1821).

24. *Mayor of New York* v. *Slack*, 3 Wheeler's Criminal Cases 237, 259.

25. See J. D. Wheeler, *A Practical Abridgment of American Common Law Cases*, 3 vols. (New York, 1834), 3:527–28; Cooley, *Constitutional Limitations*, 127, 206, 283, 595; John F. Dillon, *A Treatise on the Law of Municipal Corporations*, 5th ed. (New York, 1911), 902, 920, 1032, 2572; Theodore Sedgwick, *A Treatise on the Rules which Govern the Interpretation and Application of Statutory and Constitutional Law* (New York, 1857), 634–35.

the lessees and their assigns, paying the rent and performing the conditions, should quietly use, occupy and enjoy the premises, without any let or hindrance of [the lessor] . . . or any other person."[26] The trustees fulfilled their part of the bargain, paying the rent and building a church house and a burial ground. The city also fulfilled its part, at least until 1823, when it passed the ordinance. According to the lawyers for the church, this act breached the promise in the conveyance (the covenant of quiet enjoyment), and the church proceeded to bring an action on the covenant.

Had this been a simple property case between a private grantor and a private grantee, one can safely assume that the Brick Presbyterian Church would have won. Covenants for quiet enjoyment "run with the land." Whenever they are breached—even if they are breached sixty years after title is conveyed—a cause of action will accrue, so long as privity requirements are met, as they were in this case. Nor can there be much question but that an actionable breach had occurred, for common sense suggests that the ordinance of the corporation was hindering the church in its "enjoyment" of the premises. Indeed, the corporation's lawyers never denied the truth of the church's allegations. How to measure the damages suffered by the church for the loss of future burial rights might have presented a court with difficult although not insuperable technical issues. But had the personality (or the personalities) of the defendant been different, the church would have won.[27]

But the defendant-grantor was the corporation of the city of New York, and to the New York Supreme Court that made all the difference. As a corporation, wrote Judge John Savage for the Court, the city was authorized "to purchase and hold, sell and convey real estate, in the same manner as individuals. They are considered a person in law within the scope of their corporate powers, and are subject to the same liabilities . . . as natural persons." But as a corporation the city had no right to make any contract or agreement that would "control or embarrass" its powers and duties as an agent of the legislature.[28]

A city like New York was a schizophrenic personality, a being divided into two competing and occasionally hostile selves. As a corporation, the city of New York was just another person, subject to the same public authority that governed any other person. As an agent of the legislature, on the other hand, it was that public authority. In the struggle for dominion

26. *Corporation of the Brick Presbyterian Church* v. *The Mayor of New York*, 5 Cowen's 538, 539.

27. Kent, *Commentaries*, 4:459, 462–67; see *Min. CC, 14:601* (1825).

28. *Corporation of the Brick Presbyterian Church* v. *The Mayor of New York*, 5 Cowen's 538, 540.

between public and private identities, between legislative and corporate role, legal ascendancy had to go to the public legislative role. If such were not the case, the sovereignty of the state could be compromised and denied: "The liability of the defendants, therefore, upon the covenant in question, must be the same as if it had been entered into by an individual; and the effect of the by-law upon it the same as if that by-law had been the Act of the State Legislature."[29] If the state legislature had ordered the cemeteries closed down on its own initiative, no action for breach of covenant could have been maintained by the church against the city.[30] Nor could the city now be sued in its corporate capacity for a breach arguably committed in the proper exercise of its derivative legislative powers.

Judge Savage thus conceptualized the case as a conflict between two contrasting aspects of the city of New York. The corporation of the city of New York, which in 1766 had had its own governmental reasons for granting land to private individuals and entities, was reified as a passive and purposeless proprietor. It was the corporation, rather than the Brick Presbyterian Church, which Savage characterized as a mere *rentier*. But it was also the city, in its other, more modern aspect of a public government, which became the venturesome agent of public power. Between these two conceptions, between the private holdings of a city-as-corporate-entity and the legislatively sanctioned public actions of the city-as-government lay a gap that nineteenth-century legal thought could or would not breach.

There was no evidence to suggest that Savage's opinion shocked or surprised lawyers and city officials. In the forty-odd years between the end of the American Revolution and the *Brick Presbyterian Church* case, the legal image of New York City had undergone a profound transformation. By the mid-1820s, Judge Savage's bifurcated public entity had become part of the perceived political landscape and of normal legal discourse. His preference for public, state-delegated governmental powers over the private obligations of the corporation appears likewise representative of contemporary public opinion. Just as urban cemeteries were regarded as relics made anachronistic by growth and change, so the proprietary character of a chartered city stood revealed as an atavism in a republican governmental order. Property rights were no part of the repertoire of legitimate public action. Yet at the same time such rights served as little if any restraint on the delegated positive authority of the state.

Implicitly, Judge Savage denied the existence, let alone the legitimacy, of the legal entity that had been the prerevolutionary corporation of the city of New York. In its place he described a peculiar public agency that happened, almost by accident, to find itself encumbered by chartered

29. Ibid., 540–41.
30. Ibid., 542.

property rights. New York City, as Savage acutely saw, derived its governmental authority from its subservience to the state legislature. As a government, it could never be autonomous from a centralized state polity. As a government, it stood in opposition to all claims of vested property and private right.

And thus, in less than half a century New York City had become the opposite of what it once had been.

CHAPTER 7

A Little Republic in a Republican State

The colonial history of the corporation of the city of New York had ended not with a call to arms, or a Declaration in Philadelphia, or a state constitution, but with the defeat of General George Washington in the Battle of Long Island. On 12 September 1776, his army abandoned the city of New York to the British and retreated to Harlem Heights, on the sparsely inhabited northeastern tip of Manhattan Island. The government and much of the city's populace went into exile, and the city and the harbor were abandoned to the British army, which would not leave them for more than seven years.

When on 25 November 1783, a date later celebrated by New Yorkers as Evacuation Day, Washington returned and the British finally left, the American patriots found themselves in possession of a "ruined city." Every whig who could had left the city in 1776, and many of their houses had become the barracks of the occupying army. The British had devoted their full energy to strengthening the defenses of the town and harbor: building fortifications everywhere and converting public structures to military uses. They had not, on the other hand, maintained the ordinary facilities of a civilian city. Street surfaces had been torn up, the public wharves and slips neglected. And to make matters worse, two fires had gutted one-quarter of the settled city. Everywhere returning New Yorkers found dirt and rubble and disrepair. "A Citizen," making a plea to the legislature for debtor's relief, observed that whig merchants had arrived in 1784 with "little other property than the paper evidence of their patriotism. While in exile, they pleased themselves with the hope of one day returning to those peaceful mansions. . . . The day arrived,—and they returned:—to what? —to heaps of rubbish, and half ruined houses:—to poverty, and to the dread of future wretchedness."[1]

---

1. Sidney Pomerantz, *New York: An American City, 1783–1803*, 2d ed. (Port Washington, N.Y., 1965), 19–20; Oscar Barck, *New York City, 1776–1783* (Port Washington, N.Y.,

The prospects of the newly republican city of New York were grim indeed. Some ten thousand Loyalists had chosen to emigrate at the end of the war, including many of the leading figures in the governmental and commercial life of the prerevolutionary city. And though a large minority of tories remained to face "the fury of the democrats," the city's population was barely more than half what it had been eight years before.[2] Commerce was nonexistent, land titles in chaos. The finances of the corporation were in disarray. What the minutes of the Common Council regularly referred to as the "deranged State of the Finances of this Corporation" might better be regarded as the collapse of the traditional fiscal structure of the city.[3]

For seven years the corporation had not collected any rents from the leaseholders of its properties. Its coffers were empty, its public facilities in shambles. Moreover, it faced a bonded debt of twelve thousand pounds plus six thousand pounds interest inherited from its prerevolutionary predecessor.[4]

Yet at a time when need for corporate revenue was extraordinary, the members of the council were unwilling to enforce a general collection of the arrearages of rents for the period of occupation. In early 1784, immediately after the reestablishment of regular local government, the Common Council formed a committee to collect back rent owed the corporation. In March that committee reported that rent was by and large due from two classes of individuals. There were "many meritorious Persons," patriots, who had "taken an active and decided Part in the cause of their Country and suffered all the Inconveniences of Exile and the Loss of all their Property." But there were others, who "from Poverty and other unavoidable Misfortunes" returned to the city during the British occupation but found that they could repossess their estates only by paying rent to the vestry of Trinity Church, which had served as the agent of the occupying force. In neither case was the collection of back rents justified:

> That in the first Case it will in the Opinion of the Committee be inconsistent with the Rules of Equity to exact from such well attached returning Exiles the Rents which became in arrear from the time of their leaving the City in 1776 to the time of their occupying their respective Estates on the 25th day of November last. . . . That

1966), 207–30, and passim; Thomas V. Smith, *The City of New York in the Year of Washington's Inauguration* (Riverside, Conn., 1972), 5–7; George Dangerfield, *Chancellor Robert R. Livingston of New York, 1746–1813* (New York, 1960), 199.

2. Dangerfield, *Chancellor Robert R. Livingston,* 196–201; Alfred Young, *The Democratic Republicans of New York: The Origins, 1763–1797* (Chapel Hill, 1967), 66–67.

3. *Minutes of the Common Council of the City of New York, 1784–1831,* 21 vols. (New York, 1917–30), I : 103–4 (3 December 1784); 122 (9 March 1785); hereafter *Min. CC.*

4. Ibid., 103–4 (3 December 1784); Pomerantz, *New York,* 363.

in the second Case the Committee are of Opinion that no rent ought, in Justice, to be exacted from the Citizens who were & continued well attached to the American Cause and who returned within the British Lines during the War and actually paid Rent to Mr. Smith [of Trinity Church] for the period of time they actually paid rent.[5]

For a time there appeared to be no way for the corporation to acquire the revenue it needed to clean up and repair the public facilities of the city. The early records of the postrevolutionary Common Council are replete with gloomy references to the continuing effects of the "Ravages of War." One might have expected the corporation to shift the burden of returning the facilities of the city to working order to the "commonalty" that in the past had always assumed the costs of public action. But such could not be the case in the ravaged city, for if the corporation lacked adequate revenue to meet the needs of the time, so too did the private landowners of the city. To remove the mess, abate the nuisances, and restore public order would require public expense. In April of 1784, in fact, the Common Council even admitted that proprietors "too indigent to remove the filth and dirt which may have collected" on their private, individual lots could rely on the corporation to assume the costs of action.[6] Demands on government expanded, even as the traditional resources of the corporation contracted.

In legal and constitutional ways as well, the prospects of the corporation of the city of New York could not have been bleaker. The conservative New York Constitution of 1777 had, it is true, protected the city charter from direct legislative intervention. Like other royal grants of property secured before the Revolution, the Montgomerie Charter was formally placed beyond the reach of any socially radical legislature.[7] The charter, in Kent's phrase, had "withstood the shock of the American Revolution."[8] In theory at least the Montgomerie Charter would continue to define the propertied singularity of the corporation of the city of New York.

But in securing the government of New York City from the threat of legislative expropriation the drafters of the state's first constitution had of-

5. *Min. CC*, 1:1 (10 February 1784); 10–11 (2 March 1784); 162 (17 August 1785).

6. Ibid., 122 (9 March 1785); 29 (22 April 1784). But see 132 (15 April 1785), for a more traditional response by the Common Council to the memorial of inhabitants of the Montgomerie and Out Wards that lots filled with standing water in "the Meadows" had become a nuisance. In this case the council "Ordered that the Proprietors of the said Lots be and they are hereby respectively directed & required without Delay to fill up lots."

7. Young, *Democratic Republicans*, 20; Dangerfield, *Chancellor Robert R. Livingston*, 88–89.

8. James Kent, *The Charter of the City of New York, with notes thereon. Also a Treatise on the Powers and Duties of the Mayor, Aldermen, and Assistant Aldermen, and the Journal of the City Convention* (New York, 1836), 120.

fered the corporation a mixed blessing. Corporate property was protected, but it was also identified both with the much-contested and much-detested rights of the great land magnates of the state and with a special privilege that was anathema in a republican revolutionary culture.[9] In more pointed political terms, the Constitution of 1777 could be regarded as having created the "greatest of all political solecisms," an *imperiam in imperio*, a divided sovereignty. For insofar as the property vested by the constitution included the "property" of carrying on government itself, the corporation of the city of New York would be free of any need to acknowledge the superior authority of the newly sovereign state. A body with its continued existence protected from the will of the sovereign people contradicted cherished propositions that had guided the development of a republican political culture. And as such, the corporation would draw the attack of republican political leaders.

Postrevolutionary political culture was at best ambivalent about the traditional legitimacy and authority of local governments. On the one hand, whig legal theory had been molded in defenses of local autonomy and assertions of the constitutional legitimacy of local legal institutions. The success of the revolutionaries in neutralizing imperial authority during the 1760s and early 1770s can be largely ascribed to their ability to mobilize a vibrant local institutional structure.[10] The new political order that emerged in 1775 and 1776 had been defined by the "instructions" of local communities to their representatives, out of the perceived need of central constitution makers to consult and be guided by the wishes of more or less autonomous local publics.[11] To some of the revolutionaries, in fact, the consequence of the Declaration of Independence was neither a reversion to the state of nature nor a simple transfer of sovereign authority from the crown to the new state governments. Rather, once independent of royal authority, "*the people made a stand at the first legal state, viz. their town incorporations.*"[12]

On the other hand, in 1776 it remained a central tenet of republicanism

9. "Republicanism meant maintaining public and private virtue, internal unity, social solidarity, and it meant constantly struggling against 'threats' to the 'republican character' of the nation" (Robert E. Shallope, "Toward a Republican Synthesis: The Emergence of an Understanding of Republicanism in American Historiography," *William and Mary Quarterly*, 3d ser., 20 [1972]:49–80).

10. See John Philip Reid, *In a Defiant Stance: The Conditions of Law in Massachusetts Bay, the Irish Comparison, and the Coming of the American Revolution* (University Park, Pa., 1977).

11. Patricia U. Bonomi, "Local Government in Colonial New York: A Basis for Republicanism," in Jacob Judd and Irwin Polishook, eds., *Aspects of Early New York Society and Politics* (Tarrytown, N.Y., 1977), 29–50; Michael Zuckerman, *Peaceable Kingdoms* (New York, 1970); William Nelson, *The Americanization of the Common Law* (Cambridge, Mass., 1975); Gordon Wood, *The Creation of the American Republic* (Chapel Hill, 1969), 188–90.

12. Wood, *Creation of the American Republic*, 288.

that a successful republic depended on "a population homogeneous in its customs and concerns." A state had to be considered "one moral whole" dedicated to a unitary public good, or risk destruction in the clash of interests and factions. Although this archaic vision of virtuous homogeneity was soon overwhelmed by the reality of factional politics, the legitimacy of autonomous local constituencies only became more suspect as the revolutionaries developed the implications of their discovery of the sovereignty of the people.[13] Once the whole people had decided on a governmental structure, their decision ought not to be subjected to the conflicting choices of discrete local communities. Concomitantly, such a state government would surely insist on its authority over fragmentary and discordant local governments. The developing liberal theory of power provided little space for intermediary bodies, for institutions not clearly identified either with a monopolistic state government or an individualistic people.[14]

In the highly charged political atmosphere of republican America, chartered corporations like the corporation of the city of New York were the subjects of special scrutiny. Linked in public opinion to the luxury and dissipation identified with royal authority, they were feared as continuing repositories of privilege and corruption. Boroughs were indistinguishable from other corporations in this regard. There was as yet no principled distinction drawn between public and private corporations. And as far as some revolutionaries were concerned, none of them evidenced any guiding conception of the public good. Indeed, incorporated cities probably provided the paradigm of corporate evil. A city like colonial Philadelphia, which had excluded the large majority of its white male residents from representation and which in the early 1770s had attempted to escape any responsibility for "city charges," would not be viewed with much sympathy by republican revolutionaries.[15]

But a chartered city did not have to behave irresponsibly to be viewed with suspicion. The very possession of a charter raised questions. The grants contained in the charter, which an earlier political generation had viewed as the legitimate tools of an effective city government, would now

13. Ibid., 500, 53–65, 344–89; but see Donald S. Lutz, "The Theory of Consent in the Early State Constitutions," in Daniel Elazar, ed., *Republicanism, Representation, and Consent: Views of the Founding Era* (New Brunswick, N.J., 1979), 11–42, for an argument that consent continued to be of primary significance in state constitutional thinking through the 1770s.

14. Oscar Handlin and Mary F. Handlin, *Commonwealth*, rev. ed. (Cambridge, Mass., 1968), 94–96; Gerald E. Frug, "The City as a Legal Concept," *Harvard Law Review* 93 (1980):1057–1154.

15. Judith Diamondstone, "Philadelphia's Municipal Corporation, 1701–1776," *Pennsylvania Magazine of History and Biography* 90 (1966):200. And in 1776 that city's charter was quickly abrogated by Pennsylvania's new state government.

be characterized as "monopolies of legal privilege," bestowing "unequal portions of our common inheritance on favourites."[16] The illegitimacy of these special privileges lay both in the excessive share of the "common" wealth that grants gave to the members of a corporation and, more important for our purposes, in the power that a corporation's charter gave to its members "to effect objects on principles in a great measure independent of the people."[17]

Finally, cities suffered under the additional and familiar charge of being inherently incompatible with a virtuous republican society. Cities were not a part of what John Kasson has labeled the "ecology of liberty."[18] For republican political economists, the future growth of an American economic order properly lay with a productive agriculture and western expansion. Although this vision accepted the necessity of entrepôts to transfer agricultural goods to foreign markets, cities would remain peripheral to the legitimate economic enterprise of the new nation.[19]

It is not surprising, therefore, that the particular structural relationship between New York City and the state of New York became a matter of public debate almost immediately after the reinstitution of civilian government in the city. In 1783 the city's agents in the legislature began proposing "relief" measures—new taxes and subsidies—for the much-burdened city government. The state legislature seems to have considered the city a proper object of public solicitude. But over a two-year period in 1784 and 1785, the state Council of Revision vetoed six bills that concerned (or were perceived by the members of the council as concerning) the reconstructed government of New York City and a seventh in which the corporation may be seen as having been a subject by implication.[20] In each case the veto was accompanied by an elaborate explanation of the council's decision.

These messages were the work of a body notorious among historians for its commitment to limiting the exercise of democratic legislative power.[21]

---

16. Wood, *Creation of the American Republic*, 402; see also Stanley Katz, "Thomas Jefferson and the Right to Property in Revolutionary America," *Journal of Law and Economics* 19 (1976):467–89.

17. Lance Banning, *The Jeffersonian Persuasion* (Ithaca, 1978), 149 (quoting Madison).

18. John F. Kasson, *Civilizing the Machine* (New York, 1976), 7. See Thomas Jefferson, *Notes on the State of Virginia*, ed. Thomas P. Abernathy (New York, 1964), 157–58; Thomas Bender, *Toward an Urban Vision* (Lexington, Ky., 1975), 3–7, 21–29.

19. Drew R. McCoy, "The Republican Revolution: Political Economy in Jeffersonian America, 1776 to 1817" (Ph.D. dissertation, University of Virginia, 1976).

20. All of the messages can be found in Alfred Billings Street, *The Council of Revision of the State of New York* (Albany, 1859), 251–52, 257–58, 261–64, 266–67, 273–74, 274–75, 276.

21. On the later history of the Council of Revision, see Dixon Ryan Fox, *The Decline of Aristocracy in the Politics of New York* (New York, 1919); Jabez Hammond, *The History of*

Still, they are worthy of our attention. The messages made constant reference to general principles of republican political theory, and their language may be taken as reflecting general perceptions of the status of an incorporated city in a republic. In a political culture with a strong tradition of legislative deference to stated local wishes, only the council could act to preserve a unitary, statewide, public good. And thus the members of the Council of Revision perceived their constitutional role as requiring them to remind legislators of their republican principles by vetoing subsidies and grants to entities like the corporation of the city of New York.[22]

The central theme articulated in these messages was the impropriety of making large delegations of legislative power to a corporation. With its own source of wealth as a basis for autonomy, a corporation could not be trusted to identify its interests with those of the state as a whole. And delegating to it the ability to gather additional revenue through taxation only compounded the problem.

In 1784, for example, the Council of Revision vetoed a bill granting the officers of the city the power to raise tax revenues. In part, the disapproval of the council was founded on the ambiguity of the legislative grant, which mandated that individuals "be rated and assessed by the vestrymen according to the estates and other circumstances and abilities to pay taxes, of each respective person." The council thought that such language posed an essential threat to the "blessing" of property because it allowed assessors a measure of discretion as to the size of an individual's burden: "If the assessors are of the richer class of citizens, they will overburden the poor; if chosen from among the poor, they will endeavor to oppress the rich. Thus the first effect of this mode of taxation will be parties among the different classes of citizens, whom mutual interest and the policy of government would bind together."[23]

Obviously, this charge would apply to any government that relied on a discretionary standard for levying taxes on individuals. But it had particular force when directed at "a commercial city, where selfish views may stimulate assessors to oppress their rivals in trade, and destroy that security which makes the basis of commerce." In a message vetoing a similar bill the next year Justice John Hobart asserted that it was "inconsistent with the public good to authorize the corporation to tax the citizens in order to raise money for the very purposes for which, it is to be presumed,

---

Political Parties in the State of New York (Syracuse, 1852); and Merrill D. Peterson, ed., *Democracy, Liberty, and Property: The State Constitutional Conventions of the 1820s* (Indianapolis, 1966).

22. Wood, *Creation of the American Republic*, 191.

23. Street, *Council of Revision*, 251. Only two of the seven vetoed were ever passed into law notwithstanding the objections of the council.

the large estate they are allowed to hold was intended to provide," absent a clear demonstration that their corporate revenue was inadequate. He did not wish to be understood as insisting that the state should not provide "occasional assistance" to help the city deal with the damage of the war years. But if corporations, "which are to most purposes independent republics," should routinely be given the power to raise tax monies it would have "most alarming consequences," particularly in view of the inability of the state to ensure that the revenue raised would be spent on the purposes stated in the legislation.[24]

New York City posed a threat to the republic not just because of its ability to secure legislative aid but also because of its corrupting effect on other associations. Among the many reasons why the members of the Council of Revision thought it improper to charter an association of the tradesmen and mechanics of the city, not the least was the fact that the provisions for the proposed corporation included a formal link with the city government:

> A connection and union of views being thereby rendered necessary, either the mechanics will influence the magistrates, and the extensive powers of the corporation of the city and county of New York be made at some future day instruments of monopoly and oppression; or, which is more probable, the corporation of the city and county of New York will obtain a controlling power over the corporation of the mechanics, and thus add to the extensive influence which that rich and powerful corporation already enjoy, thereby rendering it extremely dangerous to the citizens and to the political freedom of the people.[25]

Similarly, an attempt to establish a society "for encouraging emigration from Germany; relieving the distresses of emigrants, and promoting useful knowledge among their countrymen" did not pass muster because six-sevenths of the governors of the organization would be residents of the city. The influence the corporation might exercise through these men might have "very pernicious consequences, should the supposed interest of this city at some future period interfere with that of other parts of the State."[26]

A chartered corporation like that of New York City violated republican norms not just because of the ways in which it intertwined property, power, and interest but also because the governmental structure in an incorporated city deviated significantly from the separation-of-powers theory to which Americans were increasingly committed. Speaking for the

24. Ibid., 252, 276.
25. Ibid., 261.
26. Ibid., 273.

council, Chief Justice Richard Morris determined that the act incorporating the new city of Hudson had to be overturned. In its proposed plan of government the officers of the city were authorized both to make and to enforce bylaws, "thus blending the legislative, the executive, and the judicial departments in one, which must, in its consequences, be destructive of the rights and liberties of the citizens of the State, residing within the limits of the said city." Likewise, aldermen would become judges of the mayor's court in the proposed city of Hudson, a clear violation of the state constitution because the property of nonresident citizens of the state could be made subject "to judges elected by others, in which they can have no agency."[27] In this message, the Council of Revision mentioned neither New York City nor Albany. But the perceptive reader must have known that the structures of their governments did precisely what Morris said it was improper to permit the new city of Hudson to do.

The attack on such legislation often slipped into a more general critique of the continued existence of corporations in any form in a republican society. Hudson should not be incorporated "because the increase of corporations with extensive powers is destructive of equal liberty tending to the subversion of the Constitution and government of the State." In denying the mechanics their charter Hobart wrote that "all incorporations imply a privilege given to one order of citizens which others do not enjoy, and are so far destructive of that principle of equal liberty which should subsist in every community." Respect for "ancient rights" might explain why the framers of the constitution decided to "tolerate" those corporations already in existence at the time of the Revolution, but "nothing but the most evident public utility can justify a further extension of them."[28]

The message to the corporation of the city of New York was clear. Its autonomy might have been secured by the Constitution of 1777, but its position in the polity of the state could hardly have been less secure. And thus the leaders of the city in the years after 1785 had to work to create a public institution that could be justified by "the most evident public utility." They did so, however, in a context of social change and economic transformation that made irrelevant all predictions and expectations about the proper place of city government in a republican political order.

As we have seen, the situation looked grim in 1784 for both the city of New York and its government. But New York City was on the edge of an explosion in population, wealth, and trade that would carry it in less than twenty-five years to a position of undisputed dominance in the commercial

27. Ibid., 274–76.
28. Ibid., 274–76, 261.

life of the United States. As James Hardie cheerfully reflected in 1827, "The British had scarcely left our city, when order seemed to arise out of confusion."[29] By 1786 the city had already regained its population base from before the Revolution. Between 1790 and 1810 its size tripled, rising from thirty-three thousand to nearly one hundred thousand inhabitants. In a period when the growth of Boston and Philadelphia—New York's main eighteenth-century rivals—barely kept pace with the growth of the nation as a whole, New York City's population increase approximately doubled the national rate.[30]

Blessed with a great deepwater harbor and with easy access to the rich farmland of upstate New York, it was, perhaps, inevitable that New York City would assume a position of dominance in the commercial economy of the early republic. Still, the entrepreneurs and leaders of the New York business community unquestionably made the most of their advantages. By the early nineteenth century the rest of the country was largely dependent on New York City for commercial information and for other forms of news. In the quarter century after the British withdrawal one-third of the nation's foreign commerce passed through New York City. By 1807, just before the imposition of Jefferson's Embargo, the value of the city's exports was more than ten times what it had been in 1790.[31]

If anything, these figures understate the commitment of New Yorkers to economic growth and change. On the night of the British evacuation, returning residents pledged in toasts that "an uninterrupted commerce soon repair the ravages of war!" By 1788 Brissot de Warville observed of New Yorkers, "The activity which reigns everywhere announces a rising prosperity; they enlarge in every quarter."[32] And indeed, scholars speculate that New York City grew faster than other seaport cities of the new republic because of the very consciousness of growth and of the resulting confidence that continued activity might sustain that growth. Businessmen and merchants invested their surplus capital in local enterprises; they reinvested their profits in their own ventures. As Robert Davison has written, "Because businessmen of this period perceived a major trade boom,

29. James Hardie, *The Description of the City of New York* (New York, 1827), 111.

30. Everett S. Lee and Michael Lalli, "Population," in David T. Gilchrist, ed., *The Growth of the Seaport Cities, 1790–1825* (Charlottesville, Va., 1967), 27–31; George Rogers Taylor, "Comment," in ibid., 41; S. J. Crowther, "Urban Growth in the Mid-Atlantic States, 1785–1850," *Journal of Economic History* 36 (1976): 55–84.

31. [John Adams Dix], *Sketch of Resources of the City of New York* (New York, 1827), 13–14; Allan R. Pred, *Urban Growth and the Circulation of Information: The United States System of Cities, 1790–1840* (Cambridge, Mass., 1973); Robert A. Davison, "Comment," in Gilchrist, ed., *Growth of the Seaport Cities*, 70; Thomas C. Cochran, "The Business Revolution," *American Historical Review* 79 (1974): 1449–66.

32. Pomerantz, *New York*, 148; Warville quoted in ibid., 169.

they decided on moves which greatly encouraged economic growth."[33] Local banks, insurance companies, a securities market, and rising land prices were the results. These actions appeared to validate the central premise of liberal political theory: that the pursuit of self-interest was the surest guarantee of the public welfare.[34] And the businessmen's commitment to the "entrepreneurial spirit," their confidence in the beneficent nature of change and innovation, was widely shared in New York's active political community. As Howard Rock has shown, artisans too regarded a market structure unfettered by traditional restrictions on enterprise as the only way to free themselves from "subservience to the merchant community." Masters and journeymen lacked the easy access to credit that characterized the financial situation of their merchant counterparts; they faced the constant threat that the fragile economic base of an artisan community would be destroyed by the introduction of capital-intensive factory enterprises. But they rarely wavered in their belief in the free market and in a changing and growing economic order.[35]

Concurrent with the growth of its private economy, New York City's government went through an equally radical transformation. By the beginning of the nineteenth century neither the finances nor the activities of city government resembled their prerevolutionary counterparts. The corporation of the city of New York had become a public institution, financed largely by public taxation and devoting its energy to distinctively public concerns. The emphasis on doom and gloom and the limited resources of government that characterized the minutes of the Common Council in 1784 and 1785 gave way to an expressed optimistic outlook and a willing-

---

33. Davison, "Comment," in Gilchrist, ed., *Growth of the Seaport Cities*, 69; Julius Ruben, "An Innovating Public Improvement: The Erie Canal," in Carter Goodrich, ed., *Canals and American Economic Development* (New York, 1961), 15–66; Bray Hammond, *Banks and Politics in America before the Civil War* (Princeton, 1956), 164. In 1807, the guidebook author S. L. Mitchell noted that an earlier guidebook was outdated: "But the improvements in New-York outrun the editions of his work. They are so numerous, and carry with them such an alteration of the condition of things, that the statement which was tolerably accurate seven years ago, is at present a very imperfect guide" (*The Picture of New-York; or the Traveller's Guide through the Commercial Metropolis of the United States* [New York, 1807], iv–v).

34. See Ralph Lerner, "Commerce and Character: The Anglo-American as New-Model Man," *William and Mary Quarterly*, 3d ser., 36 (1979):3–26; Joyce Oldham Appleby, *Economic Thought and Ideology in Seventeenth-Century England* (Princeton, 1978); Ronald Seavoy, "The Public Service Origins of the American Business Corporation," *Business History Review* 52 (1978):30–60. Appleby in particular has argued convincingly that a robust, materialistic liberalism quickly merged with the dominant (and originally anticapitalistic) republican political theory. See "What Is Still American in the Political Philosophy of Thomas Jefferson," *William and Mary Quarterly*, 3d ser., 39 (1982):287–309; and "The Social Origins of the American Revolutionary Ideology," *Journal of American History* 64 (1978):935.

35. Howard Rock, *Artisans of the New Republic* (New York, 1979), 149–323.

ness to experiment and innovate in both the structures and the substantive concerns of the corporation. A body that in 1785 could not consider the "kind offer" of Nicholas Ray of London to help the city purchase iron and other materials "which might be necessary for repairing the Ruins,"[36] by the mid-1790s was spending a good deal of time and money on a variety of proposals by hopeful inventors. Many, such as the "Oelopile for correcting the foul Air in crouded Court Rooms," proposed by a Doctor Ball, were not accepted for implementation by the corporation. But other inventions, such as a machine for scouring the public docks, were licensed by the council and its administrative committees. And the members of the Common Council seemed to go out of their way in the minutes to indicate their public support of useful innovations.[37]

The reconstruction of the city's private economy began as soon as the British occupation ended; the reconstruction of the "public economy" of the corporation of the city of New York took longer. As we shall see, it never reassumed the shape it had had before the Revolution. During the twenty-five years from 1783 to 1807, property declined both as a source of corporate revenue and as a resource of public action; conversely, the city grew increasingly dependent on state-delegated tax revenues and on the legislatively based regulatory authority that would later be known as the police power. A city code of ordinances, which according to Chancellor Kent "was formerly distinguished for its brevity and paucity of regulations," suddenly assumed "a new character, in the number and diversity of its regulations, better adapted to the wants of the city, arising from the great increase of business, population, wealth and extent."[38]

As early as 1784 Chancellor Livingston noticed that the government of the city, like its residents, seemed transformed by the "spirit of improvement." For such a conservative the intensity of the activity was itself cause for concern. He warned his distant relation by marriage James Duane, the first mayor of the postrevolutionary city, to "put a stop to your improvements (as they are falsely called) upon the north river," and "be cautious how you exercise the power with which the Legislature have perhaps imprudently invested you." The chancellor believed that the "Island of New York contains a sufficient quantity of ground for a much larger city than

36. *Min. CC*, 1 : 136 (30 April 1785).
37. The council was "sensible of the Ingenuity of the Invention: but cannot at present determine as to the Means of carrying it into execution" *Min. CC*, 2 : 524 (11 March 1799); see also 636 (23 June 1800), and the Petitions from Stevens and Connolly, Petition File, May–August 1787, Municipal Archives and Record Center, New York (machine to clean public docks).
38. Kent, *Charter*, 134. See also Murray Hoffman, *Treatise upon the Estate and Rights of the Corporation of the City of New York, as Proprietors*, 2d rev. ed., 2 vols. (New York, 1862), 7.

New York will ever be" and that there was no need to develop port facilities along the Hudson River.[39]

But the members of New York's Common Council did not share Livingston's pastoral vision of the proper future of the city. Instead of seeking to preserve the beauties of nature and the "pure air of the country" in "the midst of a town," as Livingston urged, the council worked to expand the usable space along the waterfront, building out streets into both rivers until they reached the "permanent line" of the city charter. And then, when the city had run out of space, it petitioned the state legislature for new grants of land further out into the Hudson and East rivers. Year by year the inland boundary of the settled city moved northward: streets were laid out, lots platted, hills flattened, all under the "leveling hand of improvement."[40] By 1807, indeed, the city would apply to the legislature for the power to implement a plan to lay out streets for an enlarged city of New York encompassing nearly all of Manhattan Island, a plan whose drafters conceded provided "space for a greater population than is collected at any spot this side of China."[41]

The irony was that even such grandiose ambition might be outrun by the rushing reality of the changing city. Consider the plans of the building committee of the Common Council, which in October 1803 recommended that the specifications for the new city hall be changed to permit the use of a more expensive marble:

> When it is considered that the City of New York from its inviting
> situation and increasing opulence stands unrivalled, when we reflect
> that as a commercial city we claim a superior standing, our imports
> and exports exceeding any other in the United States. We certainly
> ought in this pleasing state of things, to possess at least one public
> edifice which shall vie with the many now erected in Philadelphia,

39. Dangerfield, *Chancellor Robert R. Livingston*, 217–18.

40. [Mitchell] *Picture of New-York*, 2; on New York City as the paradigm case of an artificially created environment, see Rem Koolhaas, *Delirious New York* (New York, 1978). By 1807, Colonel Jonathan Williams, who had been asked by the Common Council to investigate how best to fortify the harbor against enemy attack, discovered that the channel between Governor's Island and Long Island, which at the time of the Revolution had been three fathoms deep, had increased to seven fathoms at low tide. "The cause of this is universally, and I believe truly, ascribed to the cast given to the East river ebb tide, by the docking out on that side of the city" (*Min. CC*, 4:532 [17 August 1807]).

41. William Bridges, *Map of the City of New-York and Island of Manhattan; with Explanatory Remarks and References* (New York, 1811), 24. The best source for reflections on the spirit of improvement are travelers' guides. See [Mitchell], *Picture of New-York*; Thomas N. Stanford, *A Concise Description of the City of New York* (New York, 1814); Edward M. Blunt, *The Stranger's Guide to the City of New-York* (London, 1818); Edward M. Blunt, *The Picture of New York and Traveler's Guide* (New York, 1828); Hardie, *Description of New-York*.

and elsewhere. It should be remembered that this Building is intended to endure for ages, that it is to be narrowly inspected not
only by the scrutinizing eyes of our own citizens, but of every scientific stranger, and in an architectural point of view it in fact is to give
a character to our City, the additional expense of marble will be fully
counterbalanced when we recollect that from the Elegance and situation of this Building, the public property on the Broadway and Collect [which bordered the proposed building] will much increase in
value, and that the same influence will be extended to property far
beyond these limits and that in the course of a very few Years it is
destined to be in the center of the wealth and population of this
City, a building so constructed will do honour to its founders and be
commensurate with our flourishing situation. Under these impres-
sions the Building Committee strongly recommend that the front
and the two end views of the new hall be built with marble.[42]

The building committee's arguments indicate wide-ranging perceptions of
the role of the city: the assumption that a public building ought to stand as
a symbol for an overtly privatistic city; the competitive comparison to
Philadelphia; the willingness to link the utility of a more beautiful city hall
to a rise in land values (a windfall) for neighboring public and private landowners, indeed, its willingness to justify a higher class of city hall by the
prospect of such a windfall. But the most interesting part of the argument
of the committee is the limits placed on its extravagant vision of the
growth of the city. To build a symbol that would reflect the "opulence"
and "flourishing situation" of the city, one needed only to use expensive
marble for the front and sides of the building. The rear end on the north
side could be faced in ordinary brownstone. No one would notice, for the
building would stand on the northern tip of the settled city. Years would
pass before the "scrutinizing eyes" of "scientific strangers" and citizens
could know the limited reach of municipal extravagance. But of course the
members of the committee were wrong. By the time the new city hall was
completed in 1811 the settled city was already on the verge of reaching
behind Chamber Street back toward Canal Street, leaving the city government's brownstone rear end visible for all to see.[43]

In such an environment, where public order and public planning might
be constantly upset by the workings of the private market economy, the
scope and legitimacy of public authority were uncertain and subject to
conflicting theories and demands. What did the release from the restraints
and strictures of the English mercantile economy mean at the level of local

42. *Min. CC*, 3:379–80 (24 October 1803).
43. See Charles Lockwood, *Manhattan Moves Uptown* (Boston, 1976).

governance? Ought city government to be reconceptualized as a watchman, as later *laissez-faire* theoriests would put it—an institution designed to serve limited and distinctively public purposes? How, if at all, ought city government to further the general welfare of the community?[44]

In New York City such questions were faced in the context of specific and perhaps relatively trivial government decisions. As an ideology of government, republicanism had to be consciously worked out at every level of government and for every issue.[45] If a landowner began subdividing his holdings in a "suburb" of the city, laying out streets and selling lots in the expectation that his streets would connect with those already under municipal control, did the city have any obligation to "accept" those privately developed streets; or was it free to ignore the landowner's plans and actions and to draw street lines as it chose, even to the destruction of the productive activity of the landowner?[46] How, to take a second example, could the Common Council legitimately control the use of port facilities to ensure that small market boats coming from Long Island and New Jersey would continue to find dock space to unload produce, given that the large seagoing vessels on which New York's wealth depended could easily fill most of the available space?[47] What indeed were the distinctive responsibilities of a local government? Should the city take charge of providing residents with an adequate supply of drinking water, should the need be left to the competitive market, or should a single individual (or private corporation) be given a "franchise" for the city's water supply?[48] The existence of such issues and the pressing need to arrive at workable solutions were closely connected to the city's economic and demographic growth after 1783. But the answers the members of New York City's government gave to these questions, as well as the means they chose to implement their answers, had as much to do with a new legal conception of the city and of its role in a free society as with the mere onrush of events.

44. The Handlins explained the changing conception of government as follows: "The assumptions that the government was to mediate in crimes against persons and property, and that it was to defend itself against direct assault remained constant. But the conception that political power was to further the welfare of the community, in the broader sense, by prohibiting harmful activities that might damage it spiritually, socially, and economically, passed through striking transformations in response to the altered conditions of life in the United States. As Jamestown became the tidewater South, as Plymouth became industrial New England, the very conception of community changed, and with it, the understanding of the ends that the government ought properly to pursue" (Oscar Handlin and Mary F. Handlin, *The Dimensions of Liberty* [Cambridge, Mass., 1961], 70–71).

45. I am indebted to Michael Grossberg for this formulation.

46. See Chapter 11.

47. See Chapter 8.

48. See Chapter 10.

By the beginning of the nineteenth century the corporation of the city of New York behaved as if it were a modern *public* corporation. The autonomy once found in the grant of a charter from the crown, on the reception of properties, franchises, and privileges that allowed the corporation to create an individual and inviolable personality, was at an end. The powers that would come to define the activities of the corporation during the early republic derived from the overarching legislative power of the state of New York.

New York City increasingly viewed itself as an integral part of New York State. Its fiscal structure was largely dependent on legislative authorization, its regulatory authority on delegations of legislative power. Though the city's charter would remain for many years beyond the reach of the legislature, it had become little more than an anachronistic reminder of the city's past. Writing in the mid-1830s, Chancellor Kent noted that most of the growth in the number and diversity of municipal regulations had occurred in areas in which the competence of the city to act under the charter was unquestioned and on "matters peculiarly belonging to the city, and the comfort and safety of the inhabitants." Yet before acting the corporation always looked to the state for a grant of "more specific and detailed powers." It had become difficult to determine "how far an ordinance of the Common Council rests upon the authority of the charter and how far upon the authority of some special statute." But, cautioned Kent, whenever "the latter exists, the exercise of the power is of course to be referred to the statute as the more certain and paramount authority."[49] The collected enactments of the New York State legislature were now the "true" charter of the city.[50]

By 1802, the publicist James Cheetham could look at the corporation and see only "the child and creature of the state," existing as an "instrument" to satisfy the legitimate ends of government. Such an entity was subject to the intervention of the legislature whenever "found to be inef-

---

49. Kent, *Charter*, 134–36; see also Hoffman, *Treatise*, 72.

50. In 1813, the New York State legislature passed "An act to reduce several Laws, relating particularly to the City of New-York, into one Act," as part of a systematic revision of its laws, which became for the next twenty years the general statutory basis of authority for New York City's government (William Van Ness and John Woodworth, eds. *Laws of New York*, 36th sess. 2 vols. [Albany, 1813], c. 76). This statutory "reduction" was already 120 pages long in 1813. In 1801, James Kent and Jacob Radcliff had published an edition of the laws of New York relating particularly to the city of New York. See generally, *Index to the Laws of the State of New York, 1777–1857* (New York, 1858), 430–52. Between 1786 and 1795 the legislature passed 38 acts dealing directly and exclusively with New York City; between 1806 and 1815 there were 103 such acts; between 1826 and 1835 there were 199; and between 1846 and 1855 there were 412.

fectual for the accomplishment of the purpose intended," and it was easily distinguishable in its nature from private corporations, whose rights, according to Cheetham, were founded on the sanctity of private property.[51]

Yet even as New York City became the agent of the state legislature, so, in a more practical sense, did the state legislature become the willing agent of the city. Legislative acts provided the foundation for the new structure of city government, but those acts were invariably drafted by city employees. Formally, the state had the right to intervene in the affairs of the municipality. But through the first third of the nineteenth century that remained only a formal right. From the perspective of the Common Council, the state legislature existed to provide legitimation for the initiatives of the corporation.

Indeed, by 1815 the New York Supreme Court had made it a legal presumption that state legislation touching on municipal government reflected the stated preferences of that government. The city had tried to recover a $3,000 fine from a Mr. Ordrenan for violating an ordinance against the storage of gunpowder in unauthorized places. The ordinance permitted the city to collect $125 for every hundredweight of gunpowder, and the defendant had been convicted on three counts of keeping a total of 4,400 pounds of gunpowder. Ordrenan argued, however, that the act of the state legislature on which the ordinance was founded limited the recovery of the city to $250 per count, or a maximum penalty of $750.[52]

And the court agreed, holding that even if the enabling statute contained no language to indicate that it was passed on the application of the corporation "yet we must presume that it was so passed, it being almost the invariable course of proceeding for the legislature not to interfere in the internal concerns of a corporation, without its consent, signified under its common seal."[53] The statute thus stood as a statement of the wishes of the corporation. And what really bound the city to the limits stated in the statute was not the power of the state legislature over subordinate units but rather a theory of estoppel. The city ought not deviate from terms set out in its own legislative creations.[54]

51. James Cheetham, *Annals of the Corporation* (New York, 1802), 81–85. Most other observers of city-state relations did not characterize them in such radical terms. The formal statement of a public-private split in the law of corporations still lay in the future.

52. *Mayor v. Ordrenan*, 12 Johns. Rep. 122 (1815). The city countered with the claim that its enforcement of the ordinance was based both on the statute and on the residual lawmaking power granted the Common Council under the Montgomerie Charter.

53. Ibid., 125.

54. *Ordrenan* remained good law through the 1840s. See *Matter of Seventeenth Street*, 1 Wend. 261 (1828); *Hart v. Mayor of Albany*, 9 Wend. 571 (1832); *Stokes and Gilbert v. the Corporation of the City of New York*, 14 Wend. 87 (1835). See also the Opinion Letter of Counsel to the Corporation Michael Ulshoeffer in New York City, Board of Aldermen, Committee

Like other corporations, the corporation of the city of New York shaped itself with the help of legislative enactments. City leaders thus created their public entity using some of the same legal tools others used to make private enterprises.[55] In both cases change was accomplished not through the bald assertion of the power of the central state over subordinate units but through the willingness of corporate leaders to commit their institution to the exercise of state-derived powers. In the case of New York City's leaders, it was not their powerlessness that commands our attention but their power, their ability to mold the corporation into a government that accorded with their vision of a properly public institution.

This conclusion is not meant to deny that much of the motivation for change derived from the tenuous and discordant place of chartered corporations in republican political theory. In identifying the interests of the city with the state legislature, city leaders sought to immunize the city from attack by those who viewed corporate power as inherently corrupt and who argued that there could be no legitimate institutions located between state and individual. Yet the motivations of the makers of modern municipal government cannot be encapsulated by the fear of republican opposition. They also acted out of an articulated desire to mold the corporation into a better producer of the public good. They "knew," as their predecessors had not, that government did not need to provide incentives to encourage commercial development. On the other hand, they had forgotten the significance of chartered autonomy as a bulwark against externally imposed change. For them, state legislation that modified the traditional terms of chartered government was not interference in the affairs of their private institution. It was, rather, positive and necessary action that allowed them to become planners of the public welfare.

We should not exaggerate the coherence of the republican vision of city government. There was much that city leaders disagreed over; there was much else that remained unsettled through much of the nineteenth century. It was, to take one example, never resolved to what extent the city ought to remain a licensor of trades and occupations and what the implications of licensing ought to be. At the same time, such uncertainties cannot

---

on Streets, *Report of . . . on the Subject of regulating the grounds between North and 14th Street, The Bowery and East River* (New York, 1826), 19–22. In John Dillon's treatise, however, *Ordrenan* had become authority for the different proposition that a municipal corporation was to be strictly limited in its exercise of power, without any covering assumption of consent. See *A Treatise on the Law of Municipal Corporations* (New York, 1872), 209, 292, 293. See criticisms in Hoffman, *Treatise*, 61–62.

55. See sources collected and discussed in Robert A. Lively, "The American System: A Review Article," *Business History Review* 29 (1955): 81, and Harry Scheiber, "Government and the Economy," *Journal of Interdisciplinary History* 3 (1972): 135.

hide the basic agreement of Federalists and Jeffersonians alike that city government ought to constitute a distinctively *public* sphere of human endeavor, autonomous and separate from the private, market economy, but authoritative within its own expanding purview.[56]

56. For the concept of generations as applied to American history, see Morton Keller, "Reflections on Politics and Generations in America," *Daedalus* 107 (1978): 123–35.

CHAPTER 8

The Changing Role of Property

The members of the postrevolutionary government of New York City could take a curious comfort in the Council of Revision's "messages." The corporation was resented, perhaps despised; it was regarded as incongruous in a republican polity. Yet the council conceded the inviolability of its governmental form. Its powers as a chartered corporation might be circumscribed; but its existence did not become a constitutional issue, as had that of the corporation of Philadelphia in the new state of Pennsylvania.

Yet any comfort they drew from these messages would have been lessened by the political problems of maintaining the corporate government of New York City within a republican state. A bare existence would not suffice. And if the most conservative part of the state government—a council that considered its primary role to be protection of property from the "rapacity of governors"[1]—saw the properties of the chartered city of New York as a threat to republican government, then surely the interests of the corporation would find little support elsewhere in state government.

New York City had to bind itself to New York State. It had to depoliticize its position as a privileged local government, ignore its theoretical autonomy, and make its actions appear to emanate from the power of the state legislature.[2] We cannot find any statement by the political leaders of the city saying that is what they set out to do. We cannot even hypothesize that there was a conscious program that guided their actions. All we know is that they did so.

Symbols of corporate autonomy were the first to go. The oath administered to freemen on admittance to the corporation had not been modified since 1731. In 1784 the Common Council drafted an oath that retained

1. Alfred Billings Street, *The Council of Revision of the State of New York* (Albany, 1859), 251.
2. See Donald S. Lutz, "The Theory of Consent in the Early State Constitutions," in Daniel Elazar, ed., *Republicanism, Representation, and Consent* (New Brunswick, N.J., 1979), for the thesis that republicanism was essentially identified with legislative power.

most of the statements of obligation that had characterized the 1731 version. Freemen were expected to be obedient to the mayor and other officers, to protect "the franchises and customs"—the properties—of the corporation, to protect the peace and order of the city from "unlawful gatherings, assemblies, or meetings, or of any conspiracies," and to act generally in ways that accorded with "the laws and customs of the said city." What had been dropped from the earlier oath was noteworthy: freemen were no longer expected as freemen to bear their share of the fiscal burdens of the corporation. Presumably that responsibility was now a general consequence of property ownership or residence. But the 1784 oath is more interesting for what it retained than for what it discarded. It still insisted that freemen give a measure of political allegiance to the corporation as an autonomous political entity.[3]

But two years later the oath was rewritten. Now a freeman swore only to "maintain the lawful franchises and customs thereof, and keep the same City harmless as much as in me lieth, and that I will in all things do my Duty as a good and faithful Freeman of the same City ought to do." What a good and faithful freeman ought to do no longer included obedience to the mayor, being responsible for the peace of the city, or acting in accordance with its laws and customs. Those aspects of corporate existence that had shaped the legal and governmental autonomy of New York City no longer constituted responsibilities of the freeman. His only distinctive duty as a citizen of the city as well as of the state was to care for the properties of the corporation. Those had, of course, been central to the pre-revolutionary corporation; and we should not discount this residual commitment. But even that continuing responsibility was now modified in the oath by the ominous sounding "lawful," as if the drafters of the oath were not certain that all of the city's properties would pass muster if subjected to judicial or legislative review.[4]

3. Robert F. Seybold, *The Colonial Citizen of New York City* (Madison, 1918), 24–25. See Chapter 2, above.

4. Ibid. See *Cortelyou* v. *Van Brundt*, 1 Johns. Rep. 313 (1806). A similar indication of the corporation's willingness to deny its autonomy occurred in 1786, when the Common Council formed a committee to consider various complaints that had been made regarding the weights and measures, which "by the Law of this State" ought to be the standards. In 1770, the city's agent in London had received a standard set of English weights, which were discovered to be lighter than those in use in the city. The mayor, however, had ordered the measurers and weighers of the city to continue to use the old standards. Evidently at that time the city felt free to deviate from the imperial norm. By 1786, all this was in the past. An act of the legislature of 10 April 1784 set the standard for the state (including the city), and the Common Council had to get itself a new set of weights and measures (*Minutes of the Common Council of the City of New York, 1784–1831*, 21 vols [New York, 1917–30], 1:226 [28 June 1786]; 232 [19 July]; 238 [7 August]; hereafter *Min. CC*).

How the corporation managed its estate in the years after the British evacuation becomes crucial, therefore, to our assessment of the response of the city to the republican world in which it found itself. From one perspective the answer is simple. In 1784 and in 1803, as in 1734 and 1764, the Common Council of the corporation of the city of New York devoted much of its energy and time to the conservation and management of its properties.

In the crisis atmosphere of 1784, in particular, the overriding concern of the corporation was to extract revenue from its estate. Thereafter, the number of entries in the minutes of the Common Council dealing with property matters remained roughly constant, although they made up a declining percentage of the total business of the council. By 1787, only 20 percent of the entries in the minutes were concerned with corporate properties. By 1807, the number of entries concerned with property matters had tripled, but those entries now made up less than 11 percent of the total business of the council (See Table 8.1). But throughout the postrevolutionary period, the Common Council continued to grant waterlots, lease ferries, enforce deed covenants, and prosecute those who encroached on corporation lots. And one could argue that the property practices of the early nineteenth-century corporation remained fundamentally continuous with those of its mid-eighteenth-century predecessor.

Such a perspective would miss much of what is most interesting about the practice of government in postrevolutionary New York City, however. The government of the city continued to conserve its corporate estate as best it could. But the property of the corporation was increasingly peripheral to its governmental enterprise. Members of the Common Council no longer relied on private rights to ensure public order. They were learning to separate and distinguish public power from private right. And as they clarified their commitment to a liberal theory of government, they incorporated what they learned into the management of the city's corporate estate—with significant results.[5]

The first deviations from traditional practice emerged out of the corporation's need to deal with the "deranged state" of its finances. The city government could collect only a fraction of the back rent owed it. It had been denied any of the proceeds of sales of the confiscated estates of departed Loyalists. In the wake of the messages of the Council of Revision it certainly could not feel confident of its ability to secure from the legisla-

---

5. As Edward Countryman has noted, "The problem after 1777 was not the structure of the new political order but what men did with that structure" (*A People in Revolution* [Baltimore, 1981], 286).

TABLE 8.1. *Entries into the Minutes of the Common Council by Subject Matter, 1767, 1787, and 1807*

	1767	1787	1807
Total Entries in Year	157	310	1,642
Property (management, supervision, sales, enforcement of estate)	25.5	62	180
Trade or commercial regulations	9.5	28	86
Public (noncommercial regulations)	8	71	275
Appointments and Licenses			
commercial	4	10	45
noncommercial	2	19	151
Payment of accounts, salaries, and other bills of the corporation	88	61	247
Taxes and audits of the fiscal affairs of the corporation	7.5	23	126
Certification of elections and swearing in of officers	9	17	17
Streets	–	19	284
City administration	–	–	111
Ordinances	–	–	67
Fines	–	–	43
Education	–	–	10

Source: *Minutes of the Common Council of the City of New York, 1675–1776*, 8 vols. (New York, 1905); *Minutes of the Common Council of the City of New York, 1784–1831*, 21 vols. (New York, 1917–30).

ture the right to lay local taxes. So it embarked on what might well have been the only course of action still open to it: the sale of corporation property.[6]

In December 1784 the Common Council ordered that twelve lots next to

6. See generally, George Black, *Municipal Ownership of Land on Manhattan Island* (New York, 1891), 35–50; John W. Reps, "Public Land, Urban Development Policy, and the American Planning Tradition," in Marion Clawson, ed., *Modernizing Urban Land Policy* (Baltimore, 1973), 29–40.

the Corporation Wharf on the lower Hudson be sold to the highest bidder. The 5,550 pounds which the corporation earned from the sale was sufficient to meet the government's immediate needs and to "discharge so much of the . . . Debt as at present is become absolutely necessary."[7] But the basic fiscal problems of the corporation remained.[8] Soon the Common Council ordered the surveyor of the city to conduct a survey of all "the vacant land belonging to the corporation situated between the post and Bloomingdale roads" and to divide that land into five-acre lots, with a view to their sale as soon as a reasonable price could be realized. But it was not until 1789 that 190 acres were sold to seven individuals, for a total of 5,400 pounds or about 28 pounds per acre. Much of this land lay between what is now 32nd and 42nd streets; the rest was located slightly further to the north.[9]

It seems that for the drafters of the documents that formalized these sales, as for the members of the Common Council, the sales had no purpose beyond the revenue they provided the corporation. The deeds contained no covenants or restrictions on the fee conveyed to the purchasers.[10] The sales enacted no program of development in northern Manhattan. They contained nothing that evidenced any desire on the part of the corporation to control the use of those portions of the upper commons that it had sold. All that was wanted from the sale was cash for the corporation's coffers.

During the 1790s, the economic position of the city improved dramatically. City government, like the rest of the New York community, became absorbed by the prospects of future greatness that awaited an enlarged New York City. It was apparent that growth would occur to the north, filling up an increasing portion of the island. Soon the settled city would encompass more and more of the "waste and common" lands that had once constituted the least significant part of the estate of the corporation. And most of that land was still owned outright by the city. It would seem, therefore, that the government of the city was in an extraordinarily strong position to shape and even control the growth of this enlarged city of New York, just as it had earlier helped to develop the waterfront of the lower city. Clearly, as George Black stated, "A far sighted policy could hardly fail to suggest itself as to the commons."[11]

But when it finally emerged from a committee of the council in Febru-

7. *Min. CC,* 1:103–4 (1784); Black, *Municipal Ownership,* 36–37.
8. On 27 December 1786, the Common Council resolved that all of its income from real estate would be committed to paying off the principal of the debt (*Min. CC,* 1:269).
9. Black, *Municipal Ownership,* 37.
10. Both leases and sales were inscribed on standardized forms.
11. Black, *Municipal Ownership,* 38.

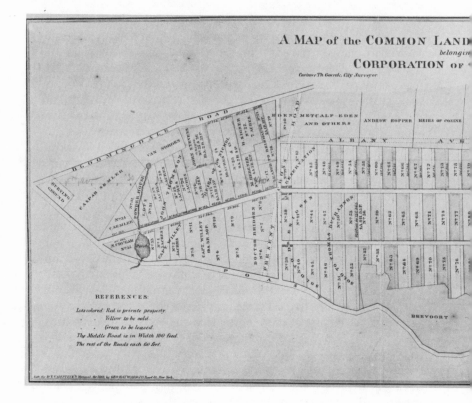

FIGURE 8.1. *Map of Common Lands between Three and Six Mile Stones, 1796*

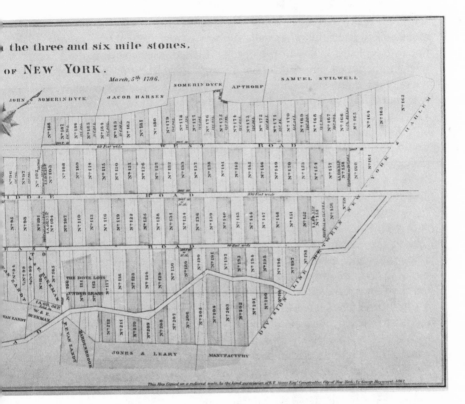

ary 1796, that policy was simply to sell half of the lots of the upper commons and to lease the other half. As before, no covenants or use restrictions were placed in any of the deeds.[12] Indeed, even the leased lots were unencumbered by any restrictions in use.[13] According to the committee, the only reason for not selling off the whole commons immediately was the fear that doing so would reduce the value of the individual lots at sale. Leasing half would give the corporation a better price for the lots it did sell. And once in private hands, both the land sold and the land leased would be quickly improved, and "the one half which is to be leased will at the end of the [lease] term be worth more than the whole now is."[14]

As a forecast of the rising value of city-owned land, the committee's judgment was astute. Through the first thirty years of postrevolutionary city government, the rental value of corporate real estate more than kept pace with the general rise in assessed valuation in New York City, even though the size of the corporation's holdings declined significantly. In 1790, municipal revenue from franchises and properties (excluding sales) was 4,504 pounds, while the total assessed valuation of property located in the city (approximately six-sevenths real property) was 2,338,000 pounds. Twenty-three years later, the city's "ordinary" revenue was $128,000, and the total assessed valuation of real estate was $27,000,000.[15]

But it is the underlying policy that deserves our closest attention. Ultimately, the committee intended to take the city out of the landholding business. The leased half of the commons was held by the corporation after 1796 with a clear expectation of future sale. Whether or not to sell was not an issue discussed by the Common Council. City leaders were concerned only with how best to secure for the corporation a good return on the land when sold. Had the corporation been a private individual, some worried parent or banker might have warned it about the addictive dan-

12. See, for example, Corporation Grant and Release to Doctor Samuel Nicoll, 1 June 1795, Grant Book E, Municipal Archives and Record Center; hereafter MARC; to Nicholas Cruger, 30 January 1797, ibid.; to Gilbert C. Willet, 25 February 1799 in Murray Papers Miscel. MSS M, New York Historical Society, hereafter NYHS; see generally the liber, "Sale of Common Lands, 1797–1810," MARC.

13. See the liber, "City Rents, 1784–1844," MARC.

14. *Min. CC*, 2:216 (10 February 1796).

15. New York City, "Records of the Board of Supervisors, 1809–1836," MARC; David T. Valentine, *Manual of the Corporation of the City of New-York* (New York, 1853), 512–20; Sidney Pomerantz, *New York: An American City, 1783–1803*, 2d ed. (Port Washington, N.Y., 1965), 357. As late as 1830 the city's corporate revenue still rose in rough proportion to assessed valuation. That year the city earned over $260,000 on its holdings as against an overall valuation of about $75 million. That pattern ended in 1844, when the council authorized the commissioners of the sinking fund to sell all uncommitted real estate still owned by the corporation (Black, *Municipal Ownership*, 60–61).

gers of dipping into capital. But it was not a private individual. And the sale of its capital assets appeared natural and inevitable.

In this attitude, of course, New York City was like other governments in republican America, notably the federal government. "By the early nineteenth century," J. Willard Hurst has written, "dominant public opinion took for granted that . . . the normal destination of the public domain should be to come to rest in private hands."[16] Yet in legal theory the corporation of the city of New York remained different from those of other governments. Only two decades before the committee's report, the commons would have been treated as a portion of the private demesne of the city. Lots might have been conveyed or leased to serve the changing governmental objectives of the corporation. No one, however, would have assumed that the commons was a form of property that could be used productively only if put without restrictions into private hands. And in legal theory, at least, nothing had changed.

But by the end of the eighteenth century, the Common Council no longer viewed the estate of the corporation as a repository of government power. From the perspective of city government, the only conceivable use of the city-owned commons was as a source of revenue. In 1806, in fact, the Common Council decided that it did not wish to continue leasing any of what by then it considered its "public property." A majority of the members of the council rejected its earlier decision to time sales to get the best possible price; they wanted only to convey the land to private owners as quickly as possible.[17] Like the national government after the passage of the Northwest Ordinance of 1787, the city was now firmly committed to a program of disposal of unrestricted grants in fee simple absolute.[18] The

16. James Willard Hurst, *Law and Social Process in United States History* (Ann Arbor, 1960), 79. See generally Paul Gates, *History of Public Land Law Development* (Washington, D.C., 1968), 121–495.

17. The closest the council seems to have come to a debate on the policy was in 1806, when the committee "appointed to recommend the mode in which the residue of the common lands should be disposed of" reported that the Dove Lots, a particularly valuable parcel of land in the remaining commons, would "no doubt meet with ready and advantageous sales either on a lease or in fee." The committee considered reserving the lots for public purposes but decided instead to recommend that the lots be leased on thirty-year leases. Their motion was defeated, however, and the council resolved that the committee should report what proportion of the lots ought to be sold immediately in perpetuity (*Min. CC*, 4:173–75 [7 April 1806]). Nearly a year later the committee returned with a plan that would leave a public square (Hamilton Square) in the middle of the "trace" but recommended that all the remaining lots should be sold in fee simple (ibid., 388–89 [30 March 1807]). See "Sale of Common Lands, 1797–1810."

18. See Thomas Donaldson, *The Public Domain: Its History, with Statistics* (Washington, D.C., 1884), 156–60. Reps, "Public Land," 29–40, covers much the same ground but came

city's part in the development of Manhattan Island would not be that of a property owner.

Compared to its disposal of the commons, there is far more seeming continuity in the corporation's management of its waterlots. During the thirty-five years after the Revolution, the corporation continued to hand out waterlots on terms that imposed obligations on grantees for the development of harbor facilities in lower Manhattan. Through the 1790s, relatively few new grants—generally no more than one per year—were made by the Federalist Common Council. After the Jeffersonian takeover in 1804, however, the pace of waterfront disposal quickened. In 1804 a record fifty-two grants were made. Thereafter, the number of grants per year varied from zero to eighteen. Throughout the period the corporation maintained an ongoing supervisory role, insisting the grantees fulfill their obligations to build the streets, slips, and piers that they had covenanted to construct. Indeed, the city government proceeded forcefully against those who did not keep facilities in repair or who did not complete their covenanted responsibilities on time.[19]

Even the changes that did occur in waterlot grants during the 1780s and 1790s seem at first glance to represent less a fundamental break with past patterns than an evolution consistent with the prerevolutionary history of the corporation. In the mid-1780s, for example, the drafters of deeds for the corporation appear to have experimented with alternative forms. Thus if the grant was conditioned by a right of entry retained by the corporation, the grantee might receive a full warranty of title. If, on the other hand, the corporation did not retain a right of entry and simply made the completion of public works the consideration for the right to collect rents and profits from the waterlot, the grantee received only a quitclaim deed.[20] That the city would transfer title by a quitclaim deed in which the corporation made no assurance of the value or validity of its holding suggests some change in the relationship between city government and the recipients of waterlot grants. But it hardly seems to represent a major break with the past.

---

to my attention after the text had been completed. For the later history of New York's public lands, see Edward K. Spann, *The New Metropolis: New York City, 1840–1857* (New York, 1981), 158–73.

19. "Corporation Property," manuscript at MARC. See *Min. CC,* 1:180 (18 October 1785); 381 (26 June 1788); 399 (17 September 1788); 456 (5 June 1789); 595 (17 September 1790); 2:245 (10 May 1797); 440 (14 May 1798); 3:233 (14 March 1803); 240 (21 March 1803); 610 (24 September 1804).

20. See Corporation Grant to Jacobus Lefferts, 1785; to Robert Watts, 1786; to the Assignees of the Estate of Andrew Van Tuyl, 1786; to Wyandt Van Zandt, 1786, all in Grant Book D, MARC.

Similarly, the corporation moved more forcefully after the Revolution to ensure that the lots ended up in the hands of those who would best and most quickly develop them. Thus a neighboring proprietor of land with an expectation in a waterlot grant might find his or her "right" cut short by the actions of the Common Council. When, to take one example, a committee reported that Dey's Dock was out of repair and unfit for the passage of carts and that there was a need for a new pier to be sunk in the Hudson, the Common Council ordered the children and residuary devisees of Deyrick Dey to apply to the council for a waterlot grant within one month "or that in Default thereof this Board do take the necessary Measures for having the said Pier built and the Dock along the Slip repaired and filled up."[21] And when, to take another example, John McComb and Daniel Neven petitioned the council for a grant of waterlots fronting land they did not own, the council decided that because the "object of the Petitioners if carried into effect would essentially promote the Improvement of the City & the Convenience of the Citizens," the actual owners of the frontage had only six weeks to "engage to make improvements equally beneficial to the Public as those which are expressed" in the proposal of McComb and Neven. Otherwise, those owners faced the loss of their interest in the waterlots.[22] By 1790, the Common Council had actually tried to extinguish some preemption claims through private negotiations in order to secure the construction of wider slips.[23] But again, these changes are hardly inconsistent with the concern of the prerevolutionary corporation for the proper development of its waterfront. The arsenal of tools available to the corporation may have been enlarged; the uses to which those tools might be put did not appear to have changed.[24]

Nevertheless, behind these apparent continuities lay a reconceptualization of the role of the city as a grantor. The willingness to consider alternative deed forms was a short-lived phenomenon. By the late 1780s the Common Council had evidently resolved to offer grantees only a quitclaim deed. Every waterlot grant now ended with the following language:

> It is hereby covenanted and agreed upon by and between all the said parties to these presents and the true intent and meaning hereof also; and it is truly so declared that the present grant or any words or anything in the same contained shall not be deemed, construed or taken to be a covenant or covenants on the part and behalf of the said parties of the first part [the corporation] or their successors but

21. *Min. CC*, 1:240 (14 August 1786).
22. Ibid., 248 (13 September 1786).
23. Ibid., 589 (2 September 1790).
24. See Pomerantz, *New York*, 295.

only so far as to pass the estate, right, title, and interest they have or
may lawfully claim by virtue of their several charters.[25]

The corporation no longer guaranteed the right of grantees to profit
from their grants; it no longer protected their "quiet enjoyment" of the
property. Warranty deeds smacked too much of monopolies and exclusive
franchises; they suggested too much continuing involvement by city government in private land development. Perhaps a warranty deed was suddenly recognized as implying that the public actions of the city might be
bound by its private commitments.[26] In any case, as a property holder the
corporation would assume no continuing obligation toward the owners of
waterlot grants after the completion of the conveyance.

Similarly, the focus of argument over the claims of neighboring proprietors to waterlot grants shifted after the Revolution. Before 1775, the right
of a landowner to a grant had been clearly identified as a customary right
founded on the practices of the Common Council. Landowners owned no
formal legal interest in a neighboring waterlot. Their claims derived neither from the charters of the city nor from the land law of the province of
New York. At most, they constituted "customs" of the corporation, expectations that might be contended for before the Common Council but did
not limit its title.

After the Revolution, by contrast, landowners argued with increasing
success that they held true preemptive interests, separate and alienable
legal rights, in neighboring waterlots.[27] They might sell a lot yet retain the
preemption of the waterlot next door;[28] or, alternatively, they might sell
the preemption alone.[29] George Codwise, to take one example, was granted

25. See, for example, Corporation Grant to Thomas Ellison, 3 January 1804, Ellison Papers, NYHS.

26. See Chapter 6 for discussion of this issue in the context of the *Brick Presbyterian
Church* case.

27. See Corporation Grant to Isaac Roosevelt, 12 March 1792, Grant Book E, MARC.

28. In 1795, Israel Wood petitioned the Common Council for a waterlot. The report of the
committee to consider his petition explained that Wood's title to the neighboring lot derived
from Richard Varick (the mayor at that time), who had expressly retained "the right of having and receiving any manner of Wharfage cranage or other profit which May at any time
hereafter accrue or arise from any part of the Wharf or Dock in front of the premises hereby
conveyed or the right of application to the Mayor Aldermen and Commonalty . . . for a
Grant of any Land under the Water . . . in front of the same premises. But that the same
shall be and remain to the use of the said Richard Varick his heirs and Assigns forever." The
committee concluded that the preemption was still vested in Varick, and Wood's petition was
rejected (*Min. CC*, 2:186–88 [12 October 1795]).

29. In 1786 the Common Council was about to grant a waterlot to Archibald Kennedy to
the east of the Fly Market Slip when it realized that Kennedy had conveyed the preemption
to John Watts. Therefore, it made the grant to Watts instead (*Min. CC*, 1:224 [15 June
1786]). The same occurred with a conveyance from the heirs of Philip Livingston to Cary
Ludlow, with the same result (ibid., 224–25).

a waterlot in 1803 as his share in the partition of the estate of John By-vanck, who had owned a lot bounded on the north by Water Street and the Hudson.[30] And landowners now claimed that their interest in a waterlot grant rested on the authority of state courts of law rather than on the customs of the corporation. When landowners were told by the council that they faced loss of their "rights" if they did not quickly promise to improve the lands under water, they could and would go to the state supreme court to seek a legal declaration of their retained rights to purchase the water-lots. The Common Council was no longer perceived as holding the power to define the basis for their rights.[31]

The most intriguing postrevolutionary changes in the property affairs of the corporation occurred in the stated terms of the waterlot grants. As before the Revolution, the members of the council continued to tie grants to the development of waterfront facilities. But from the early 1790s on, grants incorporated a changed perception of the relationship of the private landowner to the governmental affairs of the city.

In 1791, for example, Alexander Macomb was granted a huge lot between Delancey and Rivington streets in an area of the city soon to undergo rapid development. The terms of the grant were complex. The city proposed to build public slips on either side of Macomb's waterlot "for the use and accommodation of all such vessels, Boats, and craft as usually use occupy and resort to the public slips in the said city." Constructing the slips would be a city responsibility, although Macomb promised to build a street or wharf alongside each slip whenever the corporation so required. No completion date was set; indeed, groundbreaking was made contingent on a later decision by the Common Council. Nor was Macomb obliged to build a street at the rear of his grant, as would have been customary before the Revolution. Instead, the deed asserted that whenever it might "become necessary for the public convenience that there should be laid out or regulated one or more street or streets leading across the said hereby granted premises," the city should be able to take them "without paying therefor." And Macomb covenanted never to assert any right to compensation. Macomb could not profit from the actions of the city; but he was not obliged to

30. Corporation Grant to George Codwise, 7 July 1803, Grant Book F, MARC.

31. See the Riker and Remsen Claims to Burling Slip in Julius Goebel and Joseph H. Smith, eds., *The Law Practice of Alexander Hamilton*, 5 vols. (New York, 1964–81), 4: 449–50; *Peter Pra Van Zandt et al* v. *The Mayor, Aldermen and Commonalty of the City of New York*, 21 N.Y.C. Super. Ct. (8 Bosworth) 375–96 (1861); *Min. CC*, 3:232–33 (14 March 1803) (Opinion of Counsel to the Corporation, Richard Harison).

By 1808, the street commissioner worried that if the corporation did not publicly state its intention to reserve a group of waterlots for a public basin in front of land owned by Trinity Church, which the church was about to sell, the purchasers of Trinity Church lots would obtain an implied preemption in the waterlots that might oblige the corporation to compensate them for the taking (*Min. CC*, 5:377–79 [19 December 1808]).

build a street for public use. Street construction was on its way to becoming a public responsibility, the positive obligation of a public institution.[32]

Other more conventional grants had similar features. Waterlot grantees were still compelled to undertake public works for the city, but it became routine for the deeds to require only prospective street or wharf construction. Nor were time limits set at the time of the conveyance. Rather, grantees were told that they would have to comply with stated conditions within three months of a later Common Council decision, but not before then. Part of the explanation for such terms must be located in the new city practice of giving out waterlots ahead of immediate demand. City government was increasingly concerned with developing an orderly plan for street development not dependent on the timing of waterlot grant applications. But those facts indicate what is most striking about these terms: public action was regarded as entirely distinct from the "private" action of making a waterlot grant. Before the Revolution a covenanted grant had embodied a public obligation expressed in the private terms of a real estate deed. Now, in the new world of the new republic, a private deed would serve the private interests of the corporation and its grantees, and public action would await public expression by the Common Council.[33]

The terms of these grants tell us that city leaders were learning to distinguish the public from the private self of the corporation. In managing the corporate estate, the Common Council was serving interests different from those to which it responded as the government of the city. One should not exaggerate: the Common Council did not suddenly abandon a policy of securing governmental goals through the terms of property conveyances. As late as 1805 a committee of the council recommended that the corporation make it a condition of all leases of corporate property that brick buildings be erected by the tenants (to prevent fires).[34] And even in the late 1820s, waterlot grants were conditioned on the completion of public works by the grantees.[35] But after the early 1790s, one senses in the minutes of

32. Corporation Grant to Alexander Macomb, 1791, DePeyster Papers, vol. 9, 20, NYHS.

33. Corporation Grant to Thomas Ellison, 3 January 1804, Ellison papers, NYHS; to George Lindsay, 10 February 1804, Murray Papers Miscel. MSS M, NYHS; to John McKesson, 19 January 1808, McKesson Papers Box 5, 24–40, NYHS; to J. R. Murray, 24 January 1814, Murray Papers MSS M, NYHS; to Stephan Beekman, 24 March 1828, NYC Deeds, Box 14, NYHS.

34. *Min. CC*, 3:720–23 (8 April 1805). In making this recommendation the committee stated that it attempted "to reconcile 3 important Interests which presented themselves, . . . the Interests of the city generally in having substantial buildings erected, The Interests of the Corporation in point of revenue, and the Desires of the present Tennants on the Corporate Estate, who are established in business on the same."

35. See Corporation Grant to Stephan Beekman, March 24, 1828.

the Common Council an impatience with the use of property to achieve public goals.

In a large and extensive report, submitted in 1799 after a yellow fever epidemic by a joint committee made up of members of the Common Council, the Chamber of Commerce, and the local medical society, unfinished waterlots and public slips were singled out for mention as "Among the more obvious causes which contributed to produce the Disease." The committee recommended that the corporation have power sufficient to cause both to be filled up whenever it was thought necessary, with or without the agreement of the proprietors of the lots.[36] If a slip was not in regular use by market boats and other small craft, it was particularly likely to become a public nuisance because residents seemed to use such facilities as dumps for trash and offal. The committee felt that such health hazards revealed the city's need for new statutorily created powers. Indeed, it argued that whenever a market moved away from a slip the Common Council ought to have the power to pass an ordinance requiring the owner of the neighboring waterlot to fill in the slip under threat of prosecution by the street commissioner. Such a power would not depend on the previously covenanted obligations of the owner and the corporation.[37] The city-as-government would not be bound by the commitments of the city-as-property-holder.

By the early nineteenth century, this distinction between the public and private selves of the corporation began to appear in other legal contexts. An example is the peculiar course of the city's attempt to assert its authority over the New Jersey side of the Hudson River.[38] In the first years of the nineteenth century, Richard Varick, a former mayor of New York, Jacob Radcliff, a prominent attorney, and Anthony Dey, a wealthy lawyer and landowner, formed a land speculation company called the Associates of the Jersey Company to develop Powles Hook (now Jersey City). Afraid that the corporation might claim a property interest in the land under water by the New Jersey shore (which would restrict their ability to run wharves out into the river), the associates hired Alexander Hamilton and Josiah Ogden Hoffman in April 1804 to answer two questions: Did the corporation of the city of New York have any title to the land under water opposite Powles Hook? And if New York State retained a right of jurisdiction up to the low-water mark on the New Jersey side (a right contested by the state of New Jersey), would wharves and docks built into the river become sub-

36. *Min. CC*, 2:495 (21 January 1799).
37. See ibid., 3:540 (11 June 1804); 552 (25 June 1804).
38. See James Kent, *The Charter of the City of New York, with notes thereon. Also a Treatise on the Powers and Duties of the Mayor, Aldermen and Assistant Aldermen, and the Journal of the City Convention* (New York, 1836), 37–38, 122.

ject to the jurisdiction of New York City?[39] Neither Hamilton nor Hoffman answered the second query, but as to the first they entertained no doubts. "Comparing the provisions in the different parts of the Charter of New York, with each other, we are of opinion that the Corporation of this City have no right of Soil in or title to the land, under the water to and adjoining Powles Hook."[40]

On the basis of that answer, the associates advertised in New York City that they intended "to sell lots, and to build wharves, in order to promote the success of their establishment." The Common Council then turned to its own legal counsel, Richard Harison, and an outside attorney, Robert Troup, "to ascertain how far their rights will be infringed by the sale of the land under the water, and by the erection of Wharves." In separate opinion letters, Harison and Troup each agreed with the associates' lawyers that the city had no title to the waterlots off Powles Hook, but they also each concluded that the land was properly part of the state of New York and that a right of political jurisdiction was vested in the corporation under the Montgomerie Charter.[41]

The case between the corporation and the associates of the Jersey Company that resulted from these lawyers' opinions was part of an interminable boundary dispute between New York and New Jersey that was not finally settled until 1833, when commissioners fixed the boundary of New York City in the middle of the Hudson River.[42] The issue at stake for the corporation in 1804 was the extent of its political jurisdiction. Claims to title in the New Jersey land under water were never raised, for no evidence of any grant of those lands could be found in any of the city's charters. On the other hand, the Montgomerie Charter clearly defined the boundaries of the city as reaching to the low-water mark on the west side of the Hudson. Members of the Common Council emphasized that they entertained "no sentiments hostile to the interests of the proprietors" of the Powles Hook development. Indeed, they were "willing that the said Improvements should progress being of opinion that the same would greatly tend to the convenience of the Inhabitants of this City in case of the return of the Epidemic." Nevertheless, their right to determine "when, where, and in what manner wharves shall be erected with[in] its Jurisdictional limits" was undercut by the attempt of the associates to construct wharves without the prior consent of the corporation. The council therefore asked

39. Harold C. Syrett et al., eds., *The Papers of Alexander Hamilton*, 26 vols. (New York, 1961–79), 26:221, 224, 227–31.
40. Ibid., 230.
41. *Min. CC*, 3:520–23 (21 May 1804).
42. Kent, *Charter*, 122.

Troup to consider how it ought to proceed in order to gain "the most proper remedies for the injuries complained of."[43]

Troup's answer deserves close attention. He offered two alternative courses of action. The first was to consider the jurisdictional rights of the corporation as a charter right. "To infringe this privilege [the right of the corporation to regulate the construction and use of wharves] . . . is to disturb the Corporation in the Enjoyment of one of its most important franchises." Under this theory of the rights of the municipality, the right of jurisdiction was not unlike the various property grants contained in the Montgomerie Charter. The distinction between property (title) and jurisdiction remained as fuzzy and imprecise as it had been in prerevolutionary New York City. And the remedy under this theory for the injury done the corporation was a special action on the case.

Alternatively, the Common Council could treat the violation of the city's jurisdictional rights over the underwater land adjacent to New Jersey as if the corporation were an agency of the state. "As the right of Soil is vested in the People of this state . . . the wharves which have been erected, are intrusions upon the lands of the people." The corporation would file and prosecute an information of intrusion in the name of the state attorney general. And the remedy would be the dispossession of the defendants.

Troup urged the Common Council to follow this latter course of action, for a defense of the city's regulatory authority under the Montgomerie Charter was unlikely to prove satisfactory. In the first place, a judgment for the corporation on a special action on the case would be limited to the recovery of damages. A legal victory "would not extend to the abatement of the wharves, or to the removal of the Defendants from the possession of the Land." More seriously, it was altogether possible that in the course of the suit the defendants might apply to the chancellor for equitable relief, and the chancellor might enjoin the erection of wharves throughout the city while its jurisdictional rights were under challenge. On the other hand, Troup thought that there would not be any difficulty in securing the permission of the attorney general, if the council decided to prosecute an information of intrusion, because the case was "one that involves the dignity and interests of the State." And none of the risks that accompanied suing under the Montgomerie Charter were present if the city allied itself with the sovereign state.[44]

The council did as he recommended, and the state attorney general gave it permission to sue under his name, as Troup predicted he would. But the

43. *Min. CC*, 3:552 (25 June 1804); 693–94 (25 February 1805).
44. Ibid., 694–95 (25 February 1805).

suit then dragged on with inconclusive results.[45] The point to emphasize is not the acuity of the legal analysis but the assumptions on which that analysis was founded. For Troup, the governmental powers of the city—its jurisdiction—were most usefully viewed as absolutely distinct from the private rights contained in the Montgomerie Charter. The right to conduct government had not so long before been conceptualized as a property right. But for Troup and the legal culture he represented, jurisdiction was now properly an attribute of the state. A defense of the city's chartered right to regulate and control wharves was thought to be both impolitic and likely to prove inefficacious.

Of course, the corporation continued to conserve its chartered property against the claims of competing jurisdictions and resident landowners. During this period, moreover, it was particularly concerned to protect its holdings against assertions of special rights or privileges. When, for example, General William Malcolm petitioned for permission to keep a boat on the east side of Beekman's Slip, a public space that he had earlier promised to keep in repair, the council reacted sharply. It could "find no reason why the same should be granted," for "such a grant would establish a precedent very detrimental to the revenues of this Board, as no doubt there are many other individuals who are obliged to keep the Slip adjoining their property in repair, who would make claim to the like favor and there is no knowing where such claims if once admitted would stop."[46]

But the corporate estate of the city of New York increasingly was regarded as private holdings unrelated to the government of the city. Property still distinguished New York City from other local governments in republican New York State. But now it did so because it gave the corporation the appearance of being in part a private institution, not because it enhanced the governmental powers of city government.[47] According to the New York Supreme Court, a resident of the city sitting as a juror should not be presumed to be interested in a lawsuit testing the enforcement of corporate property rights. "The interest supposed to exist in favor of the success of the corporation [on the part of jurors] is too uncertain and remote. It is, in truth, seldom, if ever, felt or known; and an independent jury may as probably be obtained in this as in any other county."[48] The

45. Ibid., 712–13 (25 March 1805); 716 (1 April 1805).

46. Ibid., 1:590 (2 September 1790). When Malcolm proved obstinate and would not withdraw his petition, the Common Council rescinded an earlier promise to grant him a strip of land that would have regularized his holdings (ibid., 593 [10 September 1790]).

47. See Kent, *Charter*, 140; Murray Hoffman, *Treatise upon the Estate and Right of the Corporation of the City of New York, as Proprietors*, 2d rev. ed., 2 vols. (New York, 1862), 1:41–77 and passim.

48. *Corporation* v. *Dawson*, 2 Johns. Cases 335, 336 (1801).

concerns of the corporation as property holder did not impinge on its governmental relationship with city residents; its property was part of a private, nongovernmental personality.[49]

The legal significance of the distinction discovered between the property rights and the governmental powers of the corporation was first explored in the case of *Mayor* v. *Scott*, decided in 1804. The case developed in the context of a tangle of government activity and waterfront development, a tangle whose dimensions need to be suggested if the legal arguments raised are to be made comprehensible.

By the mid-1790s, after more than sixty years of waterfront construction, the harbor facilities of lower Manhattan along the East River had become a crowded and irregularly designed pattern of slips, piers, and wharves. Growth within the confines set out in the Montgomerie Charter was practically at an end. New facilities were badly needed. Yet the curving, inconsistent shape of the shoreline made it difficult to lay out permanent streets, and, more important, city officials were not certain whether they could compel the proprietors of lots fronting on the river to make needed improvements not mentioned in their original grants.

As the city grew, there was a concurrent need to expand the amount of public slip space in the city. Small "market boats" and larger "coasters" that together brought in the food and provisions on which the residents of New York City depended could not afford the dock and wharf charges imposed by private individuals. And by the 1790s, members of the Common Council viewed providing slip space for such boats as a responsibility of the corporation, as a government contribution to the growth and welfare of the urban community. It was, wrote one committee of the council in 1790, particularly important to preserve "every Slip as wide and Capacious as possible. . . . The increase of the City is naturally followed by a proportionable increase of the Coasting trade, the Harbours for which are at present scarcely sufficient for their accommodation and in a few Years they will

49. Corporate property was not commonly visualized as a public trust of city government. See, generally, on public trust history, Molly Selvin, "'This Tender and Delicate Business': The Public Trust Doctrine in American Law and Economic Policy, 1789–1920" (Ph.D. dissertation, University of California at San Diego, 1978). Occasionally, one sees references to such a conception of public property in the postrevolutionary minutes of the Common Council, in petitions, and in the preambles of state legislation. And it would become the focus of argument in the laying out of the city's streets after 1807. But if a public trust theory was articulable at the beginning of the nineteenth century in New York, it certainly played a very small role in the conceptualization of corporation business. Corporate property was private and therefore nongovernmental. Compare *Mayor* v. *Scott*, 1 Caines Rep. 543 (1804) with *Milhau* v. *Sharp*, 15 Barb. 193 (1853).

be under the necessity of laying off in the Stream, or submitting to pay a heavy Wharfage to the proprietors of private Wharfs which must operate as a direct Tax upon the necessaries of Life."[50]

But because of a shortage of such space, the council found itself at times in the position of having to choose between the interests of the "market" people and those of the coasting trade. The result, noted a council committee in 1803, was continuing competition between the two. One suggested solution, insisting that the coasters dock on the outer ends of the slips, did not help because of the narrowness of most of the slips. Once a coaster had docked, it was difficult for the market boats to get by and enter the slips where perishable goods would be unloaded and taken to market.[51] The only "permanent" solution was to increase the amount of dock space by widening and enlarging the slips.

In 1798, therefore, the state legislature responded to a petition of the Common Council by authorizing the construction of two new streets seventy feet in width to form an outer boundary for lower Manhattan Island. These new avenues, to be called South Street and West Street, would extend the "made land" taken from both the Hudson and the East rivers slightly beyond the four hundred feet beyond low-water mark, which had been the end point of the city's corporate title under the Montgomerie Charter. As in the past, the proprietors of the adjoining land would do the actual work of constructing the streets. And the statute also authorized the city to direct those proprietors to sink piers in front of the new streets. On completion of the public works, the developers would receive clear title to the filled waterlots and the right to collect the profits from the piers.[52]

Based on that statute, the Common Council passed an ordinance in 1801 ordering the construction of new piers. To ensure that sufficient space would be available in the public slips, the council required that some piers be built twenty feet to the side of existing slips, so that those slips would become both wider and longer. Further, the ordinance defined the side of any pier that fronted on a slip as "publick property" rather than as the property of the pier proprietor. The proprietor would have the right to collect rent for boats that docked at the front of the pier or on the side not connected to a slip. But on the slip side all profits were reserved to the corporation, for that side was defined as a continuation of the slip.[53]

It was this claim of the corporation to rights of slippage along one side of

50. *Min. CC,* 1:589 (2 September 1790).

51. Ibid., 3:255 (4 April 1803).

52. *Laws of New York,* 21st sess. (Albany, 1798), c. 80; ibid., 24th sess. (Albany, 1801), c. 129; *Min. CC,* 2:138 (7 April 1795); 214–15 (10 February 1796).

53. *Min. CC,* 2:744–45 (1 June 1801); 698–99 (12 January 1801); see also 718–19 (23 March 1801).

the newly constructed piers that raised the specific issue decided in *Mayor v. Scott*.[54] John Murray, a member of an old and wealthy family of merchants, owned a lot and a wharf on the northeastern side of the Wall Street Slip. In 1797, before the state's decision to authorize the new avenues, he received a grant of an additional waterlot from the corporation, in which he covenanted to build a twenty-five-foot access road on the west side of the premises (fronting the slip) and to build a ninety-eight-foot portion of South Street.[55] He complied with both of these covenants, although not without some grumbling,[56] and following passage of the 1801 ordinance he also built a pier, extending out beyond South Street, beginning twenty feet to the northeast of the Wall Street Slip. At its furthest point this pier extended five feet beyond the property boundary of the corporation as defined by the Montgomerie Charter; however, it did not reach beyond the space turned over to the authority of the Common Council by the 1798 statute (see Figure 8.2). Having satisfied all the conditions in his grant, Murray then claimed the right to collect the profits from the three sides of his pier, including the southwestern side, which the corporation considered merely an extension of the Wall Street Slip.

The issue turned on the corporation's power to define the five feet that

54. This reconstruction of *Mayor* v. *Scott* would be impossible without the materials detailed in *Law Practice of Alexander Hamilton*, 4:451–58, including the imprinted "Case," probably prepared by Robert Troup and Anthony Dey and then sent to Hamilton, all of which the late Joseph Smith was kind enough to share with me in the summer of 1978.

55. See Ibid., 4:453–54; Counterpart of a Release of a Piece of Ground to John Murray, Jr., 10 May 1797, Grant Book E, MARC.

56. In a petition to the Common Council in 1797, Murray asserted: "That in consequence of a regulation relative to the formation of a street to be 70 feet wide on the East River, your Petitioner hath been, and is like to be at an enormous expense in sinking Blocks &c, for the completion of his part of the said Street, which by reason of the Water being near 40 feet deep, greatly augments the charge attending the same—and as your Petitioner is possessed of a small Corner Lott, he is obliged to dock out about 28 feet, in order to form the Slip, and part of Wall Street: which is in fact working for the Publick, from which he derives no other emolument than the Wharfage arising from that small part which fronts the East River.

"These Considerations, together with that of his having been a greater Sufferer by the late Conflagration, more he believes than any one who had real Estate destroyed on that occasion, induces him to solicit such relief from the Corporation, as may be judged reasonable & proper, either in defraying a part of the expense, or in the indulgence of wharfage on the Slip Side. And when the Board reflects, that the Improvements which your Petitioner is now about making is of Public Utility, & that he derives no benefit of Wharfage, but from the Front, he indulgences a hope, the Corporation will view the Subject in a favorable Light, & from the peculiar circumstances of the Case, grant him such relief in the Premises as he may be justly entitled to, on no other ground does he ask or expect a consideration from the Board" (Petition File, January–June 1797, MARC). His petition was rejected by the Common Council, but it is important to note that Murray was already asking for what he would later receive as a consequence of *Mayor* v. *Scott* and that at least in 1797 he acknowledged the legal right of the corporation to declare the side of the pier to be part of the public slip.

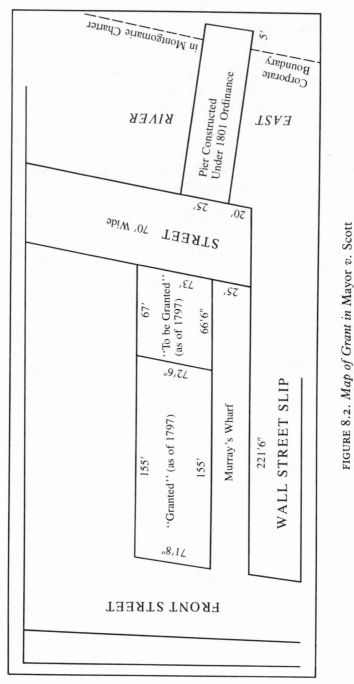

FIGURE 8.2. *Map of Grant in Mayor v. Scott*

SOURCE: "A Map of a Piece of Ground at Murray's Wharf partly granted and partly to be Granted by the Corporation of New York to John Murray jun'r. Surveyed New York March 29ᵗʰ 1797 by Casimer Ch. Goerok. City Surveyor" (bound with deed to John Murray, *Grant Book E* [MARC]).

extended beyond its chartered boundaries as "publick" property. The corporation, through its lawyers Caleb Riggs and Richard Harison, argued that it was free to define the rights of grantees as it pleased. The lawyers conceded that the 1798 act had not formally granted the city title to new land under water beyond that which had been granted in the Montgomerie Charter.[57] On the other hand, because the statute delegated to the city the power to grant title to proprietors when the waterlots were filled, a grant from the state to the city ought to be read into the statute. "They [the corporation] could not grant what they had not." And Murray in particular should be the last person capable of challenging the title of the corporation because he was the beneficiary of "an ordinance exercising the right of an implied grant."

The reservation of the slip sides of the new piers to the use of the public was hardly a governmental novelty. The insides of slips, according to Riggs, had always been reserved in grants made by the corporation, so that the "supply of market boats, &c., might not be impeded." And the ordinance challenged in this case was nothing but a typical exercise of the corporation's traditional responsibility to widen its slips "that they might be the more effectually cleansed by the tide."[58]

Robert Troup and Alexander Hamilton, the attorneys for the defendant, denied the corporation's claim that it owned the lands discussed in the statute:

> The act gave no beneficial interest to the corporation. They were simply trustees, or rather attorneys, to grant to others a right, in consideration of a service or duty performed. This duty was erecting the pier, and created a consideration for the grant. Therefore, the reserving a portion of the emoluments was so far illegal and void; for a trustee cannot take to himself, and withhold from *cestui que trust*, a part of the subject of the trust. Allowing, then, an interest to have passed by implication, it was fiduciary. Then, although the act authorizes them to grant under such restrictions, and within such limits, as they may think proper, still this is not more than a power to regulate the mode and place of enjoyment; for restriction can never signify a right of acquisition.[59]

The statute did not give the city property rights to serve its governmental purposes. The statute did not function like the Montgomerie Charter. It

---

57. Indeed, in 1801, in an opinion letter to the council, Richard Harison had already told them that they did not have formal title to that part of the piers which extended beyond the four-hundred-foot line (*Min. CC*, 2:741–42 [1 June 1801]).

58. *Mayor* v. *Scott*, 1 Caines Rep. 543, 545–46.

59. Ibid., 546.

simply delegated to the city the power to carry out a public purpose—the construction of piers. According to Hamilton and Troup, it was in the nature of such delegations of public power that their terms be strictly construed against the recipients of the power. The city government could no more reserve for itself "a portion of the emoluments" than the proprietors could lay claim to the wharfage without previously erecting a pier. In this situation the corporation was merely a trustee for the public, carrying out the wishes of the state legislature and bound to the standard of conduct of a fiduciary.

In reply, Riggs and Harison argued for a liberal construction of the statute because of the public benefit that would result. This was "a cause in which the public convenience of the city of New York was deeply interested." And the reservation of slippage in no way resembled a private advantage or right. The city would not "profit" from its ordinance. It was, moreover, vital that the side of the pier be viewed as an extension of the slip. Otherwise, a proprietor of a pier, with an understandable motive to restrict access to public docking spaces, would have the power to obstruct entry to the slip by docking several vessels on the sides of the pier and filling all the available space.[60]

But Brockholst Livingston, speaking for the New York Supreme Court, held for Troup and Hamilton. "No implied grant is contained in the act of the Legislature. The corporation are only to grant as attorneys of the public, in case piers are sunk." The capacity of the corporation to pass ordinances that regulated the construction of piers and waterfront facilities did not imply the right "to impose any terms they pleased" through such ordinances. And in any case, the corporation was mistaken in calling the side of the pier a part of the slip. A slip, Livingston declared, was "an opening between two pieces of land or wharves." By contrast, the foot of this pier remained twenty feet from the side of the slip.[61]

The direct consequences of the holding were limited. The next year the Common Council granted the petition of the lessee of the public docks for an abatement of his rent because he had been deprived of much of his expected return by the decision of the supreme court.[62] In 1806, a new statute authorized the city to make public basins (or wide slips) at its own expense. The city would have an absolute right to any slippage or wharfage that could be drawn from these basins, "any law, usage or custom to the contrary notwithstanding."[63] And New York's appellate courts always restricted the decision in *Mayor* v. *Scott* to its facts.[64]

60. Ibid., 547.
61. Ibid., 548–49.
62. *Min. CC*, 3:497–98 (16 April 1804); 4:21–22 (24 June 1805).
63. *Laws of New York*, 29th sess. (Albany, 1806), c. 126.
64. "The corporation cannot reserve or take any wharfage arising from a pier built at the

For our purposes, however, the case is less important for its influence than for its articulation of a particular conception of the relationship between the property of the corporation and the government of the city. To the conventional claim of the corporation that it had a right to reserve property for public purposes, Hamilton and Troup responded that the property rights of the corporation were distinct from its governmental responsibilities as a grantee of state power. State legislation gave the city government only the right to act as an "attorney for the public." Such legislation could not be equated with grants of property because the governmental power to restrict and to regulate "can never signify a right of acquisition." All claims by the corporation to private property rights were to be strictly construed.[65] Insofar as the corporation came to depend on delegations of state power, it did so as a public agency, without any of the authority and security of a private property holder.[66]

---

expense of individuals, nor any slippage on the side of the pier adjacent to a public slip, but not contiguous or on a line with the side of the slip" (Kent, *Charter*, 175–76).

65. This perception became legal doctrine in the 1840s. See *Bailey* v. *The Mayor of New York*, 3 Hill 531 (1842); *Milhau* v. *Sharp*. 15 Barb. 193, 212 (1853). On the other hand, after the mid-1850s the formulation of what later became known as Dillon's Rule led to a stricter scrutiny of public legislative authorizations as well.

66. This transformation of New York City into a distinctively public government stands in marked contrast with the contemporaneous history of English cities. English historians have usually concluded that most boroughs played only a passive role in the events that we think of as the industrial revolution. Instead, borough officers continued to regard their corporate estate as definitive of their responsibilities. See Malcolm I. Thomis, *Politics and Society in Nottingham, 1785–1835* (London, 1969), 4–5; François Vigier, *Change and Apathy* (Cambridge, Mass., 1970), 54–55; R. W. Greaves, *The Corporation of Leicester, 1689–1836* (Leicester, 1970), 85. Modern students of the Municipal Corporations Act of 1835, which finally forced British boroughs to manage their affairs according to uniform national standards, argue that even that late reform had far less to do with any commitment to make boroughs into effective public administrators than with a desire to break the control of oligarchies over corporate revenue. "That modern observers might suppose it to have been the functions of local government," which motivated the reforms, "is only a measure of the social and political changes that have flowed from that event" (G. H. Martin, Introduction, in H. A. Merewether and A. J. Stephens, *The History of the Boroughs and Municipal Corporations* [Sussex, 1972], x). The other side is represented in Sidney Webb and Beatrice Webb, *The Manor and the Borough*, 2 vols. (London, 1908; reprint, 1963), and *Statutory Authorities for Special Purposes* (London, 1963), chap. 6. See also G. B. A. M. Finlayson, "The Municipal Corporation Commission and Report, 1833–35," *Bulletin of the Institute of Historical Research* 36 (1963): 36–52; Finlayson, "The Politics of Municipal Reform," *English Historical Review* 81 (1966): 673–92; Elie Halevy, "Before 1835," in H. J. Laski, ed., *A Century of Municipal Progress* (London, 1935), 11–36; Ivor Jenning, "The Municipal Revolution," in ibid., 55–65; Francis Palgrave, *Conciliatory Reform* (London, 1833); Frederic W. Maitland, *Township and Borough* (Cambridge, 1897).

CHAPTER 9

The Promise of Public Power

Before the Revolution, the private property of the corporation had provided the only secure basis for local government action. Now the situation was strikingly different. As a private corporate body and a property holder, New York City's powers would be strictly construed and limited. But as a public agency, a subordinate government within a state polity, the legitimacy of its actions became virtually unimpeachable.

From the early 1790s on, there was a constant and growing stream of petitions from the New York City Common Council to the state legislature, always accompanied by draft bills. These ranged in subject matter from the major policy questions faced by the postrevolutionary city to the most trivial details of city administration,[1] from the creation of new powers unmistakably beyond those granted in the Montgomerie Charter to bills simply reaffirming power explicitly granted in charter provisions. In almost every case the city got precisely what it asked for.[2] Statutes delegating "more specific and detailed powers" replaced the Montgomerie Charter as a source of authority.[3] Yet this new dependence was not the product of an imperialistic design by state government to control the growing me-

1. See, for example, *Minutes of the Common Council of the City of New York, 1784–1831,* 21 vols. (New York, 1917–30), 2:590 (4 February 1799) (adequate power to protect the public health); ibid., 4:353–54 (16 February 1807) (plan to lay out streets of the city); ibid., 2:609 (3 February 1800) (power to aggregate smaller lots owned by the city); ibid., 3:460–61 (7 February 1804) (power to prevent the inspection of meat south of Lispenard's Meadow); hereafter *Min. CC.*

2. Even in the 1840s and early 1850s the premise of the *Ordrenan* case that legislation affecting the city was always passed at the instigation of the city remained good law. See Edmund Dana Durand, *The Finances of New York City* (New York, 1898), 66; James Bryce, *The American Commonwealth,* 3 vols. (London, 1888), 3:173–76.

3. James Kent, *The Charter of the City of New York with notes thereon. Also a Treatise on the Powers and Duties of the Mayor, Aldermen, and Assistant Aldermen, and the Journal of the City Convention* (New York, 1836), 134.

tropolis. It was, rather, a consequence of the city's own desire to identify itself with the state.

One reason for the Common Council's new attachment to legislative authorization was fear—or, perhaps more accurately, its desire to depoliticize the position of the corporation in a republican political order. The charter of the corporation may have been inviolable as a grant of vested property rights, but as a statement of political legitimacy and authority, it had a different status in a legal culture that viewed property and government as diametrically opposed.[4] To rely on the language of the Montgomerie Charter was to call attention to the distinctiveness of the corporation of the city of New York, to remind Americans that New York City found its point of origin not in popular sovereignty but in royal grant.[5]

By contrast, legislative authorizations served to place the city within a republican state polity. Questions that might have been raised regarding local action, if founded on charter rights, did not arise if the legislature had previously approved. Perhaps Chancellor Kent was correct when he observed that the charter contained "a grant of ample powers, sufficient for all the purposes of a well-ordered police, and for the good government of the city in its complicated concerns" and suggested that the city had not really needed all the supplementary legislation it had sought and received over the previous forty years.[6] But the Common Councils of the late eighteenth and early nineteenth centuries—both Federalist and Jeffersonian—rarely chose to test the proposition.

One of the few occasions when the members of the Common Council might have done so occurred in 1802. The council asked its lawyer, Richard Harison, whether it already possessed "the authority to pass an ordinance for restraining and regulating the use of fire and candles & the practice of smoking in livery stables. And also for prohibiting the lighting of fires upon the decks of vessels lying in the harbor for the purpose of preventing accidents by fire within this city." Harison quickly replied that he was unambiguously "of opinion that the Common Council possess competent powers by their charter for the purposes required. They are authorized to make by-laws for the Public good, which I think requires such regulations as tend to the prevention of Fires." Yet his confidence in the council's right

4. See Stanley Katz, "Thomas Jefferson and the Right to Property in Revolutionary America," *Journal of Law and Economics* 19 (1976):467–89; J. G. A. Pocock, *The Machiavellian Moment* (Princeton, 1974).

5. See *Respublica* v. *Duquet*, 2 Yeates 493, 494 (Penn. Sup. Ct., 1799) ("Corporations originated in feudal times amongst a barbarous people"—argument of Rawle and De Ponceau for the defendant).

6. Kent, *Charter*, 134.

to pass an ordinance without the assent of the legislature did not mean that he recommended that course of action. Indeed, as "doubts have been entertained upon the subject," he thought it "advisable (if there is no particular reason to the contrary) to obtain an act of the Legislature recognizing or confirming the powers of the Corporation in this respect."[7]

Politics and law merged in Harison's answer. Of course, legal right was with the Common Council. If it chose to ground the ordinance in the powers of the Montgomerie Charter, the authority to do so was unquestionable. But why bother? Obtaining an act from the legislature was an easy and safe alternative, and it avoided all the doubts entertained about the legitimacy of autonomous city action.[8]

What were those doubts? What led the leaders of city government to avoid reliance on the Montgomerie Charter even when its authority was unchallenged? Why, when the need for speedy action was a refrain of their reports, did they insist on the extra step of obtaining a special act from the legislature? To answer these questions requires an attempt to look at the Montgomerie Charter with the eyes of a late-eighteenth-century city official. To Chancellor Kent, writing in 1835, the charter may have read as a package of grants of "ample powers." A generation earlier, city officials

7. *Min. CC*, 3:161–62, 164–66 (20 December 1802).

8. Indeed, it is not at all clear whether the Common Council was asking Harison's opinion about the possibility of acting under the charter, or if, to the contrary, it was concerned with the sufficiency of previous state legislation as a basis for local action.

There was, moreover, a long history of ordinances and of state legislation authorizing fire regulations for the city, including previous ordinances ordering exclusive use of brick and stone in city buildings. See Sidney Pomerantz, *New York: An American City, 1783–1803*, 2d ed. (Port Washington, N.Y., 1965), 231–33, 237–38, and Joseph D. McGoldrick, Seymour Graubard, and Raymond Horowitz, *Building Regulations in New York City* (New York, 1944), 32–36, 44–45. The English traveler William Strickland noted in 1794, "By Laws of a late date for regulating the police of this City, no new houses can be built in it, or within a certain distance of it, of wood; nor any new roof made of, or old ones repaired with, shingles." He thought that "a very good regulation takes place in this town with respect to fires" (*Journal of a Tour in the United States of America, 1794–5*, ed. J. E. Strickland (New York, 1971), 61, 62.

But in fact varieties of institutional and customary constraints made it difficult to enforce such laws, which had a history of passage (and suspension) dating back to colonial times. See *The Colonial Laws of New York from the Year 1664 to the Revolution*, 5 vols. (Albany, 1894), 4:571–73 (31 December 1761); 1046–48 (31 December 1768); 5:743–46 (1 April 1775); *Laws of New York*, 9th sess. (Albany, 1786), c. 1; 14th sess. (Albany, 1791), c. 46; 19th sess. (Albany, 1796), c. 53; 24th sess. (Albany, 1801), c. 80; also "A Law for Preventing and Extinguishing Fires, in the City of New York," in *Laws and Ordinances Ordained and Established by the Mayor, Aldermen and Commonalty of the City of New York in Common Council Convened* (New York, 1793). One might interpret Harison's opinion as saying that however difficult it might be to enforce the building and fire regulations of the Common Council when accompanied by statutory mandate, it was far more difficult when the Common Council attempted to do so simply under its charter powers.

knew better. In the political theory that underlay the Montgomerie Charter, chartered power was implicitly viewed not as a source of innovation but as a restraint against externally imposed change. Regulations and other invocations of public power were valid only insofar as they rested on the consent of a local public or on absolute property rights.

To the leaders of the postrevolutionary city, the Montgomerie Charter seemed to stand in opposition to the varieties of innovative and creative action that they intended to engage in. As we have seen, earlier city leaders had viewed the charter differently. Indeed, they had found the basis for limited public action in the properties granted by the crown in the charter. But for a generation of New York public officials who lusted after growth and were impatient with all forms of restraint, the "private" governmental actions typified by the waterlot grants were far from sufficient. They thought their actions as public servants ought to be determined by the needs of their growing and changing community, not by the structures of authority laid down in a sixty-year-old document.

It was, moreover, not at all apparent that the Common Council had the right to break with settled expectations of the practices of city government, absent direct statutory authorization.[9] If the corporation had always acted in a particular way, did it have the capacity to change its mind and do things differently? Did it have the right to do anything at all that it had not done before? Even when no one objected, even when the utility of a decision was beyond dispute, members of the Common Council still worried about their right to act in the absence of legislative authorization.

In 1807, for example, various petitions were sent to the council asking it

9. As late as the 1780s it was not obvious that even with legislative authorization the Common Council could legitimately break with settled expectations of corporate practice. See Livingston's veto of "An act to invest the Mayor, aldermen, and commonalty of the city of New York with power to license and regulate the fees of hackney coaches, and to lay a tax on all wheel carriages within the city and county of New York," in Alfred Billings Street, *The Council of Revision of the State of New York* (Albany, 1859), 294–98. Among other objections to the bill, Livingston included the following: "Because it entirely changes a system which has hitherto worked no injury, and adds to the general mass of taxes, which are necessarily extremely burdensome in this city. The ground adjoining to the lots was always considered as in some sort under the direction of the proprietor of the lot; if he paved, planted, cleaned or ornamented it, he had the immediate advantage and the credit of his improvement with his fellow-citizens. For this reason, every owner of the lots submitted to tax himself, and asked no compensation from the public; no money being raised for the purpose. It was a land tax which every man expected to pay when he purchased a town lot. The bill under consideration entirely reverses this rule, and aims at exempting the owners of town lots from a duty they have never complained of, and which, now that the pavement is already made, must be comparatively light, in order to throw the burden upon others, who in numberless instances hold not one foot of land within the city."

to move the municipal powder magazine to a more "retired and unfre-
quented" place. All agreed that in its present location the magazine posed
a danger to city residents:

> That tho' the Situation of said Magazine was not improper in those
> respects when it was first established, yet at present it is surrounded
> on all sides by Inhabitants at short distances and that, in Seasons of
> general Sickness great numbers of the Poor are quartered near it by
> the City Corporation. That among the Works with which the Im-
> provement of that part of the City are necessarily carried on, is the
> blowing of Rocks from which the Magazine has already been endan-
> gered, and that all these Causes of Alarm will probably increase with
> the increase of Inhabitants and improvement, and that the Situation
> of said Magazine renders the public property less secure both in or-
> dinary times & particularly in times of public Danger, than the In-
> terest of the State seems to require.

But the Common Council hesitated to order any change in the location.
"Having assented to the keeping of the public stores therein," the members of the council did not think "themselves authorized to remove the
same without the Concurrence of the Legislature." The result was another
petition to the legislature.[10]

What was at stake was the ability of the Common Council to institute
new municipal practices. Did new conditions or mores or public demands
justify changed institutions? The members of the Common Council had no
doubt that they did, but the Montgomerie Charter was at best ambiguous
on the question, at least when read with eighteenth-century eyes.

It had been the traditional presumption of public authority that necessary public action would be carried out by private individuals. City leaders
soon realized that they could not rely on that presumption in republican
New York City. On the one hand, city residents no longer shared common
assumptions about the nature of their public obligations.[11] On the other
hand, the services demanded of local government in the 1790s and early
1800s needed a more controllable public work force. City leaders clearly
intended to create a public institution that would not be dependent on the
recurring need to mobilize the direct support of a local public.[12] Yet to do
so they needed, first, to gain legislative authorization.

10. *Min. CC*, 4:363–64 (4 March 1807).

11. From this perspective, the continuing complaints of travelers that the streets and
physical facilities of New York City were unusually dirty may reflect the failure or withdrawal
of private responsibility for public facilities as much as it also suggests the irresponsibility of
the city government. See note 17 below.

12. See, for example, *Min. CC*, 2:420–21 (12 February 1798); 486–87 (17 December
1798); 494–99 (21 January 1799); 505–8 (28 January 1799); 664–72 (6 October 1800).

In that light, consider again the petition from the Common Council asking for authorization to lay out South and West streets. In that petition the council showed itself to be far less concerned with gaining a grant of property beyond the four-hundred-foot line (which "grant" later played the pivotal role in *Mayor* v. *Scott*) than with the need to give the corporation the power to ensure that "improvements" would be constructed according to public plan. The need for "some adequate remedy" was explained by the desire both "to secure the health of the Citizens" and "to effect Ornament and regularity in the Fronts of the City and convenience and safety to the Trade and Commerce thereof." Where individual proprietors refused to sink or lay out piers as directed by the council, the council should be "authorized to sink and build those piers at the Expence of the City and receive the Wharfage without incurring a Breach of the Conditions and Covenants in their Grants to Individuals."[13]

The city still acted when possible through the indirect means of making a grant to proprietors who fulfilled stated covenants. But the petition reveals both the council's uncertainty about the extent of its capacity to compel individual proprietors to act (even with the promised consideration of a grant of wharfage and pierage) and, more important, its desire for powers that would free it from reliance on those same private individuals.

Similarly, throughout the 1799 report of the joint committee "to investigate the causes of the PESTILENTIAL DISEASE which has lately prevailed in the city," one reads a continuing refrain that without a direct grant of power by the legislature the conditions that had led to yellow fever in the summer of 1798 would recur. "The Corporation ought to have full power" to fill unfinished waterlots, such public slips "as they may think proper," and sinks and privies. There was a need for "Strong energetic laws, compelling delinquents to pay their fines for omissions or transgressions, immediately on the [presentation of] evidence of the Inspectors." The city ought to be able to employ enough individuals to remove the "filth of winter" from the streets as quickly as possible, rather than relying on those who lived along the streets. The committee regretted "that the reforms contemplated in [the report] . . . must necessarily be productive of much inconvenience to many of their fellow citizens," and they claimed to have been "extremely cautious." But they insisted that there was no alternative to growth in the delegated powers of the corporation:

> They are aware that they have recommended great and strong power to be vested in the Corporation; but they do not believe any thing short of it will restore this city to its former healthy state. The

13. Ibid., 2:420–21 (12 February 1798); similar concerns are expressed in stronger language in the committee report, ibid., 3:397–98 (21 November 1803).

sources of the afflicting pestilence with which we have been visited, are of too local a nature, to expect their removal without a strong discretionary power being somewhere lodged by the State Legislature; and we know not where it can be so properly placed, as in the hands of the immediate representatives of the city, who already have the police of it committed to them, and with which the proposed reform is very intimately connected.[14]

Perhaps the most important change contemplated in the 1799 report was that the corporation would no longer rely on "the tedious formalities of ordinary lawsuits" to compel individuals to fulfill their obligations to the city. Instead the drafters of the report contemplated that the Common Council and its agents would have the discretion to act directly to abate an unhealthy or otherwise unsatisfactory condition, with the costs of action to become a lien or assessment on the property of the responsible individuals.

The necessary implication of all its recommendations was that a public work force should be mobilized to do those tasks private residents of the city could not be expected to do. Again, the prior authorization of the legislature was seen to be an absolute necessity. But the city could get most anything it wished from the legislature, so we should not be surprised that by the early nineteenth century the Common Council was well engaged in assembling a public bureaucracy. In early 1803 it authorized a Department of Scavengers, made up of publicly employed men, "to sweep the heads of slips and all public grounds, and to clean, carry away, and sell all filth, dirt and rubbish as may be found in the streets which is not by law directed to be otherwise removed."[15] At about the same time, the council appointed two professional street commissioners "to take charge of the laying out, levelling, paving, and keeping in repair of the streets."[16]

There was, in fact, a new emphasis on the desirability of hiring full-time, salaried "professionals" to fill senior administrative positions in city government. A report in 1800 on the condition of the almshouse included a marvelous disquisition on the failure of the older system of administration and on the need for a new conception of public service:

14. Ibid., 2:501, 507–8, 498–99 (1799).

15. Ibid., 3:198 (27 January 1803); "A Law for the Appointment of a Superintendent of Scavengers," *Laws and Ordinances . . . of the City of New York* (New York, 1805), 42. Compare with "A Law for cleaning the streets, lanes, and alleys of the said city," *Laws, Orders and Ordinances* (New York, 1731); "A Law for paving and cleaning the Streets, Lanes and Alleys," in *Laws, Statutes, Ordinances, and Constitutions* (New York, 1763), 28; and "A Law to regulate the Paving and Keeping in Repair of the Streets," *Laws and Ordinances Ordained and Established* (New York, 1793), 14. For an earlier indication of the new demand for a growing public work force, see "An Act to Increase the number of Firemen in the city" *Laws of New York*, 15th sess. (Albany, 1792), c. 9.

16. *Min. CC*, 3:123–24 (6 September 1802).

The fault (if it exists) is more in the system than in the men. The doing of business by a board of commissioners, who serve without compensation, is at first plausible, as it carries the appearance of economy, and evidences a disinterested zeal for the public service; but in practice this mode has seldom been successful; very little responsibility attaches to any of the commissioners. The burthen which no one in particular is bound to sustain, is shifted from shoulder to shoulder, till at last it is left wholly unsupported: and as no compensation is to be received, no one thinks himself bound to sacrifice his own private affairs, to an object of general concern, and which there are so many others equally engaged in. The committee, however, are convinced that the success of any plan, must, after all, depend in a great measure, upon the persons who are to execute it. In everything that relates to the affairs of the poor, a rare union of system, intelligence, talents and industry is requisite; and without such union as a judicious writer (Colquhan) [sic] has observed, "Millions may be wasted without bettering their condition." In selecting therefore, the person who may be the chief conductor of the business, many difficulties will occur, and unless such a salary is allowed, as may command abilities, reward industry, and prevent the effect of small temptations, it is in vain to hope for any permanent advantages.[17]

The corporation could no longer expect individuals to sacrifice their "private affairs" for the public good. In future, paid public servants would take major responsibility for the administration of city government.

City leaders treated the corporation of the city of New York as if it were a bifurcated, almost schizophrenic institution. It remained the holder of a corporate estate, a property owner whose private rights were protected by the state constitution. But that private sphere of corporate existence was radically distinguished from its role as a government. As a private entity, its foundation continued to be the Montgomerie Charter. But as a govern-

---

17. Ibid., 2:664–72 (6 October 1800); see the similar argument of the street commissioner, who recommended that private individuals be removed from the street repair business: "It is obvious to any person who sees the Streets of the City that the pavements are generally in a very bad state of which complaints are frequently made and the occupants of the houses opposite to the places complained of have sometimes been fined for neglecting to remedy the nuisances, although they have not known to whom to apply for the purpose[;] at other times they have been imposed on by exorbitant charges and by persons incompetent to the business. . . . There is probably but one way in which an adequate remedy can be applied, and that is by the appointment of a person of a sufficient practical knowledge of the business who for a reasonable Compensation should devote as much of his time to this object as shall be adequate to produce the desired effect" (Ibid., 3:358 [25 July 1803]). See also ibid., 5:55–56 (14 March 1808) (need for more professional street surveys).

ment, New York City was a dependent agency of the state; its discretionary powers derived from the explicit mandates of the state legislature. By the early nineteenth century, some city leaders had already concluded that "it would be altogether unsafe and erroneous to resort to the charter solely, upon any question of power, or its mode of exercise."[18] As a government, its only "charter" was the accumulated relevant statutes of the New York legislature. The Montgomerie Charter still protected the city from legislative intervention into its property; but it was only a starting point for an evolving city government.[19]

In its governmental persona, the postrevolutionary corporation seems as nothing but a vessel of legislative power for city affairs. Yet even if structurally that was the case, city officials of the late eighteenth and early nineteenth centuries still showed a good deal of confusion as to the proper scope and character of city government. Was the corporation anything other than a mere delegee of state legislation? Was it to have a monopoly on governmental power within the city, or would it have to share power with other institutions?

The plea for enabling legislation that ended the report of the joint committee charged with finding ways of preventing the return of yellow fever included the more ambiguous statement that "a strong discretionary power" had to be "somewhere lodged by the State Legislature" and that it might as well be lodged with the corporation. Alexander Hamilton was asked to comment on the report and noted that, though "the Powers must be vested in a permanent body and the Corporation very naturally offers itself as that body," the corporation might not be the most appropriate recipient. Given "the attention which the Corporation is obliged to pay to its ordinary concerns" and the need for "the Prompt and vigorous execution of what is to be done," it might be "better effected by Commissioners to be appointed for the special Purpose, than by a body whose attention must necessarily be engrossed and distracted by a great multiplicity of other avocations."[20] Hamilton saw no legal obstacle to the state delegating authority to the municipality or the corporation acting under delegation. Rather, he was raising an issue of prudence: was it appropriate to give to the corporation "police" powers of the sort requested by the joint commit-

18. Murray Hoffman, *Treatise upon the Estate and Right of the Corporation of the City of New York, as Proprietors*, 2d rev. ed., 2 vols. (New York, 1862), 72; Kent, *Charter*, 151–52.

19. By 1826, Counsel Michael Ulshoeffer would advise the council that he did "not look upon the Charter power as anything more than a power given by Act of the Legislature." See his "Opinion," in New York City Board of Aldermen, Committee on Streets, *Report . . . on the Subject of regulating the ground between North and 14th Streets, the Bowery and East River* (New York, 1826), 19–22.

20. *Min. CC*, 2:519 (28 February 1799).

tee? Would it not be more effective to create what the English called a "statutory authority for special purposes"?[21]

Although the state legislature eventually vested all the powers requested by the committee with the corporation, in the wake of Hamilton's "opinion" the Common Council resolved not to insist that power be delegated to them directly: "The members of this Board have not been willing to subject themselves to great trouble and responsibility from a sense of Duty. Yet having no private Motives to wish for any peculiar Agency in this business, they will be perfectly satisfied if the objects in View are pursued in any Way that the Legislature may think proper by which their fellow Citizens may be benefitted in the most easy, safe and effectual method, and the Charter rights of the City remain inviolate."[22] The council, at least rhetorically, cared less for maintaining sole power over the governmental affairs of the city than for deriving, by any means possible, an effective basis for public action. And that depended entirely on the support of the state legislature.

It is ironic that the Federalist-controlled city government that exhibited such pragmatic disregard for the niceties of corporate autonomy has been identified by historians as the last defender of a traditional notion of corporate governance in New York City.[23] The reason is that between 1801 and 1804, in the wake of the national Jeffersonian triumph of 1800, Federalists in the city waged a rear-guard battle to retain control of the government of the city. Their only weapons were the Common Council's control of the municipal franchise and the language in the charter that "vested" government in that Common Council.

The population of the city was overwhelmingly Democratic-Republican. But by insisting on the formal freehold requirements in the charter, by refusing to make non-property holders into freemen as their prerevolutionary predecessors had routinely done, by refusing to shift ward boundaries to reflect changes in population, and by permitting landowners to vote in every ward in which they held property, the Federalists managed to retain a slender majority in the Common Council. The eligibility requirements in the Montgomerie Charter were all that stood between the Federalists and powerlessness. And so, for perhaps the first time in the history

21. See Sidney Webb and Beatrice Webb, *Statutory Authorities for Special Purposes* (London, 1963); Judith Diamondstone, "The Government of Eighteenth Century Philadelphia," in Bruce Daniels, ed., *Town and County* (Middletown, Conn., 1978), 247–53.

22. *Min. CC*, 2:250 (28 February 1799).

23. Jon Teaford, *The Municipal Revolution in America* (Chicago, 1975), 85–90; Pomerantz, *New York*, 133–46; Howard Rock, *Artisans of the New Republic* (New York, 1979), 45–51; Kent, *Charter*, 123, 127.

of municipal voting in New York City, a city government insisted on precise qualifications for admission to the franchise.

Jeffersonians attempted to meet the charter's property qualifications by jointly purchasing lots in pivotal wards (a practice known as "fagot voting," presumably because each individual voter owned no more than a few sticks of the freehold). But the Federalist majority in the Common Council scrutinized the property qualifications of all who voted in closely contested ward elections, and over the protests of the Jeffersonian mayor, Edward Livingston (who had been appointed by the state Council of Appointment), disallowed the votes of most of the fagot voters. According to the Common Council, such attempts to undermine the franchise were "contrary to the true intent and spirit of the charter of this City, and of the Act of the Legislature regulating the election of Charter Officers, and it is to be considered as a fraud upon the Election of evil and dangerous example, calculated to defeat the regular and deliberate exercise of the important privilege of voting for Charter officers by covert and sinister artifices and contrivances of a small number of individuals."[24]

The city's Jeffersonian political contestants then turned to a Jeffersonian legislature for relief. The contest between Federalists and Jeffersonians was transformed into a dispute over the power of the legislature to intervene in the affairs of the corporation and to modify the charter. In this dispute Jeffersonians and Federalists assumed characteristic roles: the former insisting on the need for change and the sovereign power of a republican legislature, the latter arguing that legislative action would violate the vested rights of the corporation and destroy legitimate republican principles. Jeffersonians claimed that the Montgomerie Charter had "been a source of complaint to our fellow citizens" for a long time. "Many of the regulations and provisions it contains for the government of the City, by lapse of time, and a total change of circumstances, [have] become useless; others improper, and some oppressive." Continued insistence on the inviolability of that charter was nothing but "a singular instance of attachment to the unwholesome regulations of former times," for much of the charter was "calculated as more congenial with a monarchical and kingly government, than with the more modern and plain republican institutions of the present day." The demand for change arose not from "the wild spirit of innovation" but "from evils and inconvenience daily felt" and "from a conviction that, in its present form, it is incompetent to ensure to the inhabitants of this city a useful and efficient government." Thus legislative action was justified even in the absence of the consent of the members (or voters) of the corporation. Indeed, Federalist insistence on the need for

24. *Min. CC*, 3:59–85, 75 (4 December 1801).

consent was "repugnant to the nature of all our civil institutions . . . tending to raise a corporate body of this nature above legislative power, and make it paramount, in effect, to the constitution under which we live."[25] As James Cheetham had earlier argued in his pamphlet *Annals of the Corporation:* "If confidence cannot be reposed in the wisdom and integrity of the legislature, then the principle must be entirely banished from society. A community must always remain competent to the superintendance of its concerns. Those general powers of superintendance must be entrusted somewhere. They can be no where more safely deposited than with the legislature. Subject to the constitution, all the rights and privileges of the citizen are entrusted with them—why not charter rights as well as others?"[26]

Federalists condemned Jeffersonian electoral proposals as the creations of demagogues, subversive of "every remnant of liberty in this country" and typical of the "destructive tendency of democratic principles." The Montgomerie Charter was more than the reminder of a discordant past that Jeffersonians labeled it. Under that charter, "the city has not only increased in size and population, but, under the fostering care of the Magistrates, improvements both useful and ornamental have been made from time to time, and are still progressing." According to the Federalists, "The rising commerce of the city, so interesting to the State at large, . . . may be ascribed in some degree to the salutary regulations contained in, and authorized by the present Charter."[27]

The Federalist majority on the Common Council did not claim that there would never be an occasion when intervention by the legislature would be justified. In fact, they promised "that as often as they shall discover *important* defects in the Charter they shall deem it their duty to communicate the same to the Legislature and ask their aid in providing a remedy." But so long as change was unnecessary, legislative interference was "altogether improper," for there was "real danger to be apprehended from frequent and important changes in Constitutions, law and charters."[28]

It might appear that Federalists and Jeffersonians were arguing over the primacy of different parts of the bifurcated corporation of the city of New York: Federalists viewing it as a repository of vested property rights, Jeffersonians as a derivative agency of the state. The Federalists, however, were more ambiguous in their language. They were less concerned that the

25. *Morning Chronicle*, 27 December 1802, and 19 February 1803, reprinted in *The Burghers of New Amsterdam and the Freemen of New York, 1675–1866.* New York Historical Society, *Collections* 18 (1885):299, 300, 319.

26. James Cheetham, *Annals of the Corporation* (New York, 1802), 82.

27. New York Historical Society, *Collections* 18 (1885):315.

28. *Min. CC,* 3:192–94 (27 January 1803).

legislature was considering changes in the government structure of the city than that change was contemplated without the accompanying consent— let alone the prior initiative—of the Common Council. They objected to the claims that change in the institutional nature of city government might be imposed as an act of sovereign power by the state legislature.[29] In their defense of the charter they made many of the same arguments that would later be refined and developed for private corporations during and after the *Dartmouth College* case. But the Federalists should not be understood as asserting that the corporation was nothing but a private entity. Their words betray an uncertainty as to the legal nature of the corporation, a confusion over the relationship of city government to the power of the state, that is one measure of the transformation already undergone by the corporation.

By the same token, Jeffersonians did not contend that local government could properly be reduced to a powerless agency of legislative authority. They did not mean to deny to city government the power to govern or the power to initiate change. Their concern, rather, was with the location of sovereignty in the legislature and with the capacity of that body to change institutional structures when the popular will mandated change. "The business of the corporation, as it respects internal police," Cheetham had written in an earlier pamphlet, "is as distant from that of the aggregate state, as legislation in one state is from that in another." In matters of local administration the corporation was "an insular polity," and legislative interference with its "ulterior regulations" was improper "except . . . where those regulations clash with the constitution." For Cheetham and other Jeffersonians, as for their Federalist opponents, the "self-management of self-concerns" was the "vital part of government."[30]

The Jeffersonians won in 1804 because they controlled the state legislature. But one wonders if even a Federalist-controlled legislature would

29. See the veto messages Kent drafted for the Council of Revision in 1803 and 1804 (Street, *Council of Revision*, 327–28, 423–25). Indeed, back in 1791 the Common Council had resolved to equalize wards within the city (*Min. CC*, 1:624 [21 January 1791]). And throughout the 1790s and 1800s the members regularly petitioned for legislation they understood as modifying provisions of the charter. Consider the preamble, drafted by the Common Council, of "An Act to alter the time for election of charter-officers . . . to reduce several laws relating particularly to the said city and county into one act, and for other purposes," passed by the state legislature in March 1800. Among other things it represented that "the Mayor, aldermen and commonalty of the said city, in common council convened, have by petition under their common seal, represented to the legislature . . . that it would be useful that several statutes of the State making alterations in the charter of the said city upon the petition of the said common council, should be incorporated into one statute" (*Laws of New York*, 23rd sess. [Albany, 1800], c. 35).

30. James Cheetham, *A Dissertation concerning Political Equality and the Corporation of New York* (New York, 1800), 42–43.

have taken seriously the pretentions of the Federalist Common Council. The actions of that same Common Council through the 1790s and early 1800s negate its claim to have defended the Montgomerie Charter as a continuing, viable repository of effective and autonomous authority. Except in their assertion of the power to set voting qualifications, the Federalists in power had not treated the Montgomerie Charter as the basis for much of anything of governmental significance. The willingness of state legislators to restructure a chartered government over the objections of the leaders of that government remains an important measure of the extent to which New York City had come to be viewed as a part of a unitary, legislatively controlled administrative structure. But arguments for the necessity of consent by the members of the corporation could not have carried much weight when city government had already so decisively committed itself to the power of the state.

The Federalists' fear of being turned out of office and the prospects of Jeffersonian political ascendance no doubt sharpened and made more radical the debate between them. But ultimately Federalists and Jeffersonians alike shared a conception of city government as largely dependent on explicit and detailed delegations of state power. Focusing on the conflict between them during the years 1801 to 1803 hides the deeper consensus that committed the postrevolutionary generation to changing the traditional legal bases for municipal government.

It is a minor measure of that consensus that in the general housecleaning that followed the Jeffersonian victory of 1804, when most of the Federalist officeholders were turned out, Richard Harison, the counsel to the Common Council and a staunch Federalist (indeed, a former tory), was retained by the reconstructed city government. And it was to Richard Harison that Jeffersonian council members would look for advice on the legitimate reach of their powers under the Montgomerie Charter and the relevant acts of the New York State legislature.[31]

Throughout the early nineteenth century, pigs wandered through the streets of New York City, "prowling in grunting ferocity." They were a

---

31. *Min. CC*, 3:656–57 (24 December 1804). In 1801 Harison had been dismissed as the official recorder of the city by the newly elected Jeffersonian state government (through the Council of Appointment). Like the mayor, the recorder was an appointive position. But on his dismissal the still-Federalist Common Council hired him as their personal counsel, in which position he remained until late 1807. On Harison, see Dixon Ryan Fox, *The Decline of Aristocracy in the Politics of New York* (New York, 1919), 11; William A. Duer, *Reminiscences of an Old Yorker* (New York, 1867): "He was the most accomplished scholar of the group [of elite New York lawyers]. He was, moreover, a sound lawyer, and a plausible if not a pleasing speaker; though at times, the native acidity of his temper would effervesce in pithy sallies and petulant contradiction" (ibid., 24–25).

municipal scandal, noted by many foreign travelers to the city. Indeed, their utility as scavengers to remove sewage and filth from the streets was viewed by middle-class New Yorkers as an indication that there was "something wrong" with the city's government.[32] It was conventional wisdom that the pigs would attack small children, and genteel ladies were regularly offended by their willingness to copulate and defecate in the streets.[33]

Still, the city government did nothing to control the pigs in its streets until 1818, when, in a test case, a grand jury indicted Christian Harriet for a public nuisance in keeping hogs in the streets of the city. The trial that followed evidently excited popular interest.[34] The defendant's lawyers claimed that the charge against their client was founded on an illegitimate exercise of public authority. The representatives of the city, by contrast, believed that not to act would have been in dereliction of their duties as public servants. Though the corporation had in the past "indulged" the practice of letting pigs run in the streets, that was no reason, argued the prosecutor, for denying it "the right of correcting the evil now." Indeed, even "if the corporation had in fact expressly authorized swine to run at large in the streets," it still would not alter the situation, "for the corporation cannot abrogate the common law."[35]

Harriet's lawyers began their defense by noting the longstanding, customary expectation that residents of the city might keep pigs:

> The practice of allowing hogs to run in the street was of immemorial duration; our ancestors had never been troubled with any excessive notions of delicacy on the subject; indeed they had ever been considered by a great many judicious people as the best of scavengers, and hundreds of people in the city now calculated on one or two hogs they might raise and fatten at little expense, for the principle supply of their families; and certainly against these substantial and important benefits it was not politic or humane to say that the few and slight inconveniences which attended the keeping of them should operate to their exclusion.[36]

32. Howard Rock, "A Delicate Balance: The Mechanics and the City in the Age of Jefferson," *New York Historical Society Quarterly* 63 (1979): 93–114; Raymond Mohl, *Poverty in New York, 1783–1825* (New York, 1971), 11.

33. *People* v. *Harriet*, 1 N.Y. Jud. Repository 258–64 (1818); to the mayor it was a scandal that "in this great and proud city, . . . our wives and daughters cannot walk abroad through the streets of the city without encountering the most disgusting spectacles of those animals indulging the propensities of nature" (ibid., 272).

34. Ibid., 258; another transcript of the case can be found at 4 Rogers City Hall Recorder 26 (1818).

35. *People* v. *Harriet*, N.Y. Jud. Repository 267.

36. Ibid., 264–65.

A social practice, argued the defense, could become a public nuisance only if it violated standards held in common by the entire population of a community. Thus, because pigs were almost a necessity of life for a large portion of the city, pigs could not be considered a nuisance: "The dandies, who are too delicate to endure the sight, or even the idea of so odious a creature, might exult; but many poor families might experience far different sensations, and be driven to beggary or the Alms House for a portion of that subsistence of which a verdict of conviction in this case would deprive them." [37]

Moreover, argued the lawyers, "by the existing state of our corporation laws, the citizens had actually a right to keep hogs, and let them run at large." Why? Because an ordinance had once been passed and then repealed regulating the keeping of hogs in the city, leaving the citizens "to the natural and only conclusion, that there was no law in existence forbidding them to keep hogs as before." [38] Finally, if allowing swine to run at large in the streets really was to be forbidden, the corporation ought to do it the right way: "Let a petition be drawn and our delegation [in Albany] instructed to have a special act passed to prevent the evil." [39] But until then, pigs should run free of city regulation.

Mayor Cadwallader D. Colden, who was sitting as judge in the case, disagreed sharply with the defendant's lawyers in his charge to the jury. Even if in the past the corporation had removed "all restraint" on the keeping of hogs, still "the corporation have no right to pass any law contrary to a statute of the state, or which shall contravene the common, or unwritten law of the land." In Colden's view, the common law was not a set of immutable principles standing above conventional authority. To the contrary, he regarded the common law of nuisance as an aspect of the public authority of the state, an alternative source of regulatory authority. In New York, according to the mayor, a public nuisance was any "offence against the public order and economical regimen of the state, and an annoyance to the public," even though "no man's health be affected." Nor "need every man in the community be offended by it." It was sufficient that a jury from

37. Ibid., 266; for evidence that artisans did depend on city swine see Rock, "Delicate Balance," 93.

38. In May 1788 the grand jury had presented the dangerous condition of swine running free in the streets. In response, a committee of the Common Council was asked to consider appropriate action. The committee drafted an ordinance, which was rejected in July by the whole Common Council, but passed on reconsideration in November (*Min. CC*, 1 : 369, 379, 385, 417; Thomas V. Smith, *The City of New York in the Year of Washington's Inaugural* [Riverside, Conn., 1972], 62–63). The ordinance was not formally repealed but lapsed from nonrenewal.

39. *People* v. *Harriet*, 1 N.Y. Jud. Repository 266–67 (1818).

within a community consider a condition a nuisance. And the mayor left no doubt in his charge that he believed pigs to be such a nuisance. The dependence of a large portion of the city's population on the swine as food made no difference. "Why, gentlemen!" he declared, "must we feed the poor at the expence of human flesh?" Although he conceded that at one time pigs might have been a "useful sort of scavengers," he insisted that "our corporation will not employ brutal agency for that object when men can be got to do it." He promised that Harriet would receive only a nominal punishment if convicted. But any expectations raised by past practices of the corporation ought to be ignored by the jury, which compliantly did as it was told and convicted the defendant.[40]

The arguments raised in the case suggest that lurking beneath the new rhetoric of public power was a class-bound and biased vision, narrower and more sectarian than the emphasis on republican ideals might have suggested. The customary "properties" that helped secure the autonomy of artisans were not to the taste of the planners of New York's urban environment. Pigs were not a private right. And the public order city leaders would have liked to create (in which they obviously failed) was one that embodied a sentimental prudishness in direct contrast to the anarchic vitality (and filth) of the premodern city.

Yet we should also consider the arguments that were not made. The lawyers for Harriet never insisted that the custom of keeping pigs was a vested right. They did not even press the position that the corporation was forbidden by its past conduct from passing a prohibition. They simply claimed, first, that the city had not passed such a regulation, and second, that it had not properly sought the authorization of the state legislature. On the other side, neither the mayor nor the prosecutor ever asserted the autonomous right of the corporation to regulate under the Montgomerie Charter. The city's powers derived only from the state, though not in this case from a statute.

By the second decade of the nineteenth century, a traditional way of thinking about the relationships between public power and private autonomy had become impossible, at least in New York City. Custom, tradition, and local authority played no significant part in the arguments. The issues raised revolved around the power of the state and around the terms by which power had or had not been delegated to a local agency. Legal positivism provided the consensual basis for legal argument.

40. Ibid., 269–72. See *Levy* v. *City of New York*, 1 Sandford 465 (1835). On the failure of this effort to reduce the swine in the streets of the city, see Charles Rosenberg, *The Cholera Years* (Chicago, 1962), 103 (presence of pigs in the epidemic of 1849).

CHAPTER 10

The Ends of Government in
Republican New York City

Changes in the practice of government in New York City during the years after the American Revolution were dramatic, justifying the claim that a "municipal revolution" had occurred.[1] The sheer scale of business became much larger than it had been before the Revolution. In 1787 entries in the Common Council's minutes were more than double those in 1767; by 1807 there were 1,642 entries in the minutes, over five times the number twenty years before (see Table 8.1). What is more, the 1807 minutes no longer accurately described the total workload of city government, for in the previous decade the Common Council had created administrative agencies and offices that assumed much of the council's routine administrative business. Thus in 1807 the largest single category of activity recorded in the minutes concerned street regulation, construction, and maintenance. But the 284 entries on that subject radically understate the actual commitment of government energy and time because much of the street work conducted by city government never appeared in the minutes of the council. Routine matters were now the responsibility of city street commissioners, and the long-term planning of streets for the growing city was a responsibility entrusted to a different group of commissioners appointed by the state legislature. There was, in fact, a tendency to view the government of the city of New York as a collection of distinctive and distinguishable activities rather than as a single entity, a tendency perhaps best demonstrated by the fact that after the turn of the nineteenth century petitions from residents for relief were normally directed to specific administrators or departments, rather than to the general Common Council.[2]

Not only had city government's workload grown, but it devoted its time

1. See Jon Teaford, *Municipal Revolution in America* (Chicago, 1975).
2. See Petition Files, 1801 and 1802, Municipal Archives and Record Center, New York. For a discussion of "componentiality" as a key element in the modernization of conscious-

to different categories of work. As Teaford has argued, there was a significant shift of concern toward health and safety regulations[3] (although one might question the effectiveness and intensity of the new commitment to "public" regulation[4]). And devotion to the management of corporate property declined as a relative proportion of the business of the Common Council.[5]

By 1807, the Common Council was engaged in activities that would have been beyond the contemplation of the prerevolutionary government. Some of these have already been mentioned: the mobilization of a public work force, the direct abatement of public hazards and nuisances, street cleaning. Other tasks undertaken by the council might seem to be of lesser importance but are evocative of the changed self-perception of New York City's government. For example, the corporation had come to view itself as a record keeper and statistician of all aspects of city life. In 1804 the council passed an ordinance requiring accurate monthly reports from the measurers of grain, lime, charcoal, boards and lumber, and weighers of hay. It was the responsibility of the city inspector to compile these reports into annual surveys of the amount and value of the articles imported into and exported from the city.[6] One year later, in the wake of an epidemic, the council ordered a census of the population.[7] One of the new public responsibilities of the city government was to measure change, to describe objectively the various quantifiable indicia of life in New York City, for such information was considered to be of "public utility."[8]

There was also a drastic shift in the finances of the corporation. By the end of the eighteenth century the receipts from corporate revenue could satisfy only a fraction of the fiscal needs of city government, which then looked to the state legislature for tax authorization. In 1799 the expenses of the corporation totaled $110,000, $90,000 of which had to be raised by taxes. In 1806, with corporate receipts of about $30,000, the ordinary expenses of city government had risen to $176,000.[9] Finally, in 1812 the cor-

ness, see Peter Berger, Brigitte Berger, and Hansfried Kellner, *The Homeless Mind* (New York, 1973). See also Daniel Calhoun, *The Intelligence of a People* (New York, 1973).

3. Teaford, *Municipal Revolution*, 91, 110.

4. See Raymond Mohl, *Poverty in New York, 1783–1825* (New York, 1971), 11; Charles Rosenberg, *The Cholera Years* (Chicago, 1962), 17–31.

5. See Chapter 8.

6. *Minutes of the Common Council of the City of New York, 1784–1831*, 21 vols., (New York, 1917–30), 3:576–78, 613 (8 October 1804), hereafter *Min. CC*; *Laws and Ordinances . . . of the City of New York* (New York, 1805), 20–21.

7. *Min. CC*, 4:94 (18 November 1805); 186–87 (28 April 1806).

8. *Laws and Ordinances*, 20.

9. David T. Valentine, *Manual of the Corporation of the City of New York*, (New York, 1859) 514.

poration committed all the revenue from its corporate properties to the payment of interest on a "permanent debt" of the city, which would be used to implement the newly drafted plan to lay out the streets of an enlarged New York City. In petitioning the legislature, the members of the Common Council noted that because of the expenses they had incurred in making various improvements "of a permanent nature," they had "found the ordinary revenues of the corporation altogether inadequate to meet the demands which those expenses have produced." They "despaired of being able to raise" the necessary sums "without legislative interference in their behalf" and looked to the legislature to authorize a sinking fund to help them "establish the credit of the corporation on a solid basis."[10]

Thus by the early nineteenth century the corporation had become largely dependent on taxes to finance its ordinary activities. Its estate still was useful in securing credit and bonding authority but had become a peripheral part of its budgetary life. Rhetorical obeisance might still be paid to a "revenue-to-avoid-taxes philosophy" of public finance.[11] But in its day-to-day operations New York City was committed to the public financing of public enterprise.[12]

Significant—even dramatic—changes had occurred in a short span of time. Yet they are less important for themselves than for the future they suggested for urban governance in America. Much had changed. But as of the first decades of the nineteenth century New York City remained legally and politically distinguishable from other local governments in New York. It still stood, like Albany but unlike other cities in the state, formally a propertied corporation with a charter guaranteed by the New York State constitution.[13]

10. *Laws of New York*, 35th sess. (Albany, 1812), c. 99.

11. See Alfred Young, *The Democratic Republicans of New York: The Origins, 1763–1797* (Chapel Hill, 1967), 235–36; Oscar Handlin and Mary F. Handlin, *Commonwealth*, rev. ed. (Cambridge, Mass., 1968), 63–77.

12. The significance of this commitment is revealed in the following remark by Max Weber: "A state based exclusively on money contributions, conducting the collection of the taxes (but no other economic activity) through its own staff, and calling on personal service contributions only for political and judicial purposes, provides an optimal environment for a rational market-oriented capitalism" (*Economy and Society* [London, 1969], 199). Weber went on to argue that other forms of government financing, including "the imposition of obligations to personal services; that is, direct personal services with specification of the work to be done" (such as characterized the earlier history of New York City), provided a less attractive environment for capitalist growth. "What is important for profit-making enterprises with fixed capital and careful accounting is, in formal terms, above all, the calculation of the tax load" (ibid., 196–200).

13. Compare the nineteenth-century charters of Brooklyn, the other explosively growing city in New York State. In 1816, Brooklyn was incorporated as a village (*Laws of New York*, 39th sess. [Albany, 1816], c. 95). It was given a corporate identity but no property, and un-

It is the political values and commitments underlying change that must be of central concern. What did city leaders wish to accomplish through their government that could be done only as a part of a state polity? To say that they both feared continued identification of the corporation as a chartered entity in a republican political culture and wanted also to identify their institution with the positive authority of the state tells us much. But we need to know their substantive goals: what they wanted government to do in the reconstructed political structure of republican America.

To city leaders—both Federalists and Jeffersonians—the corporation of the city of New York ought to become a government with complete authority over a distinctively public sphere of action. They were as committed as their predecessors had been to maintaining the autonomy of the corporation. But the concept of autonomy had changed. The relative freedom of the city from external intervention did not concern them; rather, they sought freedom from physical dependence on a local constituency. The corruption they feared was not the corruption of reliance on central authority; it was the corruption of mixing public and private spheres.[14] To rely on the initiative and support of private individuals for action made city government dependent on the public-spiritedness of its constituency. To expect individuals to divert time and attention from their private concerns was, moreover, fruitless. The very privatism which urban historians such as Sam Bass Warner have identified as the distinguishing characteristic of the American city served as an incentive to the development of an exclusively public sphere of government.[15]

In a republican and capitalistic society, government would not be the

---

like the corporation of the city of New York, its lawmaking powers were vested in trustees with responsibility for the general public welfare, who were at the same time forbidden to regulate the prices of commodities, except for bread. Eighteen years later the legislature chartered the new city of Brooklyn (8 April 1834). The charter this time added no new property rights and included no abstract statement of the powers or identity of the corporation. The city was to be nothing but an administrative agency with a long list of specific responsibilities, including a responsibility not to act in any way that would harm the chartered rights of the corporation of the city of New York.

14. See generally, Gerald Frug, "The City as a Legal Concept," *Harvard Law Review* 93 (1980):1057–1154.

15. Sam Bass Warner, *The Private City* (Philadelphia, 1968); *The Urban Wilderness* (New York, 1972), 55–84. Mid-nineteenth-century reformers bemoaned the alienation of public-spirited citizens from the American city, often sharing with modern historians an idealized image of the early American city as a place run by the "right" people. See M. J. Heale, "From City Fathers to Social Critics: Humanitarianism and Government in New York, 1790–1860," *Journal of American History* 63 (1976):21–41. What was usually forgotten was that the makers of nineteenth-century city government—the "right" people—worked to separate city government from traditional forms of citizen participation. In that sense, mid-nineteenth-century New York might have stood as the fulfillment of their intentions.

sole repository of the general public good. In their private activities and enterprises private individuals also secured the public welfare. Legitimate public authority would have as its distinctive responsibility a peculiarly public range of activities distinguishable from the concerns of private individuals.

Only in taking full responsibility for a public activity could city leaders satisfy themselves that the corporation was serving the public good; otherwise, it would be charged with serving special interests or groups. Thus the development of the waterfront of the city could not be made the hostage of the initiative of waterlot proprietors. If private landowners were not interested in widening public slips in exchange for enlarged grants, the city needed the power to widen the slips on its own.

This view of the public sphere suggests why the city always insisted on explicit legislative authorization for its actions. Legislation allowed the corporation to do not just what it might not have been able to do under the Montgomerie Charter; it also symbolized the appropriation by city government of particular areas of responsibility. Street cleaning, for example, no longer would be a task charged to private individuals under the supervision of city government in its general capacity of maintainer of public order; street cleaning would become the exclusive job of government. Individuals would not have to commit their personal time and energy to street cleaning; their tax dollars, not their labor, would be relied on to finance the venture. Cleaned streets had become a public good, a legitimate expectation that citizens would make of their government.[16]

By the first years of the nineteenth century there had emerged a consensus that at least some activities ought to be the exclusive responsibility of city government. Street construction and nuisance abatement stand out as tasks over which the corporation managed to assert largely unchallenged monopolistic control.[17] But other areas remained more controversial, and debate over whether a particular service ought to be publicly or privately provided shaped New York City's political life throughout the first decades of the nineteenth century.

Consider, for example, the problem of supplying the growing city with drinkable water. All agreed that a new and enlarged waterworks was an absolute necessity. The issue was who or what group would furnish it.

16. See Weber, *Economy and Society*, 641–42; for the modern conception of a "public good" as an unpriced or unpriceable commodity, see Paul Samuelson, "The Theory of Public Expenditures," *Review of Economics and Statistics* 36 (1954): 387–89; for a critique that argues for the priceability—the private quality—of local public goods, see Charles M. Tiebout, "A Pure Theory of Local Expenditures," *Journal of Political Economy* 64 (1956): 416–24. The latter article has spawned a huge literature, and the issue remains unresolved in modern public economics.

17. See Chapter 11.

By the end of the Revolution the Fresh Water Pond, which had once supplied the city with most of its drinking water, had become "a very sink and common sewer."[18] Only the privately owned Tea Water Pump on Chatham Street dispensed potable water. A system of well, pump, and reservoir designed before the Revolution by the engineer Christopher Colles had never been constructed. In 1785 and 1786 the Common Council invited bids from private individuals interested in reviving the project in exchange for an exclusive franchise. Three proposals were received; but when it came time to decide between them, council members balked. "It appeared to be the Sense of a Majority of the Persons they had conferred with that the Corporation ought not to grant the Privilege of supplying the City Water to Individuals; but that the same ought if possible to be undertaken by the Corporation."[19] And so the council did nothing.

Ten years later, with the example of water projects under way in Philadelphia and Albany, with the Fresh Water Pond by then viewed as "a shocking hold, where all impure things center together . . . foul with excrement, frog-spawn, and reptiles," and with even the Tea Water Pump's water tasting "sickly and nauseating,"[20] the Common Council set up a committee to consider new proposals for a publicly owned waterworks. Various proposals were submitted, including several that would have granted private individuals a franchise to run the project. But in late 1798 the committee concluded that the waterworks ought to be managed by the city directly: "Considering the immense Importance of the Subject to the Comfort & Health of their Citizens, that it will not be undertaken by a Company unless upon the Prospect of considerable Gain; and that such Gain must be acquired at the Expence of the City your Committee have at length agreed that the Undertaking ought to be pursued by and under the Controul of the Corporation as the immediate Representatives of the Citizens in general." The committee therefore recommended that a bill be drafted immediately for the legislature, "investing the Corporation with the Powers necessary to effect the great End they have in view" and granting the corporation the right to collect a tax on auction sales in the city to finance the venture.[21]

A statute to this effect was quickly prepared by then Recorder Richard Harison. By 4 February 1799 it had been sent on to the legislature, where under ordinary circumstances it would have been promptly passed into law. In this instance, however, the Federalist Common Council's innocent

18. Quoted in Sidney Pomerantz, *New York: An American City, 1783–1803*, 2d ed. (Port Washington, N.Y., 1965), 278.

19. *Min. CC*, 1:213–14 (19 April 1788).

20. *Commercial Advertizer*, quoted in Pomerantz, *New York*, 281.

21. *Min. CC*, 2:286–87 (17 December 1798).

proposal to charter a public waterworks became part of Aaron Burr's plan to charter a Republican-controlled bank, the Manhattan Company.

The story has been often told.[22] Under the guise of establishing a water company, Burr and his co-sponsors set up a corporation that could direct its "surplus capital" to "the purchase of public or other stock, or in any other monied transactions or operations not inconsistent with the constitution of this state or of the United States, for the sole benefit of the said company." Federalist legislators were either duped, bribed, or convinced to vote for a project that its sponsors intended to use for ends entirely distinct from the purposes stated in the charter: a direct and manifest violation of standard republican principles and an important event in the evolution of the business corporation form.[23]

For us, though, the event is more important for the arguments mobilized to transform public project into private enterprise. On 25 February, Aaron Burr and other members of the legislature met with Mayor Richard Varick and Recorder Harison to discuss the "great difficulties" that appear to have "arisen in the minds of the Members of the Legislature touching the Powers requested to be vested in this Board [the Common Council]."[24] This conversation was immediately reported to the council, which, with typical deference, resolved that "the Legislature should make such Provision . . . as to them appear most eligible," and the council then asked the opinion of Alexander Hamilton on the best way of proceeding. Hamilton replied not with legal arguments but with a practical discussion of the finances of the proposed "public" venture. It was unlikely, he wrote, that the legislature would grant the city the auction sales tax "for the *profit* of the Corporation." But even if it did, the revenue thereby secured by the corporation would not be enough, and the city government would have to borrow to complete the project: "To raise what may be wanted by taxes to carry on the enterprise with vigour might be found so burdensome on the Citizens as to occasion the operation to languish." Hamilton therefore recommended that the project be financed as a joint enterprise, with one-third of the stock reserved for the corporation. "By this expedient the success will become certain and the enterprise can be carried on with energy and dispatch."[25]

22. See Beatrice Reuben, "Burr, Hamilton, and the Manhattan Company," *Political Science Quarterly* 72 (1957): 578–607; ibid., 73 (1958): 100–125; George Dangerfield, *Chancellor Robert R. Livingston of New York, 1746–1813* (New York, 1960), 289–93; Pomerantz, *New York*, 187–92.

23. See J. S. Davis, *Essays in the Earlier History of American Corporations* (Cambridge, Mass., 1917).

24. *Min. CC*, 2:514 (25 February 1799).

25. Ibid., 517–20 (28 February 1799).

The Common Council accepted Hamilton's recommendation and with-drew its proposed statute, and the legislature chartered the Manhattan Company to bring fresh drinking water to the city (although the corporation was given permission to subscribe to stock in the company and a seat on the board of directors). It might appear that a more or less permanent decision in favor of private enterprise had been reached. Yet, less than a decade later, the Common Council changed its mind again. In the wake of the haphazard and intermittent activities of the Manhattan Company as a water supplier (as opposed to its more vigorous banking enterprises), the council proposed not that the franchise be shifted to another private producer or that rival water companies be chartered but that the corporation reassume entire responsibility for the city's drinking water. "It has been generally understood and believed, that the right of supplying this city with pure and wholesome water, ought to be vested in the Corporation, as the constituted guardians of its prosperity," reported the committee appointed to confer with the Manhattan Company, and it recommended that the council obtain the sanction of the legislature to buy out the company.

By 1808, the reasons for public ownership had been clarified. Providing an adequate supply of potable water was properly a public responsibility of the corporation, part of its public sphere of activity. "When the Committee consider the importance of this power, in supplying the citizens with good water for domestic purposes, in guarding against the ravages of fire and disease, in purifying the Streets, and in accommodating the public buildings, they cannot but earnestly recommend to the Corporation, the most prompt and efficient measures for obtaining it."[26] It would take another quarter century before a public water supply system was authorized for New York City, but in 1808 city leaders had finally decided that water was a public good, to be provided and produced publicly, like streets and the public health.[27]

Clearly, the postrevolutionary corporation of the city of New York was not offering a full range of modern city services. Much of what we might consider traditional and necessary public responsibilities of city government were not provided at all or only in emergencies when there was a clear failure of private initiative.[28] Nor did New York City's government do

26. Ibid., 4:715–16 (18 January 1808).
27. On the later history of the city water supply, see Nelson M. Blake, *Water for the Cities: A History of the Urban Water Supply Problem in the United States* (New York, 1956); "The Memoirs of Stephen Allen," transcription at New York Historical Society.
28. During the widespread distress that followed the 1808 imposition of Jefferson's Embargo, the corporation became something of an employer of last resort. As a committee reported, "It is incumbent on the Corporation to use such means as may be in their power,

a particularly effective job of the services for which it did take responsibility. Streets remained filthy, and pigs still competed with public scavengers for the waste and garbage on the city streets. Succeeding epidemics appear to have left members of the Common Council only rhetorically more prepared to take action to protect the public health.[29]

Still, it is proper to center our attention on the creation of direct public enterprise in republican New York City, for it was that which most clearly differentiated the postrevolutionary corporation from its colonial antecedents. On the other hand, not everything that the corporation of the city of New York did was new. It continued to manage its corporate estate. It also continued to act as a regulator of commerce.[30]

The postrevolutionary Common Council somewhat reduced its formal control over city markets (although, as we have seen, it would be a mistake to think that the prerevolutionary corporation had ever been an enthusiastic commercial regulator). It is evident, moreover, that members of the postrevolutionary Common Council were uncomfortable with their residual responsibilities for enforcing market regulations, bread assizes, and so forth. In 1789 the Common Council decided to permit all butchers who wished to keep slaughterhouses in their own homes to do so, as long as they lived north of the most settled part of the city. According to the committee sent to study the use of the public slaughterhouse, the requirement that all butchers rent stalls there was "attended with considerable Inconvenience to the Butchers, productive of little or no good consequences to the Community & the actual Revenue arising therefrom to the Corporation is considerably less than what might be expected." The council concluded that the only reason to continue to maintain a public slaughterhouse was to accommodate those butchers not immediately provided with private facilities. Similarly, in the wake of several years of protests by bakers, the Com-

---

particularly at this inclement season, to alleviate the evils which must result from a suspension of the ordinary avocations of the laborious part of the Community of this City" (*Min. CC*, 4:693–94 [5 January 1808]; 728–29 [25 January 1808]). For a discussion of the unwillingness of Cincinnati to commit its municipal resources to a wide range of public services, see Alan I. Marcus, "In Sickness and in Health: The Marriage of the Municipal Corporation to the Public Interest and the Problem of Public Health, 1820–1870" (Ph.D. dissertation, University of Cincinnati, 1979).

29. Compare the 1799 joint committee report, *Min. CC*, 2:494–99, 500–508, with Rosenberg, *Cholera Years*, 17–33, 103, 110–14.

30. Indeed, a reading of the minutes of the Common Council suggests to me at least that the city became a more active regulator of commerce in the quarter century after the Revolution than it had been in the quarter century before (see Table 8.1). Jon Teaford, of course, argues the opposite in *The Municipal Revolution in America*, but for the reasons detailed in Chapter 3, I remain unpersuaded. See Howard Rock, *Artisans of the New Republic* (New York, 1979), 149–323.

mon Council decided in 1800 that the assize of bread would no longer be used to set the price of bread but only to regulate the quality of the flour used. Allowing competitive pricing would "create an emulation among the Bakers and would of course produce good Bread and . . . at a reasonable Price."[31]

From the early 1790s on, the minutes of the council contain frequent statements of the members' commitment to a free market. Still, there was a certain ambiguity in their actions. They may have been uncomfortable in the role of regulators, but it was not a role that could easily be sloughed off. The same Common Council that had dropped the bread assize soon changed its mind. The insistence on separating public and private spheres that fueled their discomfort with price regulations and market rules made it impossible for them, as the guardians of a public sphere, to refuse to maintain institutional structures identified with the public welfare. If removing price regulation did not in fact reduce the price but instead allowed it to climb beyond the means of the poor,[32] if relaxation of market rules led to attempts by larger grocers to charge monopolistic prices by "forestalling"—buying out—the smaller "country people" whose goods might have undersold them,[33] then traditional price and market restrictions would be enforced, however distasteful they might be. Members of the city government seemed more concerned with the legitimacy of an autonomous public sphere than with the purity of their political economy.[34]

But the Common Council was unambiguously insistent that the corporation itself not promote or encourage monopolistic or anticompetitive behavior. It repealed ordinances that kept hucksters—unlicensed peddlers—from selling their wares in the public markets and the streets of the city.[35] Concurrently, the rights of corporate lessees were shorn of monopolistic implications. In 1799, the butchers leasing stalls in Fly Market were told that, contrary to their claims, they did not hold their stalls in per-

31. *Min. CC*, 1:451–52, 455 (13 May 1789); 517–18 (29 January 1790); 2:640, 642 (14 July 1800); 3:42–43 (26 October 1801).

32. Ibid., 3:53–54 (18 November 1801); see Howard Rock, "The Perils of Laissez-Faire: The Aftermath of the New York Baker's Strike of 1801," *Labor History* 17 (1976):372–87; Rock, *Artisans*, 183–201. Not until 1821 did the city permanently abandon the practice of fixing bread prices.

33. *Min. CC*, 3:202 (14 February 1803).

34. A guidebook to the city for visitors published in 1807 repeatedly emphasized the continuing regulatory authority of city government, ([S. L. Mitchell], *The Picture of New-York; or the Traveller's Guide through the Commercial Metropolis of the United States* [New York, 1807]). A similar work published in 1814 reported that "an endless variety of fruits and vegetables are sold by the hucksters and country people, who, as well as the butchers are restricted in the sale of unwholesome articles by the severest penalties" (Thomas N. Stanford, *A Concise Description of the City of New York* [New York, 1814], 16).

35. *Min. CC*, 3:310–11 (14 June 1803).

petuity subject only to the obligation to pay rent to the corporation. The council committee that dealt with them recommended that to avoid controversy each butcher be granted the right to keep his stall until 1820 or his death, whichever should come first. But it was irate that previous councils had routinely permitted butchers to claim title to more stalls than they could personally use, "receiving an emolument therefrom which they do not appear entitled to & making a sort of monopoly of the Stalls, calculated to destroy that competitor-ship in the Sale of meat which is always beneficial to the public."[36]

The corporation began in a halting way to make even openly exclusive franchises like the city-owned ferries to Brooklyn and New Jersey more competitive in their operations. In 1803, when a Mr. Budd applied for the right to run a ferry between the city and his wharf near Powles Hook, the Common Council took only passing note of the fact that there already was ferry service across the Hudson. The members of the reporting committee "did not think it necessary to express an opinion whether Mr. Budd will be able to derive a profit from the Ferry . . . *that* as an individual pursuing his own interest is his own concern." To them, the only relevant "fact" was the "public will probably be better served" by competition.[37] Similarly, in 1805 the council offered a ferry lease in direct competition with existing lessees (who indeed had thought they were receiving an exclusive franchise). The committee that recommended this course of action rationalized that "the only effectual method of accommodating the public is by the creation of rival establishments." And finally, in early 1808 the council directed the Committee on Ferries to consider what the city ought to do to promote competition between rival lessees.[38]

We should not assume that the Common Council's search for less restrictive forms of regulation and for a more competitive franchise policy signified a commitment to laissez-faire political values. The leaders of the city were concerned less with the obliteration of government or its reduction to watchman status than with the creation of a legitimate and proper sphere for government in a free society. Nothing in the available records suggests that they sought to minimize that sphere.

Government, at least in New York City, was expected to be neither a competitor nor a direct partner with private enterprise in the development of the city's economy. To the contrary, its most important function was to create a predictable and consistent environment within which that private market economy would flourish. Planning and the exercise of police powers, for all their violations of purportedly vested private rights, were cen-

36. Ibid., 2:592–93 (30 December 1799).
37. Ibid., 3:347 (18 July 1803).
38. Ibid., 4:25–36 (1 July 1805); 734 (25 January 1808).

tral to that role. In the next chapter we will consider in greater detail how the government planned the laying out of the streets of Manhattan Island north of the older settled city, a development expected both to reflect and to enhance the market economy of the city. Here, we examine the immediate ends that New York City's government pursued as a planner.

Before the Revolution, government action had not occurred ahead of demand. If the proprietor of land bordering a waterlot did not wish to develop that waterlot, there was nothing that the city government could do. Without the consent of affected private parties, the corporation of the city of New York was essentially powerless. Indeed, one power the prerevolutionary corporation did not possess was the power of eminent domain. It could not take land for its "public" purposes without the consent of the proprietor.[39] It could bargain and trade, and often did, and it had a variety of coercive tools, but it was dependent on its position as a property holder in a world of property holders rather than on its power as a government.

In contrast, early nineteenth-century public officials viewed the sources of municipal authority as entirely distinct from the bases for private action. Individuals secured the public good by seeking their private advantage, however they chose to define it. But a public institution could define its goals only in response to the dictates of its varying constituencies. In many cases popular demands might be conflicting and inconsistent, as in whether or not to deregulate the price of bread. City leaders believed, however, that they could find general assent to the proposition that government ought to be an autonomous planner creating a stable context for private decision making. That such planning would necessarily interfere with private property interests and would involve a significant extension of public power was not of concern, for members of the city government believed that they were acting under the banner of popular sovereignty.

Consider the ferry committee's long response in 1805 to the proposed development of a new ferry route from Morrill's Landing in Brooklyn to the foot of Grant Street on the northern end of the settled city. This was, declared the committee, "not only the best place for a public ferry but . . . it would be unwarrantably hazarding the interests of the public to permit the present opportunity of securing it to pass by." The only problem was that the corporation had recently leased another ferry to Brooklyn. The lessees had spent a good deal of money improving the wharves and other accommodations of the old ferry, in exchange for which they thought the corporation would ensure that they ran the only ferry to Brooklyn during the term of their lease.

39. James Kent, *The Charter of the City of New York, with notes thereon. Also a Treatise on the Powers and Duties of the Mayor, Aldermen, and Assistant Aldermen, and the Journal of the City Convention* (New York, 1836), 109.

To the committee, however, the investments and improvements of the lessees were irrelevant: "Your Committee believe it perfectly immaterial and totally foreign to the principles which govern the decision of this board to enquire whose property is benefited . . . or is not benefited by those institutions. Such enquiry might lead to favoritism and partiality, but never could advance the general interest." The only worthwhile considerations were the "convenience, safety and accommodation of the Community," for the corporation's ferry franchise was "in the nature of a trust which they are bound to exercise in such a manner as shall best promote the convenience and benefit of the public." The committee had "patiently attended to the Claims of individuals whose private interests are supposed to be concerned." And it was "always a subject of regret when individuals lose by an enterprise. Yet that circumstance cannot operate as a substantial ground of argument."[40]

In spite of the aggressiveness of its language, the alternatives considered by the committee did not include simply transferring the ferry lease to the petitioners' new route. The present lessees owned a vested right in their leasehold, and even the strength of the public interest could not overcome that right. One alternative (which in the end was implemented by the Common Council) was to secure the lessees' permission or consent to grant the Morrill's Landing–Grant Street line a franchise to compete directly with the older route. But if the lessees refused that offer, the committee urged the Common Council to decide immediately and publicly that on the expiration of the present lease the franchise would be moved to the new location.[41]

The committee detailed a number of "reasons" why it was important to act quickly to fix the public's interest in the new route: the consent of affected landowners might be withdrawn, the land might fall into the hands of infants unable to cede the ground to the public, and others. Moreover, if the present lessees were correct in their claim that the effect of a ferry change would be to lower the value of their property, "justice and duty to the public" dictated that notice of the change be given as soon as possible to keep the lessees from making any fraudulent representations as to the continuing value of their franchise. Not to act would "render the board instrumental in the deceptions which might ensue."[42]

Finally, the committee vehemently denied that the plans it proposed constituted "legislating for a future board." The committee insisted that it recommended only "such provisions for the permanent welfare of the public as is not only justifiable but strictly necessary." Not acting now would

40. *Min. CC*, 4:25–36 (1 July 1805).
41. Ibid., 52–53 (29 July 1805).
42. Ibid., 4:25–36 (1 July 1805).

"destroy the usefulness of this Corporation" by making it impossible to accomplish undertakings of "an extensive or durable nature." Even though the membership of city government was elected annually, "in its public relations it is always the same body and is bound to consult the *permanent* interests of the Community—a future board is properly bound by the Acts of its predecessors when those acts are judged expedient for the public benefit." Concerning the "durable Interests of the public," it was "necessary to look beyond the present hour." Otherwise, the powers of the corporation would be confined "within a very narrow sphere."[43]

The themes developed in the committee report fairly represent the thinking of public officials about the emergent character of public planning in republican New York City. The city was to provide a long-term, predictable context for action. Whatever the influence of Jeffersonian ideas in other areas of government practice, the notion that legislators ought to act only for their generation of constituents carried little weight in the planning of the New York Common Council. City government was not to be part of the market economy, nor was it to be influenced by transitory notions of individual benefit or loss. The "incidental effects of public action on private property" were of no concern to the makers of public policy. As part of a republican polity, city government was interested only in serving an identifiable public interest.

The postrevolutionary political structure described in these pages bears little resemblance to the "Commonwealth" model of joint enterprise and shared public and private responsibility.[44] True, some of the corporation's actions—such as its manipulation of the ferry franchise—might be made to fit such a model. But the quarter century after the end of the revolutionary war saw the development of a rigid differentiation between public and private spheres in the political theory of city government and a fairly unambiguous acceptance of the primacy of a market economy.

After about 1790, there were few expressed worries as to the prospects for the growing city. City leaders had confidence in private enterprise and willingly made the city the servant of free market values. They directed their attention to the problem of government power and to the elaboration of a legitimate autonomous public sphere rather than to the structure of economic affairs. Public action—what it should be, how it should be accomplished, how to justify it in a republican society—was their main concern.

43. Ibid. (1 July 1805); for the later history of the ferry franchise, see Chapter 15.
44. Handlin and Handlin, *Commonwealth*; Louis Hartz, *Economic Policy and Democratic Thought* (Cambridge, Mass., 1948); Harry Scheiber, "Government and the Economy," *Journal of Interdisciplinary History* 3 (1972): 135.

Under the Montgomerie Charter those concerns had not been raised, indeed could not be raised, for government had been a private property right defined and shaped by the terms of the grant. If one wanted to characterize the corporation in public terms before the Revolution, it could only have been as an instrument of the customary concerns and values of its local public. It was not an institution in command of a public sphere of authority. But it was then, in the years between the reception of the Montgomerie Charter and the coming of the American Revolution, that the corporation of the City of New York best approximated the commonwealth model of shared enterprise and blurred public and private spheres.

By the turn of the nineteenth century, on the other hand, New York City's government concerned itself less with economic growth, its corporate estate, or the changing customs of "the community" than with the perceived need for a planned and predictable public environment and for particular public goods and services. It may well be that that is what its local publics wanted from their government, although we lack the survey research data to know for sure. It may well be that a republican political culture "compelled" city government to define itself as an entity independent of its citizenry, as a distinctive goods producer, although republicanism can be read to compel many different things. What we do know is that the choices city leaders made instituted a pattern of change, a line of development that led directly to the modern conception of a city as a subordinate unit of state administration.

New York City may not yet have been a municipal corporation, but by the second decade of the nineteenth century there was no longer much else that it could be. In molding a public institution fit for the free, growing, republican society in which they found themselves, in shaping an institution capable of making the permanent improvements and providing the particular services that would be its distinctive contribution to the public good, city leaders created what their prerevolutionary counterparts had most feared—a body lacking in autonomy from external authority, a dependent tool of central power.

CHAPTER 11

The Triumph of a Public Sphere

Early in 1807 the Common Council asked Richard Harison, who was still its counsel, to draft a bill for submission to the state legislature. The bill authorized the appointment of commissioners to draw a map that would fix the future development of the streets and roads of Manhattan Island north of the settled city. The memorial that accompanied the bill confessed the past failure of the council to act as an effective planner in the face of both "the diversity of Sentiments and opinions . . . among the members of the Council" and the incessant remonstrances of proprietors against "plans . . . wherein their individual Interests do not concur." If left to the council there would never be a permanent regulation of the streets; anything adopted by one council might be annulled or disregarded by its political successors.[1]

The legislature, as usual, acceded to the corporation's request, and in April Gouverneur Morris, Simeon DeWitt, and John Rutherford were appointed commissioners with power to enter onto any lands to be surveyed throughout the city.[2] The map they were to produce was expected to serve two sets of needs long felt by city officials. In the first place, it would confirm government authority over the location and construction of city streets. Private land developers had laid out the streets in ways, according to the council's committee on streets, that served only their "private advantage, without a just regard for the welfare of others, and to the almost total neglect of public convenience and general usefulness."[3] Without a permanent public plan, however, city officials were uncertain whether they had the power to close privately developed streets. There was general agreement that once the state had vested title to the streets in the corpora-

1. *Minutes of the Common Council of the City of New York, 1784–1831*, 21 vols. (New York, 1917–30), 4:353–54 (16 February 1807); hereafter *Min. CC.*
2. *Laws of New York*, 30th sess. (Albany, 1807), c. 115.
3. *Report of the New York City Common Council Committee on Streets upon the Subject of New Streets* (New York, 1803), 1.

tion (as it had in the 1790s), private individuals lost the right to lay out streets without the approval of the municipal government. But what constituted approval? In 1797, for example, the city had contracted with two surveyors to produce a map of the streets of the city. The map included private streets. Did publication of that map constitute public approval of those private streets? Without new state legislation, city officials could not be sure. Probably the corporation had all the powers it needed. But, as the city's street commissioner noted in 1806, even though the council had long since decided that it was wrong to permit private street development, still it "made use of so little coercion in that respect, that individuals *even at this period* continued to project their streets in their own way, and dispute with the Common Council upon their uncontroulable right to do so."[4]

Alongside this characteristic concern with the absence or ambiguous nature of municipal powers was a particular frustration with the shape of the growing city. Power was needed, not just to establish the authority of a public city government over private land development, but also because only a public plan could organize the city in the regular and predictable manner city leaders considered necessary. A plan would offer direction to private landowners "in laying out and disposing of the[ir] property."[5] The directions it provided were intended to be aesthetic as well as utilitarian. The commissioners' map would create an attractive alternative to what nineteenth-century New Yorkers saw as the chaos and irregularity of the old city of New York. To them, "the arrangement of the original or lower part of the city . . . is essentially defective. Beauty, order and convenience seem to have been little valued by our ancestors."[6] Most of the streets were constructed "according to the fancy or interest of some obstinate or inexperienced landholders . . . without regard to uniformity, health, or beauty."[7]

An attractive city was, above all else, an orderly city. And thus it is hardly surprising that the fruit of the commissioners' labors was a rectangular grid imposed uniformly over nearly the whole of Manhattan Island. One hundred fifty-five east-west streets, sixty feet in width and two hundred feet apart, were crossed by twelve north-south avenues, each one hundred feet wide. Topography was ignored. The map published by the

4. New York City Street Commissioner (John Hum), *Observations on the Improvement of the City of New York South of Grand Street* (New York, 1806), 4; *Report of the . . . Committee on Streets* (1803), 7; see also Richard Harison's opinion on the authority of the corporation to close up Peter Stuyvesant's streets (*Min. CC*, 4:397–401 [13 April 1807]).

5. *Min. CC*, 3:434–36 (3 January 1804).

6. Thomas N. Stanford, *A Concise Description of the City of New York* (New York, 1814), 7.

7. Street Commissioner, *Observations*, 3.

FIGURE 11.1. *A Map of the City of New York, 1807*

commissioners pretended that the land had no contours. The commission-ers evidently assumed—correctly as it turned out—that the many hills and gullies of the island would be flattened out in the course of the plan's implementation. Frederick Law Olmsted, who detested the map, com-mented that there was "good authority for the story that the system of 1807 was hit upon by the chance occurrence of a mason's sieve near a map of the ground to be laid out. It was taken up and placed upon the map, and the question being asked, 'what do you want better than that?' no one was able to answer."[8] Although there was probably more to the commissioners' decision, it is evident that "plain and simple reflections" led them quickly and inexorably to adopt the famous (or infamous) grid.[9]

In the "Remarks" that accompanied the publication of the map in 1811, the commissioners noted that even after they had settled on a grid plan

8. Frederick Law Olmsted and J. James R. Croes, "Preliminary Report of the Landscape Architect and the Civil Topographical Engineer, upon the Laying Out of the Twenty-third and Twenty-fourth Wards," in Albert Fein, ed., *Landscape into Cityscape: Frederick Law Olmsted's Plans for a Greater New York City* (Ithaca, 1967), 352.
9. "Commissioners' Remarks," in William Bridges, *Map of the City of New York and Is-land of Manhattan* (New York, 1811), 24. A grid had earlier been adopted by the Common Council (*Min. CC*, 4:434–36 [3 January 1804]).

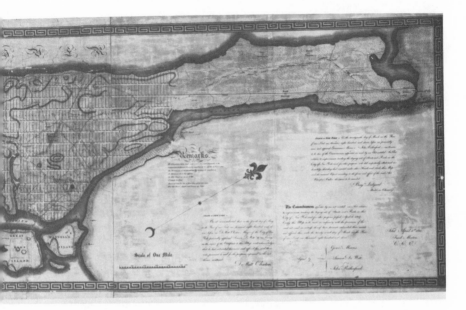

they still hoped that their map could also incorporate the varying plans and streets already opened or adopted by private landowners. To do so would have mollified opposition and reduced costs and, as a result, became "a favourite object with the Commissioners." But, for reasons unspecified, they ultimately abandoned the attempt to incorporate private projects into the public map. Their grid would be imposed uniformly, without regard to private boundaries or subdivisions.[10]

This latter decision ensured that there would be a good deal of resistance as the commissioners proceeded to survey all the lands of northern Manhattan Island. In one case an old woman threw artichokes and cabbages at the surveyors.[11] And John Randall, who served as chief engineer and surveyor for the project, later recalled that one of the hazards of his position was the continual risk of arrest "for trespass and damage committed by my workmen." In 1809, in fact, the commissioners threatened to resign if something were not done to protect their agents from "such vexatious interruptions." The corporation then went to the legislature with a request for a statute affirming the authority of the employees of the

10. "Commissioners' Remarks," 24–25.
11. John Reps, *The Making of Urban America* (Princeton, 1965), 297.

commissioners to enter onto private lands and to cut down trees when necessary for the surveying.[12]

No sooner was the map published, however, but significant opposition disappeared.[13] Those who had fought it soon realized that the fixed street plan offered a bonanza for uptown landowners who could now predict with fair precision the course of the city's growth.[14] And for the next forty years boosters would describe the commissioners' map as "the most important in its effect on the welfare of the city, of any [action] ever adopted by public authority."[15] It formed "an important legacy to posterity, from which the most solid advantages may be anticipated."[16] In the words of Chancellor Kent, the map "laid out the highways on the island upon so magnificent a scale, and with so bold a hand, and with such prophetic views, in respect to the future growth and extention of the city, that it will form an everlasting monument of the stability and wisdom of the measure."[17]

Later students of the history of city planning have often been vehement in their criticisms of that "monument." Like Olmsted, they have regarded the grid as the antithesis of a proper public plan, as nothing more than a shortsighted gift to land speculators. John Reps in particular has argued that the map was a disaster for urban form throughout America because it served as a model for many new nineteenth-century cities. "The lack of suitable sites for public buildings, the traffic congestion at the frequent intersections, the lack of enough north-south arteries, the overbuilding on narrow lots that inevitably resulted from the shallow blocks—these are but a few of the shortcomings" of the Manhattan grid by the professional standards of modern city planning. But, Reps continued, the map failed as a plan even by nineteenth-century standards, imposing a monotonous uni-

12. John Randall, "City of New York, North of Canal Street, in 1808 to 1821," in David T. Valentine, *Manual of the Corporation of the City of New York* (New York, 1864), 848–49; *Laws of New York*, 32nd sess. (Albany, 1809), c. 103.

13. But see Clement Clarke Moore, *A Plain Statement, addressed to the Proprietors of Real Estate in the city and County of New York, by a Landholder* (New York, 1818), and·A Poor Citizen, *An Appeal to the People of the City of New-York, on the Proposed Alteration of the Charter of the City* (New York, 1821), both of whose criticisms were directed more at the implementation of the map than at its design.

14. See Randall, "City of New York," 848–49.

15. Edward M. Blunt, *The Picture of New York and Traveller's Guide* (New York, 1828), 88.

16. Stanford, *A Concise Description*, 8.

17. James Kent, *The Charter of the City of New York, with notes thereon. Also a Treatise on the Powers and Duties of the Mayor, Aldermen, and Assistant Aldermen, and the Journal of the City Convention* (New York, 1836), 144. See also Charles King, *Progress of the City of New York, during the last Fifty Years; with Notices of the Principal Changes and Important Events* (New York, 1852).

formity on the city that excluded topographical relief and made no provision for open spaces or recreational facilities.[18]

By contrast, early nineteenth-century observers usually regarded the topographical uniformity mandated by the plan as among its greatest achievements. Not everyone thought that the disappearance of Manhattan's "original asperity . . . before the potent arm of improvement" was a good thing.[19] One Greenwich Village landholder argued that those changes were "lamented by persons of taste, as destructive to the greatest beauties of which our city is susceptible."[20] And even a writer who praised the map confessed that he found the uniformity "tiresome."[21] But all agreed that there was something awesome about the resolve of the city "to spare nothing that bears the semblance of a rising ground; nothing is to be left unmolested which does not coincide with the street commissioner's plummet and level."[22]

The reconstruction of the natural environment to fit the requirements of republican authority might be termed the hidden agenda that underlay the commissioners' seemingly modest proposal. In the 1807 map, latent and manifest functions were reversed. The commissioners wrote as if all they cared about was protecting the investments of land developers and maintaining government-on-the-cheap. The plan that resulted, however, served to transform space into an expression of a public philosophy. The grid, as Rem Koolhaas has recently suggested, "is, above all, a conceptual speculation. In spite of its apparent neutrality, it implies an intellectual program for the island; in its indifference to topography, to what exists, it claims the superiority of mental construction over reality."[23]

The commissioners presented their map as the antithesis of a utopian or futuristic plan.[24] Unlike most city planners, they did not seek to impose a particular, idealized way of life on the community through the manipulation of space. Their remarks glorified "ordinary" ways of life and justified the map as an expression of ongoing processes in the city. Imposition of

18. Reps, *Making of Urban America*, 294–99; Olmsted and Croes, "Preliminary Report"; Laura Wood Roper, *FLO: A Biography of Frederick Law Olmsted* (Baltimore, 1973), 363–64; Lewis Mumford, *City Development* (New York, 1945), 9–11.

19. Stanford, *Concise Description*, 8.

20. Moore, *Plain Statement*, 49.

21. Blunt, *Picture of New York*, 141.

22. Ibid., 88, 137–42; Moore, *Plain Statement*, 49; King, *Progress of the City of New York*, 9, 57–58; Stanford, *Concise Description*, 8; [S. L. Mitchell], *The Picture of New York; or the Traveller's Guide through the Commercial Metropolis of the United States* (New York, 1807), 2.

23. Rem Koolhaas, *Delirious New York* (New York, 1978), 15. The interpretation that follows closely parallels that of Koolhaas's remarkable study but was developed independently.

24. See Delores Hayden, *Seven American Utopias: The Architecture of Communitarian Socialism, 1790–1975* (Cambridge, Mass., 1976).

the map would change nothing because it simply reflected dominant social forces.

In their analysis of how best to arrange city space, the basic question was what the space was actually going to be used for. To the commissioners, the answer was obvious. A city is "composed principally of the habitations of men." Thus because public action justified itself by the ways it made individuals' private lives easier, the proper arrangement of streets in the city had to be one that made housing cheaper and more convenient for the residents. And thus, public spaces, squares, parade grounds, and such "supposed improvements" as "circles, ovals, and stars," which might reduce the supply of housing, were inconsistent with a proper public plan.[25]

To Reps this analysis seems pervaded with an unrelenting obsession with saving money. Yet it is unfair to charge the commissioners with a nearsighted cheapness. When they revealed that they had admitted "the principles of economy to greater influence than might, under circumstances of a different kind, have consisted with the dictates of prudence and the sense of duty" they did so not to justify a land grab or an abdication of public responsibility. Rather, their goal was to make as much land as possible available for housing. Their starting point was the fact that land prices were "uncommonly great." By reducing the quantity of public space in the city and by committing more land to housing, they expected the price of such land to decline. The "principles of economy" that they raised in justification of the unrelieved grid were, in fact, the principles of (political) economy.[26]

Their rhetoric might be regarded as a model for the justification of republican public authority: deferential toward private initiative, concerned to remain within the limits of proper public authority, yet insistent on the legitimacy of public control of a public sphere. The commissioners left largely unstated their own preferences as to the most proper, appropriate, or attractive development of city streets, for those were all areas of private choice. But they made it absolutely clear that private landowners had no right to expect the map to incorporate their particular plans or streets, for that was an area of public choice. "It will, perhaps, be more satisfactory to each person who may feel aggrieved, to ask himself, whether his sensations would not have been still more unpleasant, had his favourite plans been sacrificed to preserve those of a more fortunate neighbor."[27]

At the same time, constructing the map meant that the commissioners had to make some choices as to how the city ought to develop, and those

25. "Commissioners' Remarks," 24.
26. Ibid., 26; see Reps, *Making of Urban America*, 299.
27. "Commissioners' Remarks," 24–25.

choices put a strain on their rhetoric. Consider their explanation for leaving a large space for a new wholesale market. As the city grew, the commissioners predicted the "controlling power of necessity" would soon teach residents the advantages of shopping in neighborhood stores rather than in public retail markets. Dispersing grocers and butchers—allowing them to sell from private shops—would be a great convenience for consumers: "By this mode of supplying the wants of large cities, there is a great saving of time and of the articles consumed. To a person engaged in profitable business, one hour spent in market is frequently worth more than the whole of what he purchases." And once this new style of retailing was established, retailers and wholesalers would find it convenient to meet at one large public market. "In short," the commissioners concluded, "experience having demonstrated to every great aggregation of mankind the expediency of such arrangement, it is reasonable to conclude that it will be adopted hereafter, and therefore it is proper to provide for it now."[28]

In the commissioners' rhetoric, the choices contained in the map were not impositions of public power but, rather, extrapolations from trends. How people shopped was not something the city government could or should control. But public officials could learn from private practices and habits how best to mold a public sphere that satisfied the wants of their public. Where change had become the norm, however, the way people shopped at any particular moment did not provide an adequate basis for public action. Action was necessary. And action had to be founded on social practice. But when the commissioners described the empirical basis for a decision, they inevitably looked to emerging patterns and "the controlling power of necessity" rather than to simple social description. Legitimate public action was necessarily an act of prediction.

To this empirical methodology the commissioners added one presupposition drawn from republican political theory. Government ought not to act in such a way as to create inequality or special privilege. Again, only a uniform grid could possibly meet this standard. Any other plan would have prompted some spatial inequality by allowing particular individuals to live on squares or circles created by governmental act and unavailable to others.

At one level this presupposition only ensured public neutrality toward the social evolution of Manhattan Island. The commissioners' map did not impose districts or neighborhoods on those who built on New York City's streets. The map did not reveal which blocks would become high-class residential neighborhoods and which would become the quarters of laborers. Indeed, the map did not reveal whether there would be any resi-

28. Ibid., 28–30.

dential segregation. Each block was a blank slate to be filled in by private action. "If a building site is wanted, whether with a view to a church or a blast furnace, an opera house or a toy shop, there is, of intention, no better a place in one of these blocks than in another."[29] Private initiative differentiated city space, not the commissioners' map. The commissioners might be freed from the charge of creating or reinforcing inequality, but their map did little to prevent the use of space to manifest private wealth and power.[30]

But it is possible to "read" the map as implying a more thoroughgoing egalitarianism. Behind the veneer of government neutrality lay the blunt limits which the grid placed on private initiative, limits planners since Olmsted have regarded as the best demonstration of the bankruptcy of this style of city planning. Even within blocks the map prescribed a general equality in building lot size. To Olmsted the ironic consequence was that a plan designed to maximize the availability of housing resulted in a limited supply of "decent, wholesome, tidy dwellings for people who are struggling to maintain an honorable independence. . . . The rigid uniformity of the system of 1807 requires that no building lot shall be more than 100 feet in depth, none less. The clerk or mechanic and his young family, wishing to live modestly in a house by themselves, without servants, is provided for in this respect not otherwise than the wealthy merchant, who, with a large family and numerous servants, wishes to display works of art, to form a large library, and to enjoy the company of many guests." But for Olmsted the greater scandal of the map lay in the intractable quality of the block itself: "If a proposed cathedral, military depot, great manufacturing enterprise, house of religious seclusion or seat of learning needs a space of ground more than sixty-six yards in extent from north to south, the system forbids that it shall be built in New York. On the other hand, it equally forbids a museum, library, theatre, exchange, post office or hotel, unless of great breadth, to be lighted or to be open upon streets from opposite sides."[31] In a city shaped by rectangular blocks, all structures and activities would look roughly the same. Individual distinctions, whether cultural, charitable, economic, or whatever, would have to find their place within a fixed, republican spatial organization.

Eventually builders realized that individuality and spatial discrimina-

29. Olmsted and Croes, "Preliminary Report," 353.

30. Residential segregation did not actually become the norm in the city until the 1830s. See Betsy Blackmar, "Re-walking the 'Walking City': Housing and Property Relations in New York City, 1780–1840," *Radical History Review* 21 (1980):131–48; Edmund Willis, "Social Origins and Political Leadership in New York City from the Revolution to 1815," (Ph.D. dissertation, University of California, Berkeley, 1967).

31. Olmsted and Croes, "Preliminary Report," 352–54.

tion could be created three-dimensionally, by building upward (thus the skyscraper). But in the fundamentally two-dimensional world envisioned in the 1807 map, the grid ensured at least a measure of uniformity and equality.[32]

The commissioners presented their map as a resolution to the problem of how to lay out a city without disturbing private initiative or the ordinary processes of life. Yet even in carrying out that program, they created a formal plan, an attempt "to make the future conform to some present vision of it."[33] Their "remarks" were modest in the extreme; yet they revealed a plan to imprint a particular structure of values on the evolving city of New York. The 1807 map was drafted to give the city a public, republican shape that would reflect, not the particular vision of the planner or the fears of the ruler, but the individual decisions of all the many equal citizens living in New York City.[34]

The commissioners' map was not just a physical plan to which the city committed itself under legislative sanction. It was also a legal instrument molding both the rights of the corporation and those of innumerable landlords and tenants of the city. We might safely assume, in fact, that after 1811 no sale or lease of property in the newer parts of the city was consummated without attention being paid to the effects of the 1807 map on the expectations of the parties.

In 1813 the state legislature established a process for the taking of land for city streets. Whenever the members of the Common Council decided to open any street or avenue in accordance with the commissioners' map, or to "improve" a street in the older part of the city, they applied to the New York Supreme Court to appoint "commissioners of estimate and assessment" to measure the value of both the land taken for the street and the benefit accruing to the surrounding property owners from the completion of a public street. These assessors reported their findings to the court,

32. See Koolhaas, *Delirious New York*, especially 67–109.

33. Marx Wartofsky, "Telos and Technique: Models as Modes of Action," in Sanford Anderson, ed., *Planning for Diversity and Choice* (Cambridge, Mass., 1968), 262.

34. Compare these values with those of the Ringstrasse in Vienna as described by Carl Schorske in *Fin-de-siècle Vienna* (New York, 1980), and of Paris in Walter Benjamin's "Paris, Capital of the Nineteenth Century," in *Reflections* (New York, 1978). One might suggest, ironically, that the commissioners' plan was shaped by values not unlike those Thomas Bender has identified with the work of Frederick Law Olmsted (*Toward an Urban Vision* [Lexington, Ky., 1975], 160–87). I am not, on the other hand, convinced by Bender's claim that these values emerged from an "alternative planning tradition" that can be distinguished from the mainstream, bureaucratic, "progressive" tradition. On space as an expression of culture, see Henri Lefêbvre, *Le droit à la ville* (Paris, 1968), and the essays devoted to the spatial dimension of history in the special issue of the *Radical History Review* 21 (1980).

which, sitting as an administrative body, either confirmed those findings, in which case they became "final and conclusive," or referred them back to be revised.[35]

The foundation for this combined process of land valuation and assessment was the assumption that the corporation would spend none of its public revenues on street development.[36] Compensation for the lands taken for streets was to be raised as an assessment on the surrounding property benefited by the laying out of streets. And because benefited lands were often owned by the same individuals whose property was to be taken for the streets, the statute permitted the assessors to set off the value of the takings against the overall improvement in the property owner's land value.

The 1813 statute remained the basic form of public land acquisition in New York City throughout the first half of the nineteenth century. And it, no less than the commissioners' map, stands as a "monument" to the practice of public power in the city (in fact, commentators usually merged the two). It is an early example of that vast exercise of expropriation powers Harry Scheiber has identified as a distinctive feature of nineteenth-century public law.[37] And out of the many opinions that the New York Supreme Court wrote in review of the decisions of the assessors and the Common Council emerged a body of rules fairly described as the forerunner of modern administrative law.[38]

Not surprisingly, many landholders considered that statute a most radical measure.[39] According to one proprietor, it caused "bitter complaint

35. *Revised Laws of New York*, 36th sess. (Albany, 1813), c. 136, sections 177–92. On plans as legal instruments see also P. M. Smith, "Planning as Environmental Improvement: Slum Clearance in Victorian Edinburgh," in Anthony Sutcliffe, ed., *The Rise of Modern Urban Planning, 1800–1914* (New York, 1980), 99–133.

36. *Revised Laws of New York*, 36th sess. (Albany, 1813), c. 136, section 185. Corporation property, on the other hand, if located within an assessment area, would be assessed like other private property, as decided in *Ross v. Mayor of New York*, 3 Wend. 333 (1829).

37. See Harry Scheiber, "The Road to *Munn*: Eminent Domain and the Concept of Public Purpose in the State Courts," *Perspectives in American History* 5 (1971):329–402; Scheiber, "Property Law, Expropriation, and Resource Allocation by Government, 1789–1910," *Journal of Economic History* 33 (1973):232–48.

38. See Victor Rosewater, *Special Assessments: A Study in Municipal Finance* (New York, 1893). See generally, Stephen Diamond, "The Rise and Fall of Benefit Taxation: The Case of Special Assessment," *Journal of Legal Studies* (forthcoming).

39. Rosewater, *Special Assessments*, 27–29; see A Poor Citizen, *Appeal*, and Moore, *Plain Statement*. In 1828, Peter Lorillard wrote Daniel Webster asking him to come to New York to act as Lorillard's counsel in a full-scale constitutional challenge to the assessment law. He guaranteed that he would finance the suit even to the U.S. Supreme Court. There is no record of Webster's answer (manuscript at the New Hampshire Historical Society). I would like to thank Andrew King of the Legal Papers of Daniel Webster, who brought this letter to my attention.

among the owners and occupants of real estate," who regarded the 1813 "betterment" system of financing as compelling an individual "to become a capitalist for the public." He concluded that New Yorkers lived "under a tyranny, with respect to the rights of property, . . . no monarch in Europe would dare to exercise."[40] The process was repeatedly but always unsuccessfully challenged in the courts as unconstitutional. And many landholders spent much time and effort trying to reopen the "final and conclusive" decisions of the state supreme court (sitting as an administrative body).[41]

What saved the process legally was the existence of the 1807 map as a permanent and predictable statement of the plans of the corporation. The timing of city action might remain a matter of Common Council discretion (although more on that in a moment); but after 1811 a landholder knew— or, at least should have known—where streets would be laid across his or her property. And all property throughout the city was commonly burdened with a right of way in favor of the city, notice of which was regarded as having been established by the publication of the map.

The process, in fact, was justified by its permanence. According to Michael Ulshoeffer, who was counsel to the corporation through the 1820s, "When the Act of April 3, 1807, was passed, all that part of the island, the laying out of which was provided for in that Act, was in fields and gardens; and it was considered an object of great importance that a certain permanent plan . . . should be fixed." The makers of that plan, Ulshoeffer reported to the council, had intended to avoid the inconsistent decisions of the Common Council and the "caprices" of private developers by creating "one grand permanent plan, not thereafter to be altered, except (of course) by an Act of the Legislature."[42] And in opinion after opinion the New York Supreme Court held that it was legitimate to charge individual property owners with the costs of street development because the publication of the 1807 map raised the value of affected property. Knowing that streets were coming and where they were coming meant that property owners could incorporate those benefits immediately into their asking prices whenever they leased or sold property. In exchange, it was only fair that affected

40. Moore, *Plain Statement*, 5.

41. *Livingston v. The Mayor of New York*, 8 Wend. 85 (1831). For landowners' actions, see, for example, the labors of Mrs. Champlin in *Champlin v. Laytin*, 1 Ed. Ch. 467 (1832); *Champlin v. The Mayor of New York*, 3 Paige 573 (1832); *Champlin v. Laytin*, 6 Paige Ch. 189 (1836); *Champlin v. Laytin*, 18 Wend. 406 (1837); and *Wyman v. The Mayor of New York*, 11 Wend. 486 (1833). See also *Gillespie v. Thomas*, 15 Wend. 464 (1836); *Gillespie v. The Mayor of New York*, 23 Wend. 643 (1840); and *Gillespie v. The Mayor of New York*, 3 Edw. Ch. 512 (1841).

42. *Report of Street Committee on the subject of Regulating the Grounds between North and 14th Streets, the Bowery and East River* (New York, 1826), 20–21.

landowners pay for the costs of land acquisition and street construction.[43]

This perception of the permanent street plan as a valuable legal right meant, conversely, that the ways the Common Council managed that right would be scrutinized closely by the court. The timing of street construction remained for the most part within the discretion of the Common Council. But the underlying issue was always the question of when a legal right was vested in favor of particular landowners. And once the council had reached a decision to act and had petitioned the supreme court for the appointment of assessors, individual expectancies might ripen into vested rights, foreclosing further action by the council.

In the early 1820s, for example, the corporation acquired land on which it decided to build the new Fulton Market. To do so, however, necessitated changing a "proceeding" the council had already instituted to enlarge and extend Beekman Street. Evidently, that earlier proceeding had raised opposition from some neighboring landowners who now supported the city's petition to discontinue the old proceeding.

But the supreme court held that the city had no power to change its plans. The court was not even certain that it had the power to discontinue a proceeding once assessors had been sent out. But even if the court did, this was not a case where that power ought to be exercised. "Upon the faith of the stability of that plan, several persons have made purchases of lots, which will be materially depreciated in value if the new plan should be adopted and the old one superseded." The corporation had no right to violate its "plighted faith," absent "strong and cogent reasons," which did not exist here according to the court. Legal rights had vested. And if the city wanted to go ahead with the construction of the Fulton Market it would have to pay for the necessary street charges out of public coffers, a result the court considered only fair because the market was intended to serve "the citizens at large," not "merely those residing in that vicinity."[44]

While the corporation's petition to discontinue the old proceeding was still under consideration by the supreme court, the corporation went to Chancellor Kent and asked him to issue an injunction to keep two property owners from erecting a row of buildings on their lands. One of the two landowners had been a member of the Common Council when the first plan for Beekman Street was adopted, and the two had bought the lots they were busily improving in anticipation of a widened Beekman Street. But under the new plan, whether financed by the city directly or by special

43. See in particular *Matter of Lewis Street*, 2 Wend. 472, 474–75 (1829); *Matter of Seventeenth Street*, 1 Wend. 262 (1828).

44. *Matter of Beekman Street*, 20 Johns. 269, 272–73 (1822); see also *Matter of Dover Street*, 18 Johns. 506 (1821). On the parallel issue of giving notice to all interested parties, see *Matter of Dover Street*, 1 Caines Rep. 498 (1824).

assessments, all of their property would be taken in condemnation proceedings for the new market. And, according to the corporation's lawyer, their only reason for continuing construction on the lots was to increase the value of the property when taken for public use.

Kent, however, refused to grant the injunction. In this case, the land was in lower Manhattan and therefore not covered by the 1807 map; indeed, the city was not yet operating under any legally binding plan to build Fulton Market. Thus, while the city could not be compelled to take the individual's land, neither could those individuals be stopped from improving their land's value.[45]

As this last case suggests, both the courts and the Common Council found it generally impossible to distance their decisions from the actual market for land and the behavior of land developers and speculators. The shifting values that the assessors placed on particular plots of land were a source of bemusement for the members of the supreme court, who by and large were quick to concede their own incompetence to evaluate the assessors' valuations.[46] When, for example, Justice Esek Cowen was asked by petitioners to reject an award of a huge sum for a tiny piece of land needed for widening Pearl Street in lower Manhattan, he answered that he saw no basis for action so long as "no positive rule of law has been violated." The statute specifically authorized his administrative power to overrule the assessors, but he felt he had no way to judge such decisions:

> I was gravely appealed to on the argument to say that the demand . . . is inflated on its face; and I am, it seems intuitively to provinence that it is shockingly out of proportion to all ideas of valuation. I am free to say, that it exceeds any thing which I should have thought of as a mere price of land for any part of the habitable globe. I have seen and heard enough, however, to learn that *high* and *low* in such matters, are terms of very complicated relation; and above all, I know too much of my own capacity on this head to trust myself as an expert. I have not even been in the city except at long intervals; and about all I have learned of the market when my visits were most frequent, did not extend beyond the price of books at a few of the stores.[47]

It is, of course, part of the folklore of the city—and perhaps none the less true for so being—that real estate interests have always had a domi-

---

45. *Corporation of the City of New York* v. *Mapes and Schermerhorn*, 6 Johns. Ch. 45 (1822); *Matter of Furman Street*, 17 Wend. 649 (1836).

46. But see *Matter of Fourth Avenue*, 3 Wend. 452 (1830).

47. *Matter of Pearl Street*, 19 Wend. 651, 655 (1839).

nant place in public decision making.[48] The 1807 map produced a subsidy to investors, who could buy land cheaply in the still unsettled northern reaches of the island knowing that city growth was guaranteed by public statute to encompass their holdings.[49] And whatever else that map was designed to do, surely one goal was to provide security for those who developed their holdings.

Still, there was a limit to the willingness of both the New York Supreme Court and the Common Council to provide public subsidies to private land developers. And such a limit was reached when land developers attempted to treat their right to compensation for street takings as a personal right separable from their ownership of surrounding property.

Typically, a land developer subdivided his or her property into lots that would be sold to individuals who then built houses on them. Those lots would be platted on maps, which invariably incorporated the streets and avenues of the commissioners' map. And lots were bought in the expectation that they bordered on streets to be laid out by the city.

But after the developer had subdivided and sold the lots, who owned the land on which the street would be laid? More precisely, who owned the right to compensation when land was taken? At common law, courts had assumed that every lot owner owned to the center of the street bordering his or her property. And throughout American history land has usually been sold with that presumption.[50] In the 1820s, however, developers in New York City evidently came to the conclusion that that customary way of doing things constituted a needless transfer of a valuable property right. And so they began drafting deeds that specifically retained the fee in the streets. When, for example, the trustees of the estate of Elizabeth de Peyster sold lots near Washington Square, the conveyances passed title "without any intention of abandoning any right to compensation for the soil or ground over which the streets would pass when they should be opened." And in 1828 the trustees even sold their retained "rights" (to receive compensation whenever Fifth Street should be opened) for $12,800.[51]

After an initial period of hesitation, the New York Supreme Court came to the unambiguous conclusion that such retained fees in the streets did

48. See Edward Pessen, "Who Has Power in the Democratic Capitalistic Community? Reflections on Antebellum New York City," *New York History* 58 (1977): 129–56. For a sharply contrasting image of pluralistic politics and dispersed power, see Wallace S. Sayre and Herbert Kaufman, *Governing New York City* (New York, 1960).

49. See Kenneth Porter, *John Jacob Astor: Business Man*, 2 vols. (Cambridge, Mass., 1931), 2:910–52.

50. See A. James Casner, ed., *American Law of Property*, 8 vols. (Boston, 1952), 3: 427–32; *City of Albany* v. *State of New York*, 28 N.Y. 2d 352, 321 N.Y.S. 2d 877, 270 N.E.2d 705 (1971).

51. *Wyman* v. *The Mayor of New York*, 11 Wend. 486, 488 (1833).

not entitle developers or their assigns to full compensation when the street lands were taken.[52] And in 1831 and 1832 that conclusion was affirmed by the Court for the Correction of Errors, which in the process turned back challenges to the constitutionality of the whole street development process.[53] Thus, when Fifth Street was opened and assessors sent out to estimate the benefits and burdens of the various landowners, the three purchasers of the de Peyster estate's retained fee were each awarded five dollars nominal compensation.

According to the members of both courts, the fee retained by the developer was subject to an implied easement of a perpetual right of way held by those who purchased the developer's lots. The developer was welcome to retain the fee in the street land if he or she so chose, and nothing prevented the developer from alienating that fee to individuals unconnected to the development. But the implied easement to which that fee was subject encompassed most all of the value of the land; the retained fee was a "bare" fee, a merely formal title, worth only nominal compensation when taken.

This legal analysis required the courts to distinguish city lands—to which purchasers acquired an implied easement—from lands elsewhere in the state—where there were no such judicially implied expectations. The reason given for implying this "urban" easement was straightforwardly economic. In selling lots to the public, land developers received an enhanced price because of the city's street plan. Permitting them to retain the full right to compensation would be sanctioning double-dipping, permitting them to take a single entitlement twice—once in the purchase price and a second time in the street proceeding.[54]

Notions of fairness may have played a part in the decisions. But the courts were not really standing in the way of contractual freedom. Fundamentally, the defect in the claims of the developers and their assigns lay in their assumption that they had a right to treat the right of way (as opposed to the bare fee) as their personal property. "In whom did the right of way vest?" asked the court in one case. "In the public, if any one, and if so, it is not, . . . an object of individual release."[55] Developers were treating a public process as if it existed to provide them with a private advantage.

52. *Matter of Mercer Street*, 4 Cowen's Rep. 542 (1825); *Matter of Seventeenth Street*, 1 Wend. 262 (1828); *Matter of Lewis Street*, 2 Wend. 472 (1829); *Wyman* v. *The Mayor of New York*, 11 Wend. 486 (1833).

53. *Livingston* v. *The Mayor of New York*, 8 Wend. 85 (1831); *Wyman* v. *The Mayor of New York*, 11 Wend. 486 (1833).

54. *Wyman* v. *Mayor of New York*, 494 (opinion of Chief Justice Savage), 497–98 (Chancellor Walworth); *Livingston* v. *The Mayor of New York*, 8 Wend. 85, 98–99 (Walworth); *Matter of Lewis Street*, 2 Wend. 472, 474–75.

55. *Wyman* v. *The Mayor of New York*, 11 Wend. 486, 503 (Senator Sherman).

Street development was a public process. It might, incidentally, help create great private wealth for those fortunate individuals who owned land in the right place at the right time. But the benefits it provided were distributed according to a public formula, which courts had to protect from private manipulation. Speculation based on the commissioners' map was one thing, speculating in public entitlements quite another.

Underlying this process rested the assumption that the streets were a monopoly of a public sphere. That had, indeed, already been the claim of the Common Council before the publication of the commissioners' map in 1811. And according to their counsel, Richard Harison, public control of the streets by the municipality preceded any statute. But the 1807 statute confirmed that claim in "a language clear and unequivocal." After 1807 it was indisputable that "the streets and avenues to be laid out are to be the only streets and avenues."[56]

Landowners learned, as we have seen, to live with this public monopoly. Peter Stuyvesant, a descendant of the Dutch governor and next to John Jacob Astor the richest landowner in the city, had earlier fought the Common Council's right to draw new street lines across his already subdivided lands in what is today the East Village.[57] In 1796 his father had had the large family farm (called Petersfield) surveyed and a map drafted dividing the tract into streets, blocks, and building lots. None of the streets laid out on that map were ever adopted by the corporation. But building lots were leased in the early nineteenth century with covenants requiring the lessees to level and pave the streets that bounded their lots, in accordance with the 1796 map.

But then, along came the commissioners' map, which laid out streets across Petersfield without any regard to the Stuyvesant map. Instead of possessing a lease to a lot bordered on a street, lessees suddenly found that portions of their lots and houses would be taken for streets whenever the city decided to open them.[58] And to make matters worse, in August 1814 Peter Stuyvesant erected a fence across one of his "private" streets and then built a house standing partly on that street, obstructing the right of way of his lessees.

Those lessees therefore sued for damages for the loss of the right of way. But Stuyvesant's lawyers argued before the New York Supreme Court that there was no basis for their claim. The covenant to repair the street that the lessees had signed "contemplated the contingency of [the street] . . . being accepted by the Corporation, otherwise the covenant was to have no

56. *Matter of 26th Street*, 121 Wend. 203, 205 (1834).
57. *Min. CC*, 4:397–401 (13 April 1807).
58. *Underwood* v. *Stuyvesant*, 19 Johns Rep. 181, 182 (1821); see also *Astor* v. *Miller*, 2 Paige Ch. 68 (1830); *Astor* v. *Hoyt*, 5 Wend. 603 (1830).

effect. A street means a public way." And the court agreed. Both sides had simply guessed wrongly when they had assumed that "government would . . . sanction the streets proposed by the proprietor." It was, in fact, not only the right of the defendant to fence up the private street but even his duty to conform his holdings to the new regulations imposed by the government.[59]

There was little of republican virtue in this tale of one landowner's willingness to acquiesce to public authority. Neither the commissioners' map nor the street acquisition process did much to moderate the rapacity of land developers like Peter Stuyvesant.[60] And there is much evidence suggesting that that process may have provided a spur to speculative conduct.

Yet in separating public street construction from private land development, the process clarified the public-private split that city leaders had worked to incorporate into the postrevolutionary corporation. Land was private property, but the streets belonged to the people. The formal design of the city was public; but that design remained only a context for private decision making. We can say, retrospectively, that New York City chose a modest and easily corruptible role for itself. Still, as has been emphasized throughout this chapter, contemporaries saw the choice differently. The result of statutes like those passed in 1807 and 1813 was that "persons owning property which is to be diverted from its original destination, or applied for the purpose of building up the City, stand in a new relation to each other arising from new interests, and the necessity of taking a comprehensive view of the whole in order to legislate wisely and discretely as to a part."[61] To them, the city's control of its streets exemplified a proper and expansive exercise of power founded on the authority of the republican state.

59. *Underwood* v. *Stuyvesant*, 19 Johns Rep. 181, 183, 186, 188 (1821).

60. When Peter Stuyvesant died in 1847, George Templeton Strong wrote, "Everybody—that is, some thirty people at least, that I heard speak of the matter—delivered themselves to the following effect: 'What a great thing for the improvement of uptown.' Except one, who remarked that it was a very imprudent procedure for a man who was worth two millions to take a cold bath directly after dinner. He was an awful old screw . . . [The New York] Historical Society is to turn out in force at Stuyvesant's obsequies. George Gibbs suggests an eulogy at the grave after the manner of the French Academy. I'm in favor of funeral games after the manner of the Greeks, with real estate brokers for the combatants" (Allan Nevins and Milton Halsey Thomas, eds., *The Diary of George Templeton Strong*, 4 vols. [1952; reprint, New York, 1974] 1:298).

61. *LeRoy* v. *The Mayor of New York*, 20 Johns. 430, 439 (1823).

PART III

The Corporation in the
Grip of the Law

CHAPTER 12

The Laws of Communities

Frederic Maitland believed the history of the city in Anglo-American law began when medieval English towns became distinguishable as legal and governmental entities from the generality of organized communities— villages, parishes, manors, and so forth—that dotted the English landscape.[1] In a sense, as he traced the beginning of that history, we are dating its end, at least in the United States. With the emergence of the modern law of municipal corporations as an inclusive legal subject, the basis for differentiating chartered communities like New York City disappeared. The legal history of boroughs was over.

Maitland, like the student of the early history of New York City, regarded corporate property as being of signal importance in establishing the legal nature of a city. What made a place like medieval Cambridge a city and not a village was not the presence of an identifiable urban economy; for that might not have existed, at least not as we would understand it. Indeed, in *Township and Borough* Maitland emphasized that all "who would study the early history of our towns . . . have fields and pastures on their hands." Nor did he conclude that a city's distinctiveness rested on the reception of a corporate charter from the crown. Until the fourteenth century there were few such charters, and yet there were already places governed as cities. "Corporateness came of urban life,"[2] not the other way around. To Maitland and other so-called jurisprudential "realists," the history of the medieval city disproved an important tenet of the legal

1. Frederick Pollock and Frederic William Maitland, *The History of English Law before the Time of Edward I*, 2d ed., 2 vols. (Cambridge, 1968), 1:634–88; Maitland, "Moral Personality and Legal Personality," *Collected Papers*, 3 vols. (Cambridge, 1911), 3:233–39; Maitland, *Domesday Book and Beyond* (Cambridge, 1897); Maitland, *Township and Borough* (Cambridge, 1897). Maitland's formulation of how and when the break between boroughs and townships occurred has been contested by two generations of historians. See Carl Stephenson, *Borough and Town* (Cambridge, Mass., 1933); James Tait, *The Medieval English Borough: Studies on Its Origins and Constitutional History* (Manchester, 1936).

2. Maitland, *Township and Borough*, 9, 23.

positivism dominant in Western legal thought at the end of the nineteenth century.[3] It was not by "fiction" of law that Cambridge became a person in the law. The state did not bring a community into legal existence. It was, rather, in the nature of such a place that it came to be viewed as a singular individual. And it was the presence of recognized corporate property that gave it such a nature, the presence of an estate that was not the "common" property of all the community's residents.[4] Corporate property thus became both a symptom of the emergence of an urban identity and an explanation for the development of places like Cambridge and New York City into incorporated communities or boroughs.[5]

We have seen the vital role property played in the creation of a corporate personality in New York City under the Montgomerie Charter. Throughout the prerevolutionary history of the corporation, its behavior as a property holder defined its distinction within a universe of differing local governments.[6] In the last decade of the eighteenth century and continuing on into the nineteenth century, however, the governmental behavior of the corporation began to change. The city's earlier reliance on property rights as both a basis of authority and a mode of action was discarded as city government learned to look to the state for legitimacy. City leaders came to view the holdings of the corporation as separated from its duties as a public government. And that perception would make it difficult for those city leaders to sustain the identity of New York City as a particular government within a republican polity.

By the third quarter of the nineteenth century the legal individuality of the corporation no longer existed. Courts and legislature alike regarded the government of New York City as a "fiction" of the law. Between 1856 and 1863, the New York Court of Appeals ruled that city property was held entirely in trust for the public, that the city had no inherent discretionary authority over even such mundane "local" matters as the control of the streets, that the legislature could interfere at its pleasure in the affairs of the corporation and, indeed, could shift portions of the chartered juris-

---

3. See in addition to the sources cited in note 1, H. S. Maine, *Ancient Law* (London, 1861); Otto Friedrich Von Gierke, *Political Theories of the Middle Ages*, trans. F. W. Maitland (Boston, 1958); Lewis Krader, ed., *Anthropology and Early Law* (New York, 1967); M. G. Smith, *Corporations and Society* (London, 1975); Sally Falk Moore, *Law as Process* (London, 1978); and Leo Pospisil, *Anthropology of Law* (New York, 1971).

4. Maitland, *Township and Borough*, 18–36.

5. "At their first introduction, they were little more than an improvement on the communities which had grown up imperceptibly, without any positive institution; and for a considerable period, the shade which separated the one from the other, was of a touch so delicate as to require the most minute attention, and the most discerning eye, to distinguish" (Stewart Kyd, *A Treatise on the Law of Corporations*, 2 vols. [London, 1973], 1:2).

6. See Chapter 6.

diction of the city to other institutional structures. There was nothing in its nature, said the court, to distinguish the corporation of the city of New York from the smallest village in upstate New York.[7] However different one locality might be from another when viewed as social or economic institutions, legally all local governments were the same. All existed only to the extent that a state legislature granted them governmental authority.

We know what had once defined the distinctiveness of the corporation of the city of New York. We also know now how the city would be characterized in the latter half of the nineteenth century. What, though, was the legal place of an entity like the corporation during the intervening half century?

To say that we can describe both past and future perceptions of the city is not enough. Nor is it sufficient to assert that whatever New York City had been in the past, by the 1820s it was fast becoming a municipal corporation. Had someone told the government leaders of that city that their institution was nothing but an agent of the state legislature—which could intervene at its pleasure in city affairs—they would probably have considered the statement nonsense. They had, of course, applied repeatedly to the legislature for additional powers to meet the needs of a growing city. But that, they would have insisted, did not mean that transitory legislative authority had replaced the Montgomerie Charter as the basis for city government. A case like the *Brick Presbyterian Church*, which we might regard as insisting on a strict separation between corporate property and government authority (thereby robbing the government of the city of much of its historical distinction), carried a different meaning for contemporaries. To them, it stood for the narrower proposition that the corporation should not be restricted in the exercise of legislatively derived powers because of the incidental involvement of corporate property. As the owner of private property, New York City was indistinguishable from other private individuals.[8] In republican America, all alike held their private property subject to the residual authority of the state to control and restrict their use of that property in the public pursuit of the public good.[9]

7. *Davis* v. *Mayor of New York*, 14 N.Y. 526 (1856); *People ex rel. Wood* v. *Draper*, 15 N.Y. 532 (1857); *People* v. *Kerr*, 27 N.Y. 188, 200 (1863).

8. "Unwholesome trades, slaughter houses, operations offensive to the senses, the deposit of powder, the building with combustible materials, and the burial of the dead, may all be interdicted by law, in the midst of dense masses of population, on the general and rational principle, that every person ought so to use his property as not to injure his neighbours, and that the private interest must be made subservient to the general interest of the community." (James Kent, *Commentaries on American Law*, 4 vols. [New York, 1826–30], 2:276, citing the lower court decision by Judge Irving approving New York City's 1823 cemetery prohibition).

9. As late as the early 1850s, the treatise writer and judge Murray Hoffman could still

Our goal must be to place the nineteenth-century corporation of the city of New York within a changing structure of local government authority. What was the status of the city vis-à-vis other local governments? What difference did it make that New York City, unlike most others, found its legal origins in a charter still explicitly protected by the New York Constitution of 1821? If the corporation could no longer regularly lay claim to a theory of government autonomy founded on private rights, could it as yet be fitted within a general legal category of derivative agencies of state power?

Answers to these questions are necessarily tentative, and we must beware of imposing greater consistency or coherence on the law than in fact existed. It is possible to sketch a legal description of the corporation of the city of New York as it appeared to judges and other legal figures of the first third of the nineteenth century. But it may not be possible to subject that description to detailed critical analysis.

Throughout the antebellum history of New York, for example, it was conventional wisdom that the city contained within it both a public and a private self. "The Corporation of New York unites in itself a great variety of powers, peculiarly appropriate to a political corporation, and a great extent of rights, interests, and franchises, held in a private capacity," went the typical refrain.[10] But where was the line to be drawn between public and private, and what did it mean to say that some aspect of city government was held in a private capacity?

A section of the Montgomerie Charter granted the city the "offices" of gauger of wine and other liquors, measurer of grains, surveyor and packer of "bread, flour, beef, pork, and other provisions, and all other merchandises, and commodities," and licensor of "cartage, carriage, and portage, of all goods, wares, merchandises, and other things to be carted or carried in or through the said city." This was hardly a simple delegation of political responsibility, for the "offices" included the right to take "all fees, profits and perquisites . . . and all the fines amerciaments and forfeitures to be laid and forfeited concerning the same."[11] From the perspective of

---

construct a plausible case for the proposition that the foundations of New York City's government lay in the private property rights granted in its early charters and that those foundations were protected from legislative or judicial intervention (*Treatise upon the Estate and Right of the Corporation of the City of New York, as Proprietors* [New York, 1853]). Nine years later, in the second, revised edition Hoffman was a good deal less sure of the autonomy or the security of the corporation as a property holder. See Murray Hoffman, *Treatise upon the Estate and Right of the Corporation of the City of New York, as Proprietors*, 2d rev. ed., 2 vols. (New York, 1862).

10. Ibid. (1853), 48.

11. James Kent, *The Charter of the City of New York, with notes thereon. Also a Treatise on the Powers and Duties of the Mayor, Aldermen, and Assistant Aldermen, and the Journal of the City Convention* (New York, 1836), 60.

the rules of private property, these offices were vested, private rights of the corporation. But were they a part of the private sphere of the corporation? By 1836, Kent could not be sure.

In 1832, the legislature enacted a law regulating the measuring of grain in the city and eliminating the chartered right of the city to appoint and control measurers. A case was brought before the Superior Court of the city to test the legitimacy of the statute, and Chief Justice Samuel Jones ruled that the grant to the corporation was merely "a grant of political power, coupled with no interest, save the fees as a compensation for measuring; and that the grant in question was not to be considered in the light of property."[12] Kent commented that if this were the correct construction of the power of the legislature over the charter, then there were "very few provisions in the charter that can stand the test. . . . It is therefore a strong case to show the dependence of charter franchises on legislative discretion, except in those cases in which the franchise is a matter of private interest."[13]

But what made a franchise "a matter of private interest"? A cynic might answer, only that the legislature had not yet taken an interest in the matter. But that is too easy. For, so long as the legislature did not take an interest in a particular area of municipal concern, a private sphere of city government continued to exist.

Similarly, it is possible to examine a terminology, a set of definitions, used by judges and lawyers at the beginning of the nineteenth century to make sense of issues involving the authority of local governments. Cases then as now turned on the presence or absence of corporation "capacity," on the terms of a delegation from the legislature, or on the need for government to secure the public good. Yet it is clear that that terminology had not coalesced into an identifiable "law" of municipal corporations.

In order to settle particular cases various local governments might be analogized with one another, but they were not thereby placed into a common legal category. Some places were legally speaking just corporations, although for some purposes those same places suddenly became delegates of legislative sovereignty. Other local governments were not corporations at all, although at times they might act as if they were. Even when we find all localities treated alike by courts in particular circumstances we should beware of assuming that at last we have found the first expressions of an emerging field of local government law. We may instead have found only rules designed to bind all institutions chartered by the state—including businesses, charities, and banks.[14] There was a vocabulary for decision

12. Ibid., 150. See also *All the Proceedings in Relation to the New South Ferry between the Cities of New York and Brooklyn, from December 1825 to January 1835* (New York, 1835), 76.
13. Kent, *Charter*, 151. See also Hoffman, *Treatise* (1853), 48–50.
14. The rule requiring that courts strictly construe delegations of legislative power to local

making, but it was not one to inspire much confidence in its predictive or analytic content.

Through the first third of the nineteenth century, appellate courts heard relatively few cases raising issues about the nature or scope of local government authority. Courts were rarely pressed to engage in doctrinal clarification; nor did their occasional decisions appear to play a terribly important role in municipal affairs. Common Councilmen in New York never spent time in their deliberations considering the effects of appellate court decisions.[15] Indeed, if one puts aside cases in which the judges of the New York Supreme Court served as commissioners to confirm the assessments charged the city for the construction of city streets, New York City appeared as a litigant in the published reports only seven times between 1810 and 1825.[16] Other cities and towns, in New York State and elsewhere, raised claims to appellate courts even less frequently. And when they did, courts usually did not consider the issues litigated as requiring sustained inquiry into the proper relationships between public and private spheres or the sources of local government power.[17]

In sum, the law of municipal corporations had not been invented. When we consider New York City's place within a legal world of local governments, we are not evaluating the relative deviance of a single institution

---

governments (John F. Dillon, *A Treatise on the Law of Municipal Corporations* [New York, 1872], 101–5) began its life as a rule applied to all corporate charters. The author of the rule is usually considered to be Kent, who wrote in volume 2 of his *Commentaries*: "The modern doctrine is, to consider corporations as having such powers as are specifically granted by the act of incorporation, or as are necessary for the purpose of carrying into effect the powers expressly granted, and as not having any other. . . . No rule of law comes with a more seasonable application, considering how lavishly charter privileges have been granted. As corporations are the mere creatures of law, established for special purposes, and derive all their powers from the acts creating them, it is perfectly just and proper that they should be obliged strictly to show their authority for the business they assume, and be confined in their operations to the mode, and manner, and subject matter prescribed" (239–40). But Kent said he drew the rule from the decision of the U.S. Supreme Court in *Head and Amory* v. *The Providence Insurance Company*, 2 Cranch 127 (1803). See also *The People* v. *Utica Insurance Company*, 15 Johns. 358 (1818).

15. The Common Council, however, did devote considerable time to the determinations of the New York Supreme Court sitting as commissioners of review on street assessment awards. See Chapter 11.

16. *Mayor of New York* v. *Cashman*, 10 Johns. 96 (1813); *Mayor of New York* v. *Ordrenan*, 12 Johns. 122 (1815); *Varick* v. *Mayor of New York*, 4 Johns. Ch. 53 (1819); *Stryker* v. *Mayor of New York*, 19 Johns. 179 (1821); *The Corporation of New York* v. *Mapes and Schermerhorn*, 6 Johns. Ch. 45 (1822); *LeRoy* v. *Mayor of New York*, 4 Johns. Ch. 352 (1820); *Mayor* v. *Everston and Westerlo*, 1 Cowen 36 (1823).

17. Although I will argue later in this chapter that *Dartmouth College* was of fundamental importance in changing the terms of understanding of local government issues, until the 1850s relatively few local government cases cited *Dartmouth College*.

within a fixed normative structure. There was no "law" for New York City to fit or be fitted into, let alone to reject. There were only a variety of rules that might regulate and shape the conduct of a variety of local governments. With hindsight we may know that in only a few decades those rules would be woven together to shape a unitary doctrinal structure. But before the 1830s, visions of structural coherence were evanescent.

One reason why there was no "law" of municipal corporations was because chartered cities were already part of an undifferentiated "law" of corporations. Indeed, in the 1820s treatise writers still considered the borough the paradigm of corporation existence, echoing the traditional common law perception of a corporation as "properly investing the people of a place with its local government."[18] Boroughs shared a common rule structure with businesses, colleges, guilds, and mutual aid societies. For Stewart Kyd, whose *Treatise on the Law of Corporations* remained the leading work on both sides of the Atlantic until the 1830s, boroughs were simply one type of civil corporation. Nothing distinguished public from private entities; those terms played no part in his analysis (see Figure 12.1).

Kyd explained the profusion of corporations by the natural tendency of

---

18. Nathan Dane, *A General Abridgment and Digest of American Law, with Occasional Notes and Comments,* 9 vols. (Boston, 1824), 5:144. Although Dane's structure was archaic and reflected an undivided conception of the law of corporations, he also argued that courts ought to recognize the fundamental differences between local governments and other corporate entities. For that reason, he criticized Spencer Roane's opinion in *Currie's Administrator v. Mutual Assurance Society;* 4 H. and M. 315 (Va. 1809) as "clearly wrong": "There is a material distinction between property corporation[s], as insurance, bank, turnpike, canal, &c. and mere governmental corporations, as towns, cities, &c. These are established merely for the purposes of political and municipal government, and may be made or altered by the legislature without individual consent, as is every day's practice, and often altered without corporate consent, because they are only a mere incorporation of powers for the convenience of those immediately incorporated and of the government. They do not vary individual rights, nor are they founded on any contracts previously made by the incorporated. They may settle on the same tract of land, independently of each other, and be incorporated into a town, without entering previously into any contract whatever among themselves. The case is very different with such property corporations. In the very nature of the case the first act of the members is an express contract among themselves to create their capital stock, to manage it and to share the profits: by this they fix exactly what each one is to do and receive. In making this, each individual is an independent part, who can sue and be sued, and while few in numbers they can well, and often do execute the contract without any incorporation, and when incorporated, their incorporation is a mere corporation of powers, a grant or gift of the legislature to enable them to manage their property with more convenience" (Dane, *Abridgment,* 1:473–74). (See below, at note 46, for further discussion of *Currie's Administrator*). The location of Dane's argument at the end of a section on "By-laws of Corporations" in which citations to "private" and "public" entities were mixed indiscriminately, suggests something of the transitional quality of the work.

groups of men in society "to feel a common interest, acquire a common property, become subject to common burthens and common duties, assume a known character and description, and become objects of political regulation." Relying on the arguments of the lawyers who defended the Corporation of London against the crown's *quo warranto* action in the 1680s, Kyd declared that any corporation—whatever its functions or purposes—was more than a mere aggregation of granted powers. A corporation could not be equated with the political act of incorporation. Rather than a collection of capacities defined by a charter, a corporation was "a political person, in which many capacities reside." The right of acting as a corporation might be a franchise disbursed by central authority, but a corporation was more than a granted franchise: "The latter is a privilege, or liberty, which can have no existence without reference to some person to whom it may belong; the former is a political person, capable, like a natural person, of enjoying a variety of franchises; it is to a franchise, as the substance to its attribute; it is something to which many attributes belong; but is itself something distinct from those attributes."[19]

In contrast, many American lawyers and legislators viewed corporations with distrust even as they relied on them as instrumentalities of public initiative. All were considered grants of special privilege, perhaps justifiable by the exigencies of the times but indefensible as a natural part of a political order.[20]

Yet the terms by which republican America defined corporations were indistinguishable from Kyd's, however different the value judgment may have been. Decision makers like the New York Council of Revision might insist that corporations ought not to be encouraged, that the legislature ought not to create new ones or grant additional powers to those already in existence. Implicit in their diatribes, however, was a recognition that once created, corporations existed as autonomous beings. A corporation—whether a society for useful manufactures, a German Society, a college, or a chartered city—was dangerous precisely because it was "a political person, in which many capacities reside," rather than a docile agent of subordinate government. In this, all corporations were "independent republics," out of place in a unitary republican state.[21]

On the other hand, unchartered local governments—towns, counties, and school districts—were not recognized as real corporations. The term

19. Kyd, *Treatise on the Law of Corporations*, I, 14–15.
20. See *Respublica* v. *Duquet*, 2 Yeates 493, 494–96 (Pa. Sup. Ct., 1799) (Du Ponceau and Rawle, for def.). See Louis Hartz, *Economic Policy and Democratic Thought* (Cambridge, Mass., 1948), and discussion, in Chapter 7.
21. Alfred Billings Street, *The Council of Revision of the State of New York* (Albany, 1859), 276.

"municipal corporation" was rarely used before the 1830s, and it would never have been applied to a government like that of New York City. Rather, it seems to have been reserved for administrative entities that existed to provide state-defined public goods at a local level.[22] Such entities might be invested with particular corporation powers for particular purposes,[23] but they were "not bodies politick and corporate with the general powers of corporations." However extensive their delegated powers might be, they remained "deficient in many of the powers incident to the general character of corporations."[24]

American courts, therefore, followed English practice in refusing to recognize the juristic personality of rural towns and counties. Unlike true corporations, "towns and other municipal societies" had no control over their memberships or their boundaries. In the opinion of the Maine Supreme Court, such bodies "have ever been considered as subject to be arranged and modified by the legislative power at its pleasure."[25] Their ability to enter into contracts might be restricted to specific purposes,[26] their capacity to take property by private grant limited. In 1811, for example, the New York Supreme Court decided that the supervisors of Oneida County could not hold property in trust for the benefit of a town located within the county.[27] To act at all such governments were usually bound by strict procedural standards.[28]

22. See *Welles* v. *Battelle*, 11 Mass. 476, 480 (1814).

23. *Denton* v. *Jackson*, 2 Johns. Ch. 320 (1817); *Jackson ex dem. Lynch* v. *Hartwell*, 7 Johns. 422 (1811); *Hornbeck* v. *Westbrook*, 9 Johns. 73 (1812).

24. *Jackson ex dem. Cooper et al* v. *Cory*, 8 Johns. 385, 388 (1811); *Inhabitants of the Fourth School-District in Rumford* v. *Wood*, 13 Mass. 192, 197, 198 (1816).

25. *Bradford* v. *Cary*, 5 Me. 339, 342 (1828).

26. *Inhabitants of the Fourth School-District in Rumford* v. *Wood*, 13 Mass. 192 (1816); *Worcester* v. *Eaton*, 13 Mass. 369 (1816). In *Parsons* v. *Goshen*, 28 Mass. 396 (1831), the court described such limitations upon the power of local governments to enter into contracts as "a wise and salutary provision of law, not only as it protects the rights and interests of the minority of the legal voters, but as it may not unfrequently prove beneficial to the interests of the majority who may be hurried into rash and unprofitable speculations by some popular and delusive excitement, to the influence of which even wise and considerate men are some times liable" (399).

27. *Jackson ex dem. Lynch* v. *Hartwell*, 8 Johns. 422 (1811). See also *Hornbeck* v. *Westbrook*, 9 Johns 73 (1812); *Jackson ex dem. Cooper et al* v. *Cory*, 8 Johns. 385 (1811).

28. See, for example, *Hayden* v. *Noyes*, 5 Conn. 391 (1824) (passage of a bylaw regulating oyster bed fisheries by town meeting invalid if notice of the meeting did not include specific notice of the proposed bylaw). On the other hand, the Massachusetts Supreme Judicial Court, by Chief Justice Parker, noted: "We have had frequent occasion to perceive the great irregularity which prevails in the records of our towns and other municipal corporations; and the courts have always been desirous to uphold their proceedings, where no fraud or wilful error was discoverable. Too much strictness on subjects of this nature would throw the whole body politick into confusion" (*Welles* v. *Batelle*, 11 Mass. 476, 480 [1814]).

And always their ability to act was judged by the specific terms of a legislative delegation. Thus, in the great case of *Gardner* v. *Newburgh*, Chancellor Kent held that the trustees of the town of Newburgh could be enjoined from diverting a stream that flowed through the plaintiffs' land, even though the trustees had previously obtained an act authorizing them to go on lands adjacent to the town where there were springs of water to pipe water for the use of the town. The act ordered the town to compensate the owners of the springs but said nothing about compensating landowners through whose lands the streams had previously run. The trustees of the town were willing to compensate those landowners anyway, but Kent ruled that they had no right to act until the defect in the statute was remedied.[29]

State governments permitted localities to raise money by taxation for only a limited number of purposes. According to the Massachusetts Supreme Judicial Court, "providing for the poor, for schools, for the support of public worship, and other necessary charges" constituted the only concerns that could be financed through local taxes.[30] Conversely, localities also had no power to refuse to expend taxes for purposes or activities that superior authorities had decided were properly their responsibility. In 1821, for example, the small town of Mooers in Clinton County in upstate New York voted to offer a bounty of twenty dollars for any wolf killed within the town by a town resident. Mooers acted under the authority of a statute that gave county supervisors the right to add to each town's proportion of the county tax "such further sum as any town should have voted to be raised for the destruction of noxious animals." But Clinton's supervisors decided that the town should pay the bounty to nonresidents as well as residents of the town, in spite of the specific terms of the town vote. The result was a charge of $2,040 levied against the town at the end of the year, most of which evidently went to professional hunters from out of town. The town tried to rescind its prior vote, but this the county would not permit. The taxpayers of Mooers then applied to Chancellor Kent for relief. But he regretfully told them that no relief was available to them in equity, even though the state supreme court had already denied their motion for legal relief. "This was not the case of a private trust, but the official act of a political body." And for such acts, except in cases of

29. *Gardner* v. *Newburgh*, 2 Johns. Ch. 161 (1816).

30. *Stetson* v. *Kempton*, 13 Mass. 271, 278 (1816). This case arose because the town of Fairhaven had voted a tax of $1,200 during the War of 1812 to pay additional wages to the members of the local militia. The English were off the coast, within sight of the town, and had already made an attempt to land. But, according to the Massachusetts court, no rule of necessity existed to justify the town's actions, for "it is not a corporate duty to defend the town against an enemy" (279; see also *Van Eps* v. *Schenectady*, 7 Am. Dec. 330 (N.Y., 1815).

fraud or corruption, there could be no remedy in equity. The town would have no choice but to pay the bounty for all the wolves killed within its boundaries.[31]

Nothing better exemplifies the sharp distinction drawn between incorporated and unincorporated local governments in early America than the ways courts analyzed the liability of local governments for defects in highways. For boroughs the rule was clear: an action would lie against the corporation for not repairing a public facility.[32] For unincorporated communities the rule was equally clear, but it cut in precisely the opposite direction. In both England and America courts agreed that towns, counties, and local officials lacked an identity as legal individuals that could be differentiated from the interests of the public as a whole. Thus such governments ought to be protected by the doctrine of sovereign immunity. It was, in Lord Ashurst's famous phrase, "better that an individual should sustain an injury than that the public should suffer an inconvenience."[33]

The justifications offered by courts to protect local governments from liability had more to do with the apparent contrast between corporations and other local governments than with any seeming identity of interest between locality and sovereign, however. In the leading English case of *Russell* v. *The Men of Devon*, decided in 1788, Lord Kenyon held first that an action could not be maintained against the county because there was no statute that specifically gave litigants a remedy against the county as an incorporated entity. This did not mean that Parliament could not incorporate the county of Devon "to some purposes." But even if the county were viewed as a corporation, damages could be recovered only out of a corporate estate (rather than against the corporators in their individual capacity). And because the county lacked such an estate, "this experiment ought not to be encouraged."[34] Similarly, in *Mowers* v. *Leicester*, the first important American case on the same question, the Massachusetts Supreme Judicial Court held that unlike corporations, which, "created for

31. *Mooers* v. *Smedley*, 6 Johns. Ch. 28, 31, 32 (1822). Appended to Kent's opinion was the following note: "On the 12th of April, 1822, an act of the legislature was passed, relieving the town of Mooers from paying any wolf bounties allowed to non-residents of the town, or for wolves taken after the 28th of June, 1821; and directing all bounties allowed by the supervisors of Clinton county, in October, 1821, to non-residents, or for wolves taken in the town of Mooers after the 28th of June, to be assessed and paid by the county. This statute was, in effect, a legislative reversal of the decision of the supervisors, and was, probably, passed upon the ground, that there was a case of abuse, for which no remedy could be granted under the existing laws."

32. See *Mayor of Lynn* v. *Turner*, Cowper 86 (1774).

33. *Russell* v. *The Men Dwelling in the County of Devon*, 2 Term Rep. (Dunford and East), 667, 673 (1788).

34. Ibid.

their own benefit stand on the same ground, in this respect, as individuals," towns and counties were merely "quasi-corporations, created by the legislature for the purpose of public policy." Such governments could be indicted for neglect of their duties, but they were not liable to private suits for damages.[35]

The very word "municipal" was freighted with meanings in eighteenth- and nineteenth-century jurisprudence inconsistent with notions of corporate autonomy. In Blackstone's *Commentaries*, "municipal law" represented the English equivalent of the *jus civile* of continental law; what later Anglo-American lawyers would call "positive law." It was, as Blackstone repeated almost interminably, "a rule of civil conduct prescribed by the supreme power in a state, commanding what is right and prohibiting what is wrong."[36]

Such usage was adopted unchanged in American law. In Kent's *Commentaries on American Law* "municipal law" referred to the legal structure that shaped the internal affairs of a nation or state, and he saved his strongest arguments for the independent authority of the judiciary in American law for a section entitled "Of the Various Sources of the Municipal Law of the Several States."[37] Everybody realized, of course, that the word "municipal" derived from the Latin word for city. But, explained *Bouvier's Law Dictionary* in 1839, the significance of the word lay in its reference to a single legal and political jurisdiction, rather than in its reference to a city. Cities joining the Roman republic were said to retain "their law, their liberties and their magistrates." And so Americans applied to the term a "more extensive meaning, for example we call *municipal law* not the law of a city only, but the law of the state."[38]

The idea of a "municipal law" thus encompassed two central notions of nineteenth-century public law in America: the uniformity of law within a jurisdiction and the supremacy of the state as a source of power and authority. Both notions underlay the way Americans thought about municipal corporations in the years after 1830 when courts began to characterize cities as "municipal corporations." But in the first decades of the nineteenth century no such uniformity or strict positive authority could be inferred from appellate cases as a necessary attribute of city government.

A corporation like that of the city of New York remained in legal theory indistinguishable from what we, speaking anachronistically, would call

35. *Mowers* v. *Inhabitants of Leicester*, 9 Mass. 247, 249–50 (1812); see also *Riddle* v. *Proprietors*, 7 Mass. 169 (1810).

36. William Blackstone, *Commentaries on the Laws of England*, 4 vols. (London, 1765–69), 1 : 44–53.

37. Kent, *Commentaries*, 1 : 419–508.

38. John Bouvier, *A Law Dictionary* (Philadelphia, 1839).

"private" corporations. New York City had already gone far toward re-defining itself as a public entity, and the state legislature had already intervened in the chartered affairs of the city, both with and without the consent of local authorities. Yet there was still no way to categorize the corporation as nonprivate. And although courts drew a sharp line to distinguish towns, counties, and school districts—quasi-corporations—from real corporations, as yet they had done little to bifurcate the world of corporations.

The controversy and confusion that surrounded the law of corporations throughout the early years of the republic is, of course, a familiar part of our legal and economic history. Statements like those made by the Council of Revision in 1784 suggested that all corporations were private, that all were the property of their incorporators and thus secure from legislative intervention.[39] In contrast, state legislatures often regarded corporations as agencies of state power, as mechanisms for the achievement of public policy.[40] A charter that involved the conveyance by the state of valuable properties into "private" hands, as almost all charters surely did, might be regarded as a contract, on which the corporators could rely.[41] And as early as 1806 the Massachusetts Supreme Judicial Court declared that they were "satisfied that the rights legally vested in . . . any . . . corporation, cannot be controlled or destroyed by any subsequent statute, unless a power for that purpose be reserved to the legislature in the act of incorporation."[42] Yet Jeffersonian lawyers and judges continued to argue that construing a corporate charter as a binding contract was inconsistent with fundamental republican principles. A charter was nothing but an act of legislation. As a law like other laws, it existed subject to the continuing power of the legislature to change its mind about how best to secure the public good. It was, wrote Spencer Roane for the Virginia Supreme Court, "the character of a legislative act to be *repealable* by a succeeding legisla-

39. See Chapter 7.
40. See Edwin M. Dodd, *American Business Corporations until 1860* (Cambridge, Mass., 1954); Oscar Handlin and Mary F. Handlin, *Commonwealth*, rev. ed. (Cambridge, Mass., 1948); Hartz, *Economic Policy and Democratic Thought*; Nathan Miller, *The Enterprise of a Free People* (New York, 1962); Morton Horwitz, *The Transformation of American Law, 1780–1860* (Cambridge, Mass., 1977), 111–14; James Willard Hurst, *The Legitimacy of the Business Corporation in the United States, 1780–1970* (Charlottesville, Va., 1970); Oscar Handlin and Mary F. Handlin, "Origins of the Business Corporation," *Journal of Economic History* 5 (1945): 1–25.
41. See James Sullivan, "Opinion of the Attorney General of Massachusetts, on the Life of the Corporation, 1802," reprinted in Handlin and Handlin, *Commonwealth*, 271–76.
42. *Wales v. Stetson*, 2 Mass. 143–46 (1806). Even the lawyers arguing against the exercise of power by the city in *Respublica v. Duquet*, 2 Yeates 493, 495 (Pa. Sup. Ct., 1799), conceded the inviolability of its charter.

ture: nor can a preceding legislature limit the power of its successor, on the mere ground of volition only."[43]

Few of these disparate opinions distinguished between public and private corporations.[44] The general understanding remained that "all corporations wielded power and all corporations protected rights."[45] To the Massachusetts Supreme Judicial Court, the existence of rights holders meant that all corporations were private; to Spencer Roane, the fact that corporations exercised state-derived powers meant that all were public. Distinctions within the world of corporations could be drawn on the basis of the presence or absence of charitable purposes or the religious character of the founder. But those traditional distinctions left businesses and cities together in the same categorical box. They exercised their powers through legislative delegations. They had similar sources of corporate revenue. They both might be regarded as designed to encourage commercial growth.[46] And whether corporations were finally labeled public or private entities, it seemed evident that both businesses and cities would be subjected to the same fate.

That did not occur, however. It was the United States Supreme Court's great achievement in the *Dartmouth College Case* in 1819 to legitimize a way of understanding the law of corporations that neither undercut the constitutional responsibility of the legislature to protect the public interest nor called into question the contractual expectations of citizens in their dealings with government. Both the power of the state and the autonomy of the individual would find validation in *Dartmouth College*.[47] The trick was to divide entities that derived power from the state from those that held rights against the state.

A generation of Americans that had already gone far to distinguish property from governance could not have found the notion of a public-private split in the law of corporations much of a surprise.[48] The absolute

43. *Currie's Administrator* v. *Mutual Assurance Society*, 4 H. and M. 315, 346–48 (Va., 1809).

44. That judges did not usually distinguish between public and private corporations did not mean that it was not possible for such distinctions to be drawn. See the arguments of James Cheetham, quoted in Chapter 7.

45. Gerald Frug, "The City as a Legal Concept," *Harvard Law Review* 93 (1980): 1102.

46. See authorities cited in note 40.

47. William Nelson has recently argued that in decisions like *Dartmouth College* John Marshall was primarily motivated to recreate a form of eighteenth-century political consensus. See "The Eighteenth-Century Background of John Marshall's Constitutional Jurisprudence," *Michigan Law Review* 76 (1978): 893. I remain unconvinced of the general argument, although I do think that Marshall's opinion in *Dartmouth College* should be viewed as an attempt to uphold both private, vested rights and the power and authority of the republican state.

48. See Chapters 7 through 11. Constitutional use of the public-private distinction is usu-

quality that the dichotomy assumed in the opinions of the justices might have represented more of a novelty, however. For the various members of the court what was public was not private; what was private could never be public. A public corporation was nothing but an agency of the state; a private corporation assumed the character of a private citizen. And the problem that John Marshall, Bushrod Washington, and Joseph Story all faced in writing their opinions was to make such a radical dichotomy seem natural and not arbitrary.

For Story, whose influential concurrence was relied on as often as Marshall's opinion for the court during the 1820s and 1830s,[49] the problem was easily solved. A public entity was one in which "the government have the sole right, as trustees of the public interests, to regulate, control, and direct the corporation, and its funds and its franchises, at its own good will and pleasure." In the "strictly legal" sense of the term, if not in common usage, a private corporation was one "subject to no other control . . . than what is expressly or implicitly reserved by the charter itself." The authority to intervene in the affairs of a corporation existed only "where its whole interests and franchises are the exclusive property and domain of the government itself." And for Story, as for most nineteenth-century Americans, only the state could constitute the "domain of government."[50]

Because Story twice referred to "towns, cities, and counties" as examples of what he meant by a public corporation, one might suppose that his definitions would have resolved any uncertainty about the legal status of a city like New York. New York City would join the villages and counties of New York State in a unified public sphere. But in fact Story's concurrence had the opposite effect. For the next forty years it would provide ammunition for lawyers defending chartered rights of the corporation against the encroachments of the state. What distinguished a private corporation in Story's lexicon was the existence of property not strictly under the domain of the state. Thus, so long as New York City was the possessor of an estate founded on a prerevolutionary charter secured from state attack by the state constitution, it could hardly be an unambiguously public entity.

Both Chief Justice Marshall and Bushrod Washington avoided Story's emphasis on the relative presence or absence of property by shaping their versions of the public-private dichotomy around a more literal description

---

ally said to find its origin in Story's opinion in *Terrett* v. *Taylor*, 9 Cranch 43 (1816), three years before *Dartmouth College*.

49. See Kent R. Newmeyer, "Justice Joseph Story's Doctrine of Public and Private Corporations and the Rise of the American Business Corporation," *DePaul Law Review* 25 (1976):825–41; Kent, *Commentaries*, 2:242–44.

50. *The Trustees of Dartmouth College* v. *Woodward*, 4 Wheaton 518, 671, 675, 672 (U.S. 1819).

of the charter as a contract. Corporations like Dartmouth College were private only because private individuals had contracted with the state in receiving a charter. Those individuals had accepted certain responsibilities in exchange for certain privileges, and in consequence the state was estopped from violating the agreement it had made with them. All corporations were public, Marshall conceded, in the sense that all were created by the state to provide services to the public. But what distinguished eleemosynary and other "private" institutions from public agencies was the existence of "charitable, or public spirited individuals, desirous of making permanent appropriations for charitable or other useful purposes," who had applied to the legislature for an act of incorporation.

> They apply to the government, state their beneficent object, and offer to advance the money necessary for its accomplishment, provided the government will confer on the instrument which is to execute their designs the capacity to execute them. The proposition is considered and approved. The benefit to the public is considered as an ample compensation for the faculty it confers, and the corporation is created. If the advantages to the public constitute a full compensation for the faculty it gives, there can be no reason for exacting a further compensation, by claiming a right to exercise over this artificial being a power which changes its nature, and touches the fund, for the security and application of which it was created.[51]

Conversely, what made local governments public institutions was that the state created them on its own initiative, that there was "no other founder or visitor than the king or government." If the charters of such institutions were amended by the unilateral acts of the legislature, Bushrod Washington argued, "such legislative interferences cannot be said to impair the contract by which the corporation was formed, because there is in reality but one party to it," and that was the state.[52]

For public entities, then, the existence of a corporate charter was beside the point in analyzing their relations with the state. Corporate status gave some local governments a surface similarity to private corporations. Like charitable corporations or private franchises, a city might have the power to hold property, to sue and be sued as an individual, to make internal bylaws, and so forth. But that did not make the city into a private entity:

> The character of civil institutions does not grow out of their incorporations, but out of the manner in which they are formed, and the objects for which they are created. The right to change them is not founded on their being incorporated, but on their being the instru-

51. Ibid., 637–38.
52. Ibid., 660–61.

ments of government, created for its own purposes. The same institutions, created for the same objects, though not incorporated, would be public institutions, and of course, be controllable by the legislature. The incorporating act neither gives nor prevents this control.[53]

It would seem to follow from Marshall's and Washington's line of analysis that the corporation of the city of New York would be clearly redefined as a public entity. Although Story's argument allowed the corporation to rely on its corporate estate to differentiate itself from other local governments, their opinions implied that the corporation was nothing but an aspect of a public, statewide polity. The "ancient" Montgomerie Charter made no difference. Corporate autonomy would be reserved for entities shaped by the presence of private incorporations.

Such an implication, moreover, could not have surprised the lawyers and political leaders of New York City, who, as we have seen, had already come to the practical conclusion that the future of the city lay in viewing it as a public institution. When, for example, the Common Council petitioned the legislature in 1808 to remove the water franchise from the Manhattan Company and return it to the city, it reasoned that because the corporation was a public entity incapable of deviating from its commitment to the public good the legislature could trust it to fulfill its responsibilities (unlike the Manhattan Company, which stood revealed as a mere private company).[54]

And yet, however ineluctable the implications of the decision in *Dartmouth College*, and however clear New York City's identification with the public side of the public-private dichotomy, in legal theory the place of an institution like the corporation of the city of New York remained unclear. Other local governments—including most chartered city corporations—might be separated from the autonomy of corporate existence by the absence of an identifiable membership of incorporators. No one could be a "citizen" of an ordinary town, for in republican America the only compulsory political communities to which the individual belonged were the state and the federal government. But New York City had a charter in which its "mayor, aldermen and commonalty" were identified as its recipients. The corporation of the city of New York, no less than Dartmouth College, had had "incorporators" who had shaped the terms of the Montgomerie Charter and who had relied on that charter in their dealings with the province and the crown. Did that not prevent the state from modifying or abrogating the commitments of its predecessors?

The notion of an identifiable corporate membership of a municipality

53. Ibid., 638.
54. See Chapter 10.

had ceased to have much meaning by 1819. But when Marshall wrote of the significance of private incorporators in the formation of a contract with the state he was not referring to the continuing membership of a private corporation. To the contrary, it was the past existence of individuals who had received a charter from central authority that revealed the private character of a private corporation. It was old Doctor Wheelock with his plans to educate the Indians—not the nineteenth-century trustees of Dartmouth College—who had made Dartmouth into a private corporation. And thus, was not the corporation of the city of New York as unambiguously a *private* corporation as Dartmouth College?[55] Changing notions of political membership did no more to change the existence of a contract between the crown and the municipal incorporators of New York City than a changing conception of the state's role in higher education changed the nature of the contract between the college and the state of New Hampshire.[56]

The point is not that the government of New York City was ever likely to claim a freedom from state intervention comparable to that asserted by Daniel Webster for Dartmouth College. Even so resolute a defender of chartered rights as James Kent knew that the battle to protect the corporation against unilateral modifications of its charter had been fought and lost.[57] The point is rather that the behavioral transformation of the government of New York City into an agency of the state was not yet reflected in legal theory. Or, more accurately, the implications of an emerging legal theory had not yet been worked out.

Throughout the 1820s and early 1830s the doctrinal role of the public-private dichotomy remained unsettled. In the second volume of his *Commentaries on American Law*, first published in 1827, Kent introduced the dichotomy into his chapter on corporations. His typology of corporations remained a simplified version of Blackstone's or Kyd's, however (see Figure 12.1). Aggregate corporations divided into ecclesiastical and lay; lay corporations divided into eleemosynary and civil; and the public-private split appeared only as a way of distinguishing between different civil corporations. His discussion of the constitutive elements of a public corporation seemed designed, in fact, to lay a foundation for the argument that

55. See Hoffman, *Treatise*, 1:passim.

56. See John S. Whitehead, *The Separation of College and State* (New Haven, 1973), 52–88; John M. Shirley, *The Dartmouth College Causes and the Supreme Court of the United States* (1879; reprint, New York, 1971).

57. Kent, *Charter*, 127–28. According to Kent, the last defense of the autonomy of the chartered corporation lay in its property rights such as the ferry franchise. Thus it is not surprising that he gave such weight to Story's concurrence in *Dartmouth College*.

The World of Corporations

Kyd (1791)

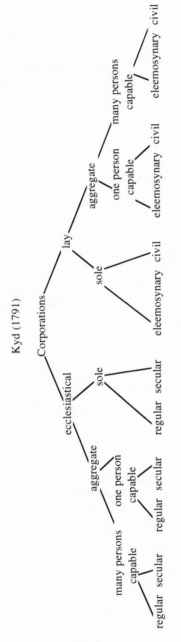

Kent (1827)

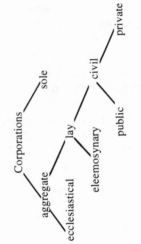

FIGURE 12.1. *The World of Corporations*

New York City was not one. "Public corporations," he began, "are such as exist for public political purposes only, such as counties, cities, towns, and villages. They are founded by the government, for public purposes, and the whole interest in them belongs to the public. But," he continued, "if the foundation be private, the corporation is private, however extensive the uses may be to which it is devoted by the founder, or by the nature of the institution." To Kent a point of origin as a private entity remained definitive of a continuing status.[58]

On the other hand, the emergence of a constitutionally based public-private dichotomy had an immediate effect on judicial analyses of the distinctions between local governments. In the 1820s the contrast between chartered corporations and quasi or municipal corporations, which had played so important a role in earlier appellate opinions, largely disappeared. Towns and counties, evidently, were really corporations and, for the most part, legally indistinguishable from cities. They were not, as New York's chancellor noted in 1824, "declared to be corporations, in the forms and terms which are usual in special grants of incorporation; but even in grants to private persons, a body politic may be created by any terms which sufficiently express the intention of the creating power."[59]

The differences earlier courts had noted between incorporated and unincorporated local governments were of reduced significance because all shared in a public quality that distinguished them from private entities. To Kent, "They have facilities which belong not to private persons and which persons cannot confer upon themselves, by any voluntary association.

---

58. Kent, *Commentaries*, 2:222. When American lawyers looked for clarification to the common law "origins" of the public-private dichotomy, what little they found left the status of an institution like the corporation of the city of New York even less settled. The great case of *Philips* v. *Bury*, 2 T.R. 353, 1 Ld. Raymond 5 (1694), on which both Bushrod Washington and Joseph Story placed much emphasis in their respective concurrences, dealt with the jurisdiction of the royal courts over the actions of a visitor to a college at Oxford who had dismissed the rector. Lord Holt held that there was no such jurisdiction because the college was a private charity. In contrast, over corporations constituted for "publick government," including guilds, trading associations, turnpike corporations, banks, as well as boroughs, the royal courts did exercise a visitorial power (ibid.). Nothing in the case, however, suggested that the power of courts to visit a corporation was in any way analogizable to the power of Parliament, let alone state legislatures, to interfere in the government of public corporations. And indeed, the one important English case to suggest that a grant of corporate powers might create a contractual relationship between the government and the recipient of the charter, *King* v. *Passmore*, 3 T.R. 199 (1789), involved the charter of a borough. See Warren B. Hunting, *The Obligation of Contracts Clause of the United States Constitution* (1919; reprint, Westport, Conn., 1976), 58–110.

59. *North Hempstead* v. *Hempstead*, Hopkins 329, 333 (1824); affirmed, 2 Wend. 109 (1828). See *Denton* v. *Jackson*, 2 Johns. Ch. 320 (1817), for Kent's different treatment of the same case.

They are little republics recognized by the constitution, defined by the laws, and invested with important powers."[60]

Their powers, though, were never "invested" with a capacity to bind the state. In 1826, for example, the commissioners of Madison County in Illinois tried to collect a penalty against a Mr. Coles for bringing into the county and freeing ten slaves, without first giving a bond to the county for their support. The county acted on the basis of an 1819 statute, which had, however, been repealed in 1825 by a second statute. Did the 1825 statute impair the rights of Madison County in denying it the penalties and the bond previously granted by the legislature? Of course not, answered the Illinois Supreme Court:

> On an inquiry into the different kinds of corporations, their uses and objects, it will appear that a plain line of distinction exists between such as are of a private and such as are of a public nature, and form a part of the general police of the state. Those that are of a private nature and not general to the whole community the legislature cannot interfere with. The grant of incorporation is a contract. But all public incorporations which are established as a part of the police of the state are subject to legislative control, and may be changed, modified, enlarged, restrained, or repealed to suit the ever varying exigencies of the state. Counties are corporations of this character, and are consequently subject to legislative control.
>
> Were it otherwise, the object of their incorporation would be defeated. It cannot be doubted that Madison County, as a county, might be stricken out of existence and her interest in a popular action thereby defeated. Upon what principle, then, can it be contended that the legislature cannot remit a penalty in a popular action brought for her benefit?[61]

Since public government bodies acted only under the aegis of state power, whether their foundation was a formal act of incorporation or not no longer mattered. Courts asked only that the exercise of power be derived from an act of the legislature. Thus when litigants challenged the ability of the newly incorporated city government of Boston to pass bylaws

---

60. Ibid. See Maitland's 1891 letter to Melville M. Bigelow in which he describes the American rule as "a sort of 'atavism,' a 'throw back' to ancient law brought about by your recognition of the corporation character of the rural township. Thus, as I take it, you came by corporations which often had no property of their own. But the whole thing is wonderfully interesting" (Cecil H.S. Fifoot, ed., *Letters of Frederic W. Maitland* [Cambridge, 1965], 89).

61. *Coles* v. *County of Madison*, Breese 154, 160; 12 Am. Dec. 161, 167 (Ill., 1826). See *Armstrong* v. *Board of Commissioners of Dearborn County*, 4 Black. 208 (Ind., 1856).

founded on an enabling statute passed for the benefit of the previous un-chartered Boston town administration, the Supreme Judicial Court held that the fact that the bylaws derived from a valid delegation from the legis-lature was enough to sustain their governmental authority.[62]

The defects that courts had earlier perceived in unincorporated local governments now became the virtues of these "public" corporations. Be-cause towns lacked either an identifiable corporate membership or control over corporate boundaries, nonresidents could be held to the same stan-dard of conduct as residents.[63] Indeed, because towns, unlike private cor-porations, were not autonomous beings intent on aggrandizing power to themselves at the expense of the legislature, rules that insisted on a strict construction of all legislative delegations could at times be relaxed. "Where there are no negative powers in a statute, the court will allow *ex necessitate* a latitude of construction."[64] Memphis, for example, passed an ordinance directing all steamboat traffic to a particular spot on the Mis-sissippi River, a spot that had originally been platted as a public prome-nade. When individuals objected, on the grounds that such a change in land use was beyond the powers of the corporation under its charter, the Tennessee Supreme Court held that a public body ought to be capable of responding to changing needs. "If this were not so, a thriving town would be exceedingly crippled in the exercise of its corporate rights. Few persons would have sufficient foresight, in laying off a town, to anticipate and pro-vide everything that was calculated to promote its prosperity and good government."[65] And likewise, when Charleston attempted to regulate the sale of British coal within the city, the South Carolina court refused to con-sider the charge that such regulation was contrary to the United States Constitution's prohibition on state duties on imports. "If the city has the power of regulating commerce between its citizens," held the court, "it must have the power of enforcing these regulations."[66]

Most important of all, courts came to the conclusion that local govern-ments were "clothed with legislative powers and prerogatives to a certain extent, and . . . [were] fully empowered to adopt measures of police, for the purpose of preserving the health and promoting the comfort, conve-

62. *Commonwealth* v. *Worcester*, 20 Mass. 462 (1826).

63. See *Vandine, Petitioner*, 23 Mass. 187 (1828), in which the court held: "The by-laws which are made by corporations having a local jurisdiction, are to be observed and obeyed by all who come within it, in the same manner as aliens and strangers within the Commonwealth are bound to know and obey the laws of the land, notwithstanding they may not know the language in which they are written." See also *Town of Marietta* v. *Fearing*, 4 Ohio 427 (1829).

64. *Hart* v. *Mayor of Albany*, 9 Wend. 571, 594 (N.Y. Ct. of Errors, 1832).

65. *Mayor of Memphis* v. *Wright*, 14 Tenn. 497, 499–500 (1834).

66. *City Council* v. *Rodgers*, 13 Am. Dec. 751 (S.C., 1823).

nience, and general welfare of the inhabitants within the city."[67] So long as their actions were in pursuit of a legislatively defined public good, localities could act, even if their actions altered or harmed private property rights. "The law will not, by any construction, advance a private interest to the destruction of that of the public, but, on the contrary, will advance the public interest as far as possible, though it be to the injury of private interests."[68] The *Brick Presbyterian Church* case was only one of several contemporaneous cases in which local governments were authorized to act in ways that divested individuals of rights previously secured from their governments.[69] Courts almost uniformly accepted the right of cities to destroy the settled expectations of citizens without paying any compensation. Boston in one case dammed and filled up a creek previously used by fishermen as an outlet to the sea, without incurring liability. According to the city, the creek had become a health hazard, but it was undisputed that the reason for the creek's changed condition was the construction of municipal sewers that drained "offensive matter" into it.[70] On another occasion Boston directed that only city employees be permitted to collect the offal and household waste thrown by city residents into the streets, thereby robbing the pig farmers of Cambridge of their traditional source of feed.[71] In neither instance did the Massachusetts court think that the city had "taken" anything that warranted compensation.

In general such cases interpreted the powers of public corporations in broad and abstract terms. The Louisiana court began its influential opinion in *Milne* v. *Davidson* with a typical affirmation of the power of the state to regulate property rights in pursuit of the public interest:

67. *Baker* v. *Boston*, 12 Pick. 183, 193 (Mass., 1831); see also *Vandine, Petitioner,* 6 Pick. 187 (1828); *Parks* v. *Boston,* 8 Pick. 218 (1829); *Gwynn* v. *City of Cincinnati,* 3 Ohio 24 (1827); *Milne* v. *Davidson,* 5 Martin N.S. 309 (La., 1827); *Towne* v. *Lee,* 8 Martin N.S. 548 (La., 1830); *Mayor* v. *Morgan,* 7 Martin N.S. 1 (La., 1828); *Green* v. *Savannah,* 6 Ga. 1 (1849).

68. *Hart* v. *Mayor of Albany,* 9 Wend. 571, 594 (Senator Allen) (N.Y. Ct. of Errors, 1832).

69. *Milne* v. *Davidson,* 5 Martin N.S. 409 (1827); *Gwynne* v. *City of Cincinnati,* 3 Ohio 24 (1827); *Green* v. *Savannah,* 6 Ga. 1 (1849).

70. *Baker* v. *Boston,* 12 Pick. 184 (1831). But see, *per contra, Barron and Craig* v. *The Mayor of Baltimore, American Jurist* 4 (1829): 203, 215.

71. *Vandine, Petitioner,* 6 Pick. 187 (1828): "The great object of the city is to preserve the health of the inhabitants. To attain that they wisely disregard any expense which is deemed to be requisite. They might probably have these offensive substances carried out of the city without any expense, if they would permit the people from the country to take them away at such times and in such manner as would best accommodate them. Everyone will see that if this business were thus managed there would be continual moving nuisances at all times and in all streets of the city, breaking up the streets by their weight and poisoning the air with their effluvia" (192).

The natural right to the enjoyment of property, in opposition to the positive regulations of society, is a subject of little utility in a court of justice. It is true, that the right to acquire property may be regarded as one of those which is inherent in man; but this right, which took its rise in the law of nature, has received its perfection, and had a permanency given to it, by municipal or civil law; and it is in relation to this law, that the right of individuals to the possession and enjoyment of things, must be examined. The modifications which legislative power may make, in the possession, use, and distribution of property, are infinite; and nearly every contest which arises in courts of justice, proceeds from the real or imputed violation of some one of those modifications; any one of which might be urged to be a violation of natural law, with as much reason as that of which the appellant now complains.

The holding in *Milne* turned on an analysis of the inappropriateness of applying common law rules to the particular powers of New Orleans, but that argument was posed by the court less in terms of civil versus common law jurisprudence and more in terms of the universal need for specific legislative grants of power to permit cities and towns to mold a decent public environment.[72]

When the public health and safety were at issue, courts throughout America tended to grant wide discretion to municipal officials. Once "clothed with legislative powers and prerogatives" local officials "necessarily" had "the power of deciding in what manner" the public health would be secured. So long as a government acted in a manner appropriate for a public institution and betrayed no identification with a private sphere, its actions were usually safe from challenge.[73]

In all of these cases, the legitimation of state power rested on a public-private analysis of the sort developed in the *Dartmouth College* case. Local governments were part of a unified public sphere because they were not autonomous private entities. When they modified or regulated (or destroyed) private property rights or customary expectations they were not viewed as gaining special privileges or rights. As parts of a statewide polity they did not compete for rights with private individuals.[74]

72. *Milne* v. *Davidson*, 5 Martin N.S. 409, 412–14 (1827).

73. Thus, although the bylaws of a private corporation would be held void if in restraint of trade, see *Sargent* v. *Franklin Ins. Comp.* 8 Pick 90 (1829), this rule was held inapplicable to municipal bylaws exercising police powers. See *Commonwealth* v. *Worcester*, 20 Mass. 462 (1826). But compare *Randall* v. *Van Vechten*, 19 Johns. 60 (1821), *Lessee of Cincinnati* v. *First Presbyterian Church*, 8 Ohio 298 (1838), *Goodloe* v. *Cincinnati*, 4 Ohio 500 (1821), in which cities were seen as engaged in "private" activities. See Chapter 14.

74. *Coates et al* v. *Mayor of New York*, 7 Cowen 585 (1827); *Vanderbilt* v. *Adams*, 7 Cowen 349 (1827).

Later treatise writers described the "police power" as if it had long roots in traditional legal theory. It appeared to them to be a synthesis of public nuisance law and the traditional regulatory authority of government bodies.[75] But previous forms of public action had always been justified by the need to prevent change, by the public value found in maintaining a fixed, customary order. In the 1820s and 1830s, by contrast, government claimed the right to institute change, to undo past practices through public actions. Such a right could not be legitimated by tradition or the common law. Instead, courts and local officials identified cities with a republican state legislature invested with monopoly powers over publicly instituted change.[76]

The appearance of these cases in Jacksonian America suggests that local governments throughout the country had learned the same lessons taught to the leaders of New York City twenty-five years before. Only the state offered legitimacy to act in ways that deviated from past practices. Only by relying on delegations of state power could local governments create a public environment that would satisfy the needs of a changing society.

The stylistic hallmark of these early police power cases was their ability to affirm the public power of municipalities without saying much about the nature of those localities. The critique of "vested" private property rights in the face of municipal action was mounted from the perspective of state legislative authority. As far as the courts were concerned, private litigants attacked the legitimacy of state power rather than the exercise of power by local units. Even when the police power was implemented by an institution as "private" as the corporation of the city of New York (perhaps, particularly, when the power was exercised by the corporation of the city of New York), courts acted as if the suit were between the state and the individual rather than the corporation and the individual:

> The sovereign power in a community . . . may and ought to prescribe the manner of exercising individual rights over property. It is for the better protection and enjoyment of that absolute dominion which the individual claims. The powers rest on the implied right and duty of the supreme power to protect all by statutory regulations, so that, on the whole, the benefit of all is promoted. Every public regulation in a city may and does, in some sense, limit and restrict the absolute right that existed previously. But this is not considered as an injury. So far from it, the individual, as well as others, is supposed to be benefited.[77]

75. See Thomas M. Cooley, *Constitutional Limitations* (Boston, 1868), 572–97; Christopher Tiedemann, *A Treatise on the Limitations of the Police Power* (St. Louis, 1886).

76. *Vanderbilt v. Adams*, 7 Cowen 349, (1827).

77. Ibid., 351–52.

One might hypothesize that courts adopted this rhetorical strategy to avoid dealing with entities they were not certain how to characterize. Local governments had been freed from the analytic confines of the law of corporations, but they had not yet found their true home in a law of municipal corporations. All local governments were clearly part of a statewide polity. Were they therefore indistinguishable from state governments? Or did they retain a local and individual identity? Courts ignored such questions in the 1820s and focused instead on the state authority that made local action possible.

Yet even as courts sidestepped the question of the legal "nature" of local governments they were developing a theory of delegation—of the ways derivative institutions received authority and of the standards courts could use to identify the substance and limits of the authority delegated—that would later serve as the legal underpinning of the law of municipal corporations.[78] State courts had not yet worked out a way of making sense of the nature of entities like the corporation of the city of New York. But by 1830 we can begin to see the outlines of a legal category to which the municipal corporation of New York would, one day, belong.

78. Compare the theory of delegation contained in the police power cases of the 1820s with the "analysis" conducted in *Respublica* v. *Duquet*, 2 Yeates 493 (Pa. Sup. Ct., 1799).

CHAPTER 13

Unifying the Public Sphere

Through the 1820s what passed for local government law in America was largely composed of a series of analogies and comparisons. Some local governments were just like corporations and therefore should be treated by courts like other corporations. Other local governments were like corporations in limited ways only and, therefore, should only occasionally be considered autonomous entities. Insofar as local governments exercised the powers of public authority they should be treated as if they were the state. Little bound together the field of local government law. As late as the early 1830s one might guess that lawyers regarded the corporation of the city of New York as having more in common legally with the Manhattan Company or a turnpike corporation than it had with a small unincorporated village or even with the much larger incorporated village of Brooklyn.

Looking backward we can say that this situation had to change. Viewed retrospectively it seems obvious that local governments would be organized into a uniform legal category. Liberal political theory, it is said, could not tolerate the existence of a variety of disparate political bodies interposed between the public authority of the state and the private freedom of the individual, could not tolerate the sheer untidiness of the local government *gestalt* of the first quarter of the nineteenth century.[1] Alternatively, we might argue that the state itself had a large stake in establishing more explicit legal control over local entities, that at least in legal theory local government had to be made subject to centralized norms.[2] It is

1. See Gerald Frug, "The City as a Legal Concept," *Harvard Law Review* 93 (1980): 1057–1154; John Higham, *From Boundlessness to Consolidation: The Transformation of American Culture* (Ann Arbor, 1969).

2. See Charles Tilly, ed., *The Formation of National States in Western Europe* (Princeton, 1975) (particularly the essays by Tilly, Gabriel Ardant, and David Bayley); Frederic W. Maitland, "Moral Personality and Legal Personality," in *Selected Essays* (Cambridge, 1936), 223–39, and *Collected Papers*, 3 vols. (Cambridge, 1911), 3:304–20; and "Trust and Corporation," in *Selected Essays*, 141–222, and *Collected Papers*, 3:321–404.

apparent, moreover, that courts were about to face an enormous increase in the number of cases dealing with local government matters, as a new scale of urban growth began in America. In the face of that explosion in legal business it made sense to develop a rationalized and simplified structure of rules. Just as the period 1830 to 1860 witnessed the emergence of free incorporation laws and rationalized standards for the conduct of incorporated business enterprise, so too was it the era for a rationalized structure of public enterprise. Was any other outcome conceivable?[3]

But if, on the other hand, we attempt to place ourselves in the position, say, of a city attorney in 1830, the picture becomes murkier. Nothing would have told such an individual that appellate judges throughout America were about to engage in a more or less systematic program to reconstitute the various elements of law dealing with local communities. The reigning Jacksonianism perhaps sharpened a traditional republican critique of special privilege and suggested that there could be fewer legal differences between local governments. But Jacksonianism also glorified decentralization and local autonomy.[4] No one declaimed about a crisis in local government law. No one seemed committed to a radical clarification of legal rhetoric.

But that is precisely what did occur in the quarter century between 1835 and the beginning of the Civil War. By the middle of the nineteenth century, a uniform image of the legal nature of the city had become part of the conventional wisdom of the American lawyer. Judges might disagree over practically everything yet share a common characterization of the legal structure of local governments.[5]

In place of local autonomy and political decentralization, the new law of municipal corporations posed the absolute centrality of state power and the insignificance of local publics in the political order. In place of the

3. For a good, recent case study of such a Weberian process of legal rationalization, see Mark Tushnet, "The American Law of Slavery, 1810–1860: A Study in the Persistence of Legal Autonomy," *Law and Society Review* 10 (1975): 119–80.

4. Consider the following comment by Theodore Sedgwick: "American freedom is based on the idea of local action, localized power, local sovereignty, and has received its best developments from the intelligence and energy of its people, fostered to the highest degree by a system which seeks, as far as safely possible, to strip the central authority of influence, and to distribute its functions among local agents and bodies" (*A Treatise on the Rules Which Govern the Interpretation and Application of Statutory and Constitutional Law* [New York, 1857], 460, citing the 1846 New York constitutional convention as "the strongest illustration . . . [which] has carried local sovereignty to a point never tried before. It cannot yet be said with confidence, whether the line of wisdom has not been passed"). On Sedgwick as a Jacksonian, see Marvin Meyers, *The Jacksonian Persuasion* (Stanford, 1960), 163–84.

5. See, for example, the various opinions in the great case of *Sharpless* v. *The Mayor of Philadelphia*, 21 Penn St. 158 (1853), *American Law Register*, old ser., 2 (1854): 27–43, 85–112.

distinctive chartered rights of cities and the particular customs of local communities—both of which earlier served to frustrate the designs of central authorities—the new "law" held localities to explicit delegations of legislative power. Within constitutional limits, all municipal corporations were whatever state legislatures said they were, and all did only what state legislatures clearly and distinctly said they could do. They possessed "no powers or faculties not conferred upon them, either expressly or by fair implication, by the law which creates them, or other statutes applicable to them."[6]

Underlying these substantive conclusions was a strikingly new image of the role of the courts in determining local authority. Starting around 1835 appellate judges began to decide cases by referring to principles that they said bound all local governments equally. Litigation turned less on the specific mandates contained in enabling statutes than on general—judicially created—rules. If a statute delegated power to a locality, for example, the statute would be interpreted against an enlarged delegation of authority, whatever the intent of the drafters of the statute. Other judicial rules provided standardized characterizations of different aspects of municipal governance. Some local activities would be part of the "private" sphere of the municipal corporation and subject to private suits for damages; other activities were public and probably protected by the doctrine of sovereign immunity. Some public duties were "judicial"; others were "ministerial." These categories were said to be equally applicable to all local governments. Judges had apprehended the Platonic essence of the municipal corporation. Seemingly different local governments would be subject to common rules and to common legal consequences.

The causes of this transformed judicial understanding of the legal nature of local government elude us.[7] It is possible, however, to identify an agent of change, at least in New York. Appointed to the New York Supreme Court in 1831, after a short but successful legal and political career and six years as circuit judge (all in western New York), Samuel Nelson is one of the many important American judges about whom we know relatively little.[8] But by 1843, when he left the New York bench to assume a seat as associate justice of the United States Supreme Court, he had produced a body of opinions on local government matters that clearly fixed

6. John F. Dillon, *A Treatise on the Law of Municipal Corporations* (New York, 1872), 29.

7. See Edward K. Spann, *The New Metropolis: New York City, 1840–1857* (New York, 1981), 45–66 and passim; and especially Paul Boyer, *Urban Masses and Moral Order in America, 1820–1920* (Cambridge, Mass., 1978), for descriptions of analogous changes.

8. For a short biographical sketch, see Frank Otto Gatell, "Samuel Nelson," in Leon Friedman and Fred L. Israel, eds., *The Justices of the United States Supreme Court, 1789–1969*, 4 vols. (New York, 1969), 2:817–39.

the contours of the new law of municipal corporations. Some of his hold-ings proved controversial, and on occasion he was criticized and reversed by the politicized New York Court for the Correction of Errors (known usually as the Court of Errors), which was composed primarily of state senators and had the right to review the decisions of the New York Su-preme Court under the 1821 state constitution. But it is one measure of the growing autonomy of nineteenth-century American legal culture that his opinions remained influential in spite of their reversal and eventually were recognized as ruling case law.

Politically, Nelson always remained a conventional Jacksonian Demo-crat. Legally, he stands out as a committed and uncompromising legal positivist. His central legal values seem to have been an unshakable belief in the authority of the state combined with a visceral dislike of claims to vested rights.[9]

Two of his earliest local government decisions demonstate both of these values. In *People* v. *The Corporation of Albany* Nelson reviewed the convic-tion of the corporation of Albany for maintaining a nuisance when it failed to clean up rubbish in the basin of the Hudson River at the termination of the Erie Canal. The trial court instructed the jury that the corporation was liable if the jury was satisfied both that the condition constituted a nui-sance and that it was the duty of the corporation to abate the nuisance. According to the trial court, part of Albany's duty would then include re-moving the bulkhead erected by the canal company. Although the bulk-head had been specifically authorized by statute, the public health was paramount and justified its removal.

Nelson's opinion separated the duty of the corporation to abate nui-sances from its responsibility to remove the bulkhead. Insofar as the city had the power to remove the cause of the nuisance by cleaning out the basin, it also acquired a duty to use that power. Nelson asserted that the powers and the duties of a municipal corporation were indistinguishable. Its powers existed only to serve the public good, and thus its officers were "bound to execute them when demanded by the public interest."[10]

On the other hand, Nelson also held that the trial court had been mis-taken in instructing the jury that the corporation could be directed to cut down the bulkhead of the Erie Canal. A principle of public health or self-preservation would, he conceded, justify cutting down the bulkhead, if such a principle were available to the corporation. But there was nothing in the city's charter authorizing it to enforce that principle. And the city had no right to do anything without explicit authorization. Albany thus was "no more bound to perform the act by a supposed law of necessity

9. See, for example, his dissent in *Taylor* v. *Porter*, 4 Hill 140 (1843).
10. *People* v. *The Corporation of Albany*, 11 Wend. 539, 542–43 (1834).

for the protection of the public health or comfort than any individual citizen."[11]

In *People* v. *Morris* this perspective on the nature of local authority was expanded into a paradigmatic exposition of the new law of municipal corporation. The defendant in *Morris* was a grocer who had been convicted of selling liquor in his store without a license as a tavernkeeper. He challenged the statute under which he had been indicted on two grounds: first, that it divested the village of Ogdensburg, where he lived, of its traditional vested right to grant liquor licenses, and second, that even if the legislature had the power to preempt the provisions of the village charter it could do so only by a statute to which two-thirds of the members of each house of the legislature had assented.

For Nelson, the first challenge constituted something of a red flag. "Vested rights," he began, "are indefinite terms, and of extensive signification; not infrequently resorted to when no better argument exists. . . . Government was instituted for the purpose of modifying and regulating these rights with a view to the general good; and under the Constitution, the mode by which it was thought this great object' might best be attained, was left to the wisdom and direction of the people themselves, acting through the medium of their representatives." Even if rights might sometimes vest against the state, they certainly did not do so in behalf of a village. And the local power to grant licenses was in any case merely "political" in character. Private rights had nothing to do with the use of such tools to arrange the affairs of local governments. "It is an unsound and even absurd proposition that political power, conferred by the legislature, can become a vested right *as against the government* in any individual or body of men. It is repugnant to the genius of our institutions, and the spirit and meaning of the constitution; for by that fundamental law, all political rights not there defined, and taken out of the exercise of legislative discretion, were intended to be left subject to its regulation." Political power could never "belong" to the members of a public corporation. "How long it shall exist, or in what manner it shall be modified" were matters outside of the control of local authority and within the absolute discretion of the legislature.[12]

The defendant's second challenge to his conviction was founded on a provision in the 1821 state constitution mandating a two-thirds vote for any bill "creating, continuing, altering, or renewing any body politic or

11. Ibid., 544. Nelson, ever the positivist, thought little of any undefined principle, believing that such was never "enforced by the authority of law. . . . The law of the land does not contemplate such an exigency and, therefore, does not provide for it—if it had, it would no longer be the undefined law of necessity."

12. *People* v. *Morris*, 13 Wend. 325, 329–32 (1835).

corporate."[13] The provision had been drafted as a restraint on the ability of
the legislature to charter corporations. And Nelson was quick to point out
the distinction in form between corporate charters and general or public
laws like the one under which Morris was convicted. A literal interpretation of the provision would exempt all corporations from all forms of public regulation, to Nelson an obviously absurd result.[14]

But the more important reason for dismissing this second challenge was
the sheer inapplicability of the constitutional provision to public corporations. American municipal corporations were not, according to Nelson,
like English corporations. In England a charter was "in the nature of a bill
of rights." Here, by contrast, it constituted merely an institution of "municipal jurisdiction" (using the word "municipal" in the sense of internal
state law). American municipal corporations, furthermore, corresponded
"only in name" to private corporations. Private corporations were "the
private property of the corporators," and there were good economic reasons for protecting their charters from legislative intervention. By contrast, towns, counties, cities, or villages were merely "political institutions" incorporated "for the good government of the people." And the state
contracted with no one "in their creation, continuance, alteration, or renewal." Acts of public incorporation were therefore indistinguishable from
other public acts, all of which needed only a majority vote to become law.[15]

Opinions like Nelson's in *Morris* and *Albany* suggest the ascendancy of a
new understanding of the public-private distinction in the "law" of corporations.[16] *In Dartmouth College*, "public corporations" and "private corporations" had been uniformly regarded as subcategories within a compen-
dious definition of "corporations." For Marshall, the dichotomy defined
the constitutional reach of the legislature over different types of corporations. But both Story and Washington had left unanswered the question of
whether all American corporations had to be either "public" or "private,"
thus permitting Kent and others to claim that the corporation of the city of
New York remained at least partially private.

By the mid-1830s, however, "public corporations" and "private corporations" were increasingly viewed as separate categorical structures. No
public corporation could ever become a private corporation, nor would
any private entity assume public status. To Nelson it seemed beyond debate that a constitutional provision drafted to control the legislature's
treatment of private corporations should not restrict its treatment of pub-

13. Article VII, section 9.
14. *People* v. *Morris*, 13 Wend. 325, 333–38; Nelson's argument here closely parallels that
of Marshall in *Providence Bank* v. *Billings and Pittman*, 4 Peters 514 (1830).
15. *People* v. *Morris*, 13 Wend. 325, 334–35, 337–38.
16. See *Spaulding* v. *Lowell*, 23 Pick. 71 (Mass. Sup. Jud. Ct., 1839).

lic entities, for the differences between the two were both obvious and irreducible. And even Kent, who in 1827 had defined the public nature of cities in the most ambiguous terms possible, had changed his mind by 1836. In the third edition of the *Commentaries on American Law*, he conceded that a city was unquestionably a public corporation whose powers were "subject to the control of the legislature of the state." If a city were empowered to hold private property for municipal purposes, such property would be "invested with the security of other private rights." But the presence of property did nothing to change the public nature of the municipal corporation.[17]

Even when cities had private aspects they remained public institutions. This did not mean that analogies to private corporations would disappear from the developing law of municipal corporations. For particular purposes or in particular situations a municipal corporation would be treated in the same way as a private corporation. But as the contrast between public corporations and private entities grew more absolute, judges began to use the law of private corporations as a way of defining by negation the nature of a public entity.

Just as Nelson did in *People* v. *Morris*, they often identified what made a corporation public by describing what made other corporations private. To learn what a municipal corporation was, it was first necessary to know what it was not. Judges often cited Joseph Angell and Samuel Ames's *Treatise on the Law of Private Corporations Aggregate* (a work whose publication in 1832 was justified by its authors on the basis of the need felt by the legal community for a treatise solely devoted to the study of private corporations) as authority for the public character of public corporations.[18]

It is possible to exaggerate the significance of the public-private dichotomy for the law of municipal corporations. The dichotomy offered a structure of argument and justification. But it is not clear, at least to me, that much was changed substantively in courts' treatment of local governments. At no time after the American Revolution would Morris have been likely to sustain his claim that the village of Ogdensburg owned its right to grant liquor licenses in the same way that a bridge company owned its right to charge a toll.

Still, we might expect that one substantive consequence of the absolute tone of a case like *People* v. *Morris* would have been the obliteration of the

17. James Kent, *Commentaries on American Law*, 3d ed., 4 vols. (New York, 1836), 2:275.
18. Joseph Angell and Samuel Ames, *A Treatise on the Law of Private Corporations Aggregate* (Boston, 1832), preface, 8, 21, 22. See, for example, *Hamilton County* v. *Mighels*, 7 Ohio St. 109 (1857); *Berlin* v. *Gorham*, 34 N.H. 266 (1856); *Paterson* v. *Society for Establishing Useful Manufacturers*, 24 N.J.L. 385 (1854); *Robie* v. *Sedgwick and Hardenbrouck*, 35 Barb. 319 (N.Y. Sup. Ct., 1861); *Bow* v. *Allentown*, 34 N.H. 351 (1857).

traditional justification for distinguishing entities like the corporation of the city of New York from other local governments. Nelson stated in dicta: "Any person who will look into the powers and privileges conferred upon towns and counties, and their qualified right of self-government in reference to their domestic regulations . . . and into the charters of the several cities and villages, will not fail to perceive that the only essential difference that exists between these corporate bodies, arises mainly from the difference in the extent of their territory, the density of their population, and the nature of their occupations."[19] The "law" regulating the corporation of the city of New York should be, if it was not already, of a piece with the law of municipal corporations generally. Once the nature of an entity became a matter of judicial definition, the presence of a charter—however private in its nature—would cease to distinguish it from other entities similarly defined.

But even as the Jacksonian Nelson argued the case for a unitary law of municipal corporations in New York State, other New York judges continued to stress the distinctiveness of the powers of New York City. In denying a bill for an injunction to stop the city from taking particular lands for streets, for example, Chancellor Reuben H. Walworth held that "it would certainly be both unwise and inexpedient for this court to stop the proceedings of a body whose powers and duties are more important to the public than those of the legislatures of some of our sister states."[20] And in an important series of decisions by the Court of Errors on the power of the corporation to assess the value of property taken for new city streets, a contrast emerged between city streets and those in more rural communities. "The rule of law applicable to the former are not so to the latter."[21]

Nothing in those decisions denied the public nature of the city of New York or its place within a state polity. To the contrary, the purpose behind the city-country dichotomy developed in street valuation cases was to create a uniform analytic framework that could be applied anywhere within New York State. New York City was seen as a particular kind of place rather than as a particular legal entity.[22] And although judges might stand in awe of the powers of the corporation, they were also careful to emphasize how different the corporation was from any private entity.[23]

19. *People* v. *Morris*, 13 Wend. 325, 330.
20. *Champlin* v. *The Corporation of New York*, 3 Paige, 573, 575–76 (1832). See also *Dening* v. *Roome*, 6 Wend. 651, 655–56 (1831); *Stokes and Gilbert* v. *The Corporation of the City of New York*, 14 Wend. 87 (1835).
21. *Wyman* v. *Mayor of New York*, 11 Wend. 486, 494 (1833); *Livingston* v. *The Mayor of New York*, 8 Wend. 85 (1831).
22. *Livingston* v. *Mayor of New York*, 98.
23. See *Denning* v. *Roome*, 6 Wend. 651, 655 (1831).

But what remained unsettled was the question of whether all public entities were necessarily alike in their relationship to the sovereign state. If *People* v. *Morris* meant what Nelson intended it to mean, the answer was clear. But other judges saw in his reasoning a general attack on private property rights and regarded his opinion as a willful misreading of the language of the 1821 Constitution.[24]

In 1840 this conflict surfaced in a *quo warranto* action brought by the state attorney general against the officers of the corporation. Those officers still had the right to sit as judges in the New York County courts, in accordance with the terms of the Montgomerie Charter. Yet a section of the 1821 Constitution directed that all judicial officers except justices of the peace had to be nominated by the state senate. According to the attorney general, that provision necessarily voided the charter. "The constitution is paramount to the charter of the city, and if there is any incongruity, the constitution must prevail, even to the entire destruction of the charter." The fact that the city's charter was covered by the constitution's continuing guarantee of the security of the prerevolutionary grants (which had been carried over from the 1777 Constitution) made no difference, because "the exercise of judicial power is a public and political right, which is incapable of becoming vested in any number short of the whole people." And the constitution should receive the same "construction" in New York City as it did in any other county.[25]

But Associate Justice Greene C. Bronson, with the silent concurrence of Samuel Nelson (who had been made chief justice in 1837), denied the attorney general's action on the legalistic grounds that the mayor and aldermen were not judicial officers. Bronson argued that the constitution mentioned only judicial officers, and the attorney general's argument was based on the faulty assumption that every person who exercised judicial powers was thereby a judicial officer. Most public officials made "judicial" decisions, yet that did not make them judges. To hold against the city, moreover, would unnecessarily bring one part of the constitution into conflict with another part and create the false impression that the 1821 Constitution took away some of the corporation's chartered powers.[26]

When the attorney general appealed to the Court of Errors, Bronson's holding was sustained, though only because the court found itself evenly divided on the question. Chancellor Walworth voted to affirm the supreme court's decision, arguing, "The adoption of a new constitution by a politi-

24. Samuel Nelson had been a member of the 1821 constitutional convention. See Gatell, "Samuel Nelson," 817–18.
25. *The People* v. *The Mayor and Aldermen of New York*, 25 Wend. 9, 27–29 (1840).
26. Ibid., 23–26.

cal body already organized and established is not, as was contended in this case, a bloodless revolution, which is to sweep away all existing institutions whose continuance is not expressly provided for in the Constitution itself. On the contrary, it leaves all existing institutions and officers not expressly abolished and continuance of which is not inconsistent with the letter or the spirit of such new constitution in the same state in which it found them." But Senators Abram Dixon and Laurens Hull both relied on Nelson's *People* v. *Morris* opinion to urge the Court of Errors to reverse the supreme court. Hull thought the 1821 Constitution's guarantee of pre-revolutionary charters should be read to protect "only such rights . . . as could be properly regarded as vested, such as rights of property, and not to establish or perpetuate beyond the reach of legislative control, rights of a mere political character."[27]

The tie vote of the Court of Errors did not end the matter, however. Within a year the state legislature passed an act creating a new court structure for New York City bypassing entirely the officers of the corporation. And now it was the officers of the corporation who filed an action *quo warranto* against the "pretentions" to office of the new local judges appointed under the act.[28]

According to Bronson, the issue raised this time had nothing to do with "the power of the legislature to alter the charters of public corporations without their consent." On that question he and the other judges of the New York Supreme Court were in agreement. The powers of government cannot, "from their very nature, be the subject of an inalienable grant. They may be recalled at pleasure." The issue the new statute raised was whether such a modification in the charter required a two-thirds vote of each house of the legislature. Nelson, of course, had argued in *Morris* that the requirement did not apply to public corporations, and he and Esek Cowen together outvoted Bronson to deny the *quo warranto*. But for Bronson, nothing in the two-thirds rule provision of the 1821 Constitution indicated that public corporations should be distinguished from private corporations. "If the clause can be so construed . . . it may then, I think, be set down as an established fact, that the English language is too poor for the framing of fundamental laws which shall limit the powers of the legislative branch of the government."[29]

And this time the Court of Errors reversed. Such a statute was held to be void, absent a two-thirds vote, and Nelson's holding in *Morris* that public corporations could be modified by a simple majority vote of the legisla-

27. Ibid., 33, 61.
28. *The People* v. *Purdy*, 2 Hill 31 (1841).
29. Ibid., 33, 35–36. See also *The People* v. *The Mayor and Aldermen of New York*, 25 Wend. 9, 26 (1840).

ture was specifically overruled. According to Senator Alonzo C. Paige, the terms of the provision in the constitution were "comprehensive, explicit and unambiguous. They express, with a distinctness and force which to my mind is irresistible, an intention to include *all* corporations, whether public or private."[30]

The opinions in *People* v. *The Mayor and Aldermen of New York* and *Purdy* v. *The People* should not be read as endorsements of the autonomy of the corporation of the city of New York from legislative control. They were, rather, skirmishes in a continuing war between the "legalistic" New York Supreme Court and the "political" Court of Errors over the proper interpretation of the section of the 1821 Constitution that regulated incorporations.[31] By the late 1830s and early 1840s, corporations—public as well as private—no longer evoked the particular fears and passions that had justified the rule requiring a two-thirds vote in each house in 1821. What had once been regarded as a virtuous restraint on the powers of a republican legislature was now characterized as "either a political blunder of men who wished to remedy an existing evil without knowing how, or it was a stratagem of interested men to perpetuate existing monopolies, by rendering the creation almost hopeless of competing new institutions."[32] The need for the provision was no longer felt. Yet the provision still remained in the constitution. How should it be interpreted? Were banks chartered under the new Free Banking Act of 1838 corporations or associations? If the latter, the provision arguably did not apply. But if the former, a general corporation statute that allowed banks or businesses to come into existence without a special vote of the legislature became unconstitutional.

The arguments bounced back and forth as case after case was appealed first to the New York Supreme Court and then to the Court of Errors. By 1845 Senator Augustus Hand of the Court of Errors concluded that there was "no escape from the charge of irreconcilable inconsistency in our decisions."[33]

30. *Purdy* v. *The People*, 4 Hill 384, 395 (1842).
31. *Thomas* v. *Dakin*, 22 Wend. 9 (1839); *Warner* v. *Beers*, and *Bolander* v. *Stevens*, 23 Wend. 103 (1840); *The People* v. *The Assessors of Watertown*, 1 Hill 616 (1841); *People* v. *The Supervisors of Niagara*, 4 Hill 20 (1842), aff'd., 7 Hill 504 (1842); *DeBow* v. *The People*, 1 Denio 9 (1845); *Gifford* v. *Livingston*, 2 Denio 380 (1845). These cases are critically analyzed in Bray Hammond, *Banks and Politics in America from the Revolution to the Civil War* (Princeton, 1957), 572–600.
32. A. B. Johnson, "The Legislative History of Corporations in the State of New York, or, The Progress of Liberal Sentiments," *Hunt's Merchants Magazine* 23 (1850):610–14, reprinted in Carter Goodrich, ed., *The Government and the Economy, 1783–1861* (Indianapolis, 1960), 396–405.
33. *Gifford* v. *Livingston*, 2 Denio 380, 394 (1845).

But in the midst of angry opinions and constitutional controversy, members of both courts agreed that *People* v. *Morris* had been wrongly decided. Aside from Nelson, who left the supreme court in 1843, no one dared argue that the meaning of the 1821 provision should be reinterpreted to save it from anachronism. According to the others, the language of the 1821 Constitution neither mandated a distinction between public and private corporations nor insisted that the legislature treat all local governments alike.[34]

But if it did not, most of the judges conceded that it should have. And when delegates met in Albany in the summer of 1846 to draft a new state constitution they found that local government gave them little to argue about.

The convention voted without much debate to remove the section of the 1821 Constitution that had protected prerevolutionary royal grants. Henry C. Murphy, a Brooklyn Democrat who took the lead in all the convention's discussions of matters local governmental, argued that the old provision had promoted "a very common error in this community—an extensive error—that there was something in charters before the formation of the constitution, so very sacred, that they might not be touched, whilst charters granted since might be touched."[35] But if it was a common error, it was one few delegates committed in 1846. As Murphy himself conceded, even in New York and Albany there were those "who did not believe that chartered rights were of such a nature as to prevent an exercise of sovereignty here, with a view to correct evils." And, according to Robert Morris, a former New York City mayor, "There had been no man anywhere . . . that would contend for a doctrine such as his friend [Murphy] had so eloquently argued against."[36] By the mid-1840s the notion that special privileges or grants might continue to protect some cities from the reach of the sovereign had become too absurd to be treated seriously.

The rule requiring a two-thirds vote by both houses of the legislature on matters regarding corporations also disappeared quietly. But when the convention's committee on private corporations reported out a draft sec-

34. Compare Bronson in *De Bow* v. *People*, 1 Denio 9, with Walworth and Hand in *Gifford* v. *Livingston*, 2 Denio 380.

35. S. Crosswell and R. Sutton, reporters, *Debates and Proceedings in the New York State Convention for the Revision of the Constitution* (New York, 1846), 82. An alternative source for the 1846 convention is Bishop and Attree, reporters, *Debates and Proceedings* (New York, 1846). On Murphy, see Henry R. Stiles, ed., *The Civic, Political, Professional and Ecclesiastical History and Commercial and Industrial Record of the County of Kings and the City of Brooklyn, N.Y. from 1683 to 1884*, 2 vols. (New York, 1884), 1:360–66.

36. Crosswell and Sutton, *Debates and Proceedings*, 119–20. See Howard Lee McBain, *The Law and Practice of Municipal Home Rule* (New York, 1916), 34. On the general consensus on questions of state-corporate relations, see Meyers, *Jacksonian Persuasion*, 260–67.

tion banning special laws and requiring general incorporation statutes, Murphy tried to amend the section to include municipal corporations as well. The section was intended to promote "the same equality of rights as well between corporations themselves as between corporations and individuals." Yet the "grossest violations of personal rights were to be found in our municipal corporations" rather than among private ones. As a good citizen of Brooklyn, Murphy then proceeded to sketch out the "feudal" structure of the corporation of the city of New York. But his main argument rested on the lack of uniformity in governments across the state as a result of their reliance on special legislation. Good legislation was always general legislation, which spoke in terms of the citizens of the whole state. By contrast, a special act or charter was usually "a piece of empiricism by the wiseacres of the place where it is to be put in force."[37]

Murphy lost the latter argument. Evidently the members of the 1846 convention thought it more important to maintain a consistent separation of public from private corporations than to include municipal corporations in a general ban on special legislation. And the final document simply made it the duty of the legislature to provide for the organization of cities and villages and "especially" to oversee the fiscal affairs of local governments "so as to prevent abuses."

The formal structure of local government and its place in the political order raised little debate within the convention, but somewhat more conflict ensued when Murphy proposed a section that abolished all municipal offices responsible for the inspection of goods and produce. To Murphy and the vast majority of delegates, this was an obvious political reform. The recorders of the convention noted that "he felt gratified that he could stand here acting in consonance with . . . public opinion and at the same time according to the dictates of his own judgment." Businessmen would assuredly be "sharpsighted" in their dealings with one another, and in a free society everyone in the community should be presumed honest. Inspections constituted "improper interferences with the private dealings of individuals" and, in any case, almost inevitably failed to achieve their goal of ensuring quality. "The great question," as another delegate put it, "was whether we could not reduce the patronage of the government" by eliminating an "army" of inspectors. Such a responsibility should not be left to the will of the legislature, for the inspectors—particularly those of the city of New York—were a well-organized interest group that would besiege the members of the legislature, and "crows would be white" and "the sky would rain larks" before any legislative reform of inspections would occur.[38]

37. Crosswell and Sutton, *Debates and Proceedings*, 739.
38. Ibid., 398–400. The inspectorial system was abolished by a vote of 94 to 10.

This proposal was, of course, intended as an attack on a franchise of the corporation of the city of New York.[39] One delegate from the city put the matter directly. It seemed to him that such proposals revealed that the goal of the convention was to prevent "in every possible way . . . the city of New York from enjoying any benefit from legislation, and of crippling its prosperity." Proponents of the measure denied the charge but in a manner suggesting that there may have been some truth to it. One delegate "repelled the idea that either the convention or committee intended any injury to the city of New York," and he asked the city's representatives "what sort of a community" they had, "if their statements were to be believed. . . . It was said that merchants had weights and scales [there] and yet no one would trust them." Another proponent insisted that "he did not wish to apply any rule to the city of New York which he was not willing to have applied to the country."[40]

City power may not have been the primary evil to be overcome by the new state constitution. But the debate in the convention over inspection laws suggests that the existence of the corporation of the city of New York raised particular problems for the delegates and others who thought about the construction of the state's political order. It was not New York City's status as a public corporation that created controversy, however; it was its position as a public body capable of getting what it wanted from the legislature. Those who argued for the constitutional abolition of inspection laws felt that such a decision could not be left to the legislature. They did not trust state legislators to secure the general public interest in opposition to the sustained efforts of an entity like the corporation of the city of New York.

The 1846 state constitution revealed New York City as a public, municipal corporation. Its charter no longer identified it as a distinctively private entity in a world of local governments. Yet the basic problem that the corporation had always presented for republican legal theory remained: How was an entity as large and politically potent as New York City to be con-

39. On the other hand, it is not clear that that franchise was still of much value to the city. See *The Mayor of New York* v. *Nichols*, 4 Hill 209 (1843).

40. Crosswell and Sutton, *Debates and Proceedings*, 399–402. George Templeton Strong called the new constitution a "bungling piece of radical legislation" and wished "no severer punishment to the fools, quacks, and demagogues who brewed that precious instrument . . . than to be compelled to write notes and commentaries on the work of their own dirty hands till they can show that it had some good points somewhere and is not shallow and slovenly and incoherent and contemptible even beyond what sensible people had a right to expect from its authors." Reading it, Strong reported, gave "one a taste for the crime of treason generally and in the abstract" (*Diary*, ed. Allan Nevins and Milton H. Thomas, 4 vols. [New York, 1952], 1:284, 296–97).

trolled? How to ensure that city government behaved virtuously within a republican political order?

The city's dependence on state legislation provided no solution, for although the city was enmeshed in it, the result was less rather than more public scrutiny. Not only did the state legislature do practically everything the city wished, but the legislature's presence as a continuing provider of authority for municipal action made judicial action difficult, if not impossible. The prevailing constitutional norms of the mid-nineteenth century insisted that public action—action under the banner of legislative power—not be subject to judicial review.

To make New York City into an entity whose powers would be subject to legal control demanded, paradoxically, that courts reaffirm not the public nature of the municipal corporation but, to the contrary, its likeness to private entities. Judges learned to distinguish the city from the sovereignty of the state in order to establish their power to scrutinize municipal affairs. And they constructed a law of municipal corporations, which emphasized the separation of local government from sovereign authority.

CHAPTER 14

The Judicial Creation of
a Municipal Corporation

Between 1835 and 1860, appellate judges created a new American law of municipal corporations. In his treatise, John Dillon, then still a judge on the Iowa Supreme Court, gave formal—one might almost say final—expression to this new legal subject. And like other treatise writers of the time he invested his subject with a pedigree that stretched back to a time to which the memory of man runneth not. But even Dillon had to concede that it was "remarkable how many changes were necessary to adapt" the old English municipal system "to our system of government and modes of administration and to the wants and situation of our people."[1] The citations in his footnotes reveal the degree to which his law of municipal corporations was the creation of mid-nineteenth-century America. In the two crucial conceptual chapters of the book—"Chapter Four: Public and Private Corporations Distinguished—Legislative Authority and Its Limitations," and "Chapter Five: Municipal Charters" (subtitled, "General Municipal Powers.—Their Nature and Construction.")—almost every assertion in the text found support in references to state court decisions of the preceding forty years. No lines of continuity bound the judicial doctrines of municipal corporation law to the ancient common law. For authority Dillon could look only to the opinions of the immediate American past.

Although the initial premise of this new legal subject was the dependence of localities on legislative authority, there remained a good deal of ambiguity in the ways courts perceived the relationship of municipal corporations to state legislatures. For the most part, nineteenth-century legal authorities placed the public, state-oriented aspect of local government at

1. John F. Dillon, *A Treatise on the Law of Municipal Corporations* (New York, 1872), 1–26, v.

the center of their conception of the institution.[2] But some insisted that
even as creations of legislative policy, municipal corporations remained the
governments of communities whose interests could be distinguished from
those of the state as a whole.[3] To at least a minority of judges, local governments existed as manifestations of unwritten or customary constitutional
values that would be respected by any conscientious legislature.[4] No one
denied that "a municipal corporation may be . . . imposed upon the corporators without their consent." But, according to the New Jersey Supreme Court,

> It would be alike against the genius of our government and the spirit
> of the British constitution. It would be, in the nervous language of
> Lord Thurlow, an atrocious violation of principle, which would cut
> every Englishman to the bone. Almost invariably in practice munici-
> pal charters have been granted or altered by our legislature, in ac-
> cordance with the expressed will of the corporators. The exceptions
> are very rare. They have occurred in seasons of high excitement;
> they cannot be reconciled to sound principle. They are to be re-
> garded as beacons to be shunned, not as precedents to be followed.
> Before imposing the burthens of a city charter upon a people, the
> legislators not only may, but ought to require the assent of the
> corporators.[5]

It was not the actual relationship between cities and the state that justified judicial intervention into the affairs of local governments. For the
most part, judges regarded that as outside their proper sphere of authority.
Rather, it was the dangers municipal governments posed to the rights
of private individuals and to the institution of private property. Mid-
nineteenth-century American judges took the protection of property as
their particular domain. In the conduct of the American city and of its
agents, they saw a serious and significant challenge to the security of private estates. As taxpayers, property owners faced the prospect of being
compelled by municipal extravagance to become involuntary contributors

2. Ibid., 96; see John Bouvier, *A Law Dictionary*, 1st to 11th eds. (Philadelphia, 1839–
65), under heading "Corporations."
3. See Bouvier, *Law Dictionary*, 12th ed., 2 vols. (1868), 2:201 (under heading "Municipal Corporation"). See also Alexander M. Burrill, *A Law Dictionary and Glossary*, 2d ed.
(New York, 1859), 2:215, which defined a municipal corporation as "a public corporation, a
corporation created by government for political purposes and having subordinate legislative
powers to be exercised for local purposes, such as a county, city, town, or village."
4. See *People ex rel. Wood* v. *Draper*, 15 N.Y. 532, 558 (1857) (Brown, dissenting); *People
ex rel. Le Roy* v. *Hurlburt*, 24 Mich. 44, 97–98 (1871) (Cooley, concurring).
5. *City of Paterson* v. *The Society for Establishing Useful Manufactures*, 24 NJL 385 (1854).

in enterprises in which they had no interest or which were actually contrary to their private interests.[6] As urban landowners, they were at the mercy of municipal governments, which could destroy the value of their holdings with a single decision.[7]

In the governmental conduct of the American city (both real and potential), judges found a legal equivalent to the moral dangers antebellum reformers perceived in urban social disorder. Just as evangelical reformers raised the specter of homeless boys adrift in the city without the moorings of Protestant faith and discipline, so American judges viewed the wastefulness and heedlessness of municipal action as a symptom of a moral breakdown of government.[8] Both urban reformers and judicial activists saw the city as a challenge to republican values. For the reformers, institutions like the Sunday School and the YMCA, which recreated the discipline and order of the rural family and of small-town America, were all that kept the urban young from a dissolute and degraded existence. For judges, judicial intervention was all that restrained corrupt city governments that had lost all sense of republican virtue.[9]

The difficulty lay in formulating a justification for judicial intervention. Local action, no matter how reckless or harmful, invariably occurred under the banner of legislative authority. But in antebellum America formal judicial deference to the legislature remained constitutional dogma. Private litigants often argued for the prima facie illegitimacy of government action that restricted or injured or devalued their property. But even the most sympathetic judge lacked the tools necessary to legitimize such an analysis of legislatively authorized action. There was as yet no Fourteenth Amendment to the Constitution, no "state action" doctrine. The Fifth Amendment did not apply to the states,[10] and state constitutional provisions were seldom viewed as restraints on government expropriations.[11] State constitutions, in fact, were never interpreted as restricting public initiatives that happened incidentally to harm private property.[12]

To fulfill their self-defined role as defenders of private rights, judges needed doctrinal language that could be used as a wedge to split apart the

6. See the dissenting opinion of Judge Lowrie in *Sharpless* v. *The Mayor of Philadelphia*, *American Law Register*, old ser., 2 (1854):29, 35.

7. See cases cited in Chapter 12.

8. See *Sharpless* v. *The Mayor of Philadelphia*, 21 Penn. St. 158 (1853) and *American Law Register*, old ser., 2 (1854):27–43, 85–112.

9. See, in particular, Paul Boyer, *Urban Masses and Moral Order* (Cambridge, Mass., 1978), 65–120, and Edward K. Spann, *The New Metropolis* (New York, 1981), 65–66.

10. See *Barron and Craig* v. *The Mayor of Baltimore*, 7 Pet. 243 (1830).

11. Harry Scheiber, "Property Law, Expropriation, and Resource Allocation, 1789–1910," *Journal of Economic History* 33 (1973):232–48.

12. See Chapter 12.

cozy relationship between municipal action and political sovereignty. Cities had to be separated from legislative empowerments and from sovereign immunities, without challenging legislative sovereignty itself. The goal, as Dillon indicated, was to resolve all doubts "whether the legislature intended to confer the authority in question . . . in favor of the citizen, and against the municipality."[13] One result was a rule of strict statutory interpretation (known to later generations as Dillon's Rule), which raised such doubts systematically.

A municipality had only such powers as were granted to it in specific and unambiguous statutory language. All legislative grants were to be interpreted against an enlarged exercise of authority by the municipality, whatever the implicit intent of the legislature in making the grant. Even traditional municipal functions would fail to secure judicial approval, absent explicit statutory authorization.[14]

Ironically, this rule was first formulated as a way of controlling the expansion of powers granted to private entities.[15] As late as 1836, Chancellor Kent, who is usually credited with originating the rule, wrote that the "broad and latitudinary powers" granted to the New York Common Council, "were given to be exercised with sound discretion, and with a liberal spirit commensurate with the growing wants and prosperity of a great commercial metropolis. The courts construe powers liberally, for such purposes."[16]

But by the 1840s a rule of strict statutory interpretation emerged as the symbolic center of the doctrinal structure of local government law.[17] It was applied to the actions of New York City as well as to those of smaller towns.[18] And its invocation resulted in numbers of anomalous decisions.[19] Its effect on the exercise of municipal power is harder to determine. Cities presumably became all the more committed to obtaining formal legislative

13. Dillon, *Treatise on Municipal Corporations*, 104.

14. Ibid., 101–5.

15. See Chapter 12.

16. James Kent, *The Charter of the City of New York, with notes thereon. Also a Treatise on the Powers and Duties of the Mayor, Aldermen, and Assistant Aldermen, and the Journal of the City Convention* (New York, 1836), 133.

17. *Spaulding* v. *Lowell*, 23 Pick. 71 (Mass. Sup. J. Ct., 1839); *Hodges* v. *City of Buffalo*, 2 Denio 110 (N.Y. Sup. Ct., 1846).

18. "These principles are so obviously in accordance with the end and object of the creation of this class of governmental agencies that their correctness must be acknowledged by every one, and yet if we were to judge from the conduct of municipal corporations alone, we would conclude that there was no limitation of their powers, at least of their power of levying taxes" (*Halstead* v. *The Mayor of New York*, 3 N.Y. 430, 433 [1850]; *The Mayor of New York* v. *Nichols*, 4 Hill 109 [N.Y. Sup. Ct., 1843]).

19. See, for example, *Dean* v. *Charlton*, 23 Wisc. 590 (1869) and *Robb* v. *The City of Indianapolis*, 38 Ind. 49 (1871).

authorization for contemplated activities. But one might hypothesize that its primary impact would have been on the size and professionalization of municipal legal departments, which now needed to take more care in the wording of the statutes they drafted.

For our purposes, though, Dillon's Rule is most important as an indication of a new judicial attitude toward local government. Rather than allowing the legislature to prescribe the terms of municipal delegations statute by statute, courts developed uniform "objective" judicial standards to evaluate the legitimacy of municipal conduct. Judges would decide what a statute gave a city, and they would do so using formal legal categories that defined the legal rights of the municipality independently of any legislation. Although stated as rules of statutory interpretation, the effect of these standards was to interpose judicial authority between the legislature and the city, leaving it to judges to determine whether a particular statute authorized particular local acts and what the consequences of legislative authorization would be.

This formal rule structure still today is what most lawyers mean when they speak of the law of municipal corporations. In its development the New York courts of the middle third of the nineteenth century played a particularly important role. Commentators such as Dillon did not always like what the New York courts did, but they had to recognize that New York decisions established much of the conceptual framework of municipal corporation law.[20] Cases involving the corporation of the city of New York as a litigant became leading cases, cited throughout the country as authoritative statements of the nature of local governments generally. And the categories the New York courts developed to analyze the peculiar legal situation of New York City were applied everywhere to define the legal rights and responsibilities of the American municipal corporation.

In the mid-1830s the corporation wrested control of the municipal water supply from the Manhattan Company, which finally acknowledged that banking was its true vocation, and the city began work on one of the great public works of the nineteenth century—the Croton Aqueduct. The waters of the Croton River in northern Westchester County were diverted to the city, where they formed the basis for a replenished and enlarged city water supply. In this case, at least, public enterprise clearly outdid private enterprise, giving the lie to Hamilton's 1799 prediction. By 1842, the aqueduct, a series of reservoirs, and a dam across the Croton River were all complete, and in October of that year the city held a huge Croton Water

20. See the extended opinion of Chief Justice Campbell in *Detroit* v. *Blackeby*, 21 Mich. 84 (1870); Dillon, *Treatise on Municipal Corporations*, 83, 723, and passim; *American Law Register*, new ser., 9 (1868):670.

Celebration, complete with parades, speeches, and an ode to water. For at least a short moment, according to Philip Hone, "The moral as well as the physical influence of water pervaded everything. Ardent Liquors were not proof against its predominating powers."[21]

At about the same time that New Yorkers were celebrating the introduction of "clear, sweet, soft water" into the city,[22] Chief Justice Samuel Nelson was delivering the opinion of the court in the case of *Bailey* v. *The Mayor*, an opinion that would be as celebrated in the history of the law of municipal corporations as the Croton waterworks would be in the history of municipal enterprise.[23] The plaintiffs in the case had had a dam across the Croton River, which they used to provide power for several mills. When the upstream dam built by the Croton water commissioners as part of the new waterworks broke, however, it allowed the river's waters to sweep down on the plaintiffs' dam, demolishing their dam, flume, sluices, mills, machinery, and buildings. And Bailey and his associates proceeded to sue the city for the negligence of its agents, the Croton water commissioners.

At trial, the lower court held that the plaintiffs had no remedy against the corporation of the city of New York because the dam was the work of the water commissioners, who had been appointed by the state and were therefore not the city's agents. On appeal, the corporation further insisted that the plaintiffs lacked a cause of action against the city, even if the water commissioners were regarded as the city's agents. The corporation was acting in a public capacity and hence was not responsible for the misconduct of those necessarily employed by it.[24] But Nelson reversed, holding the city liable for the acts of the water commissioners.

He began his opinion by conceding the corporation's contention that if it was acting in a public capacity it would be free from liability, whether or not the water commissioners were regarded as its agents. But, Nelson con-

21. Allan Nevins, ed., *The Diary of Philip Hone, 1828–1851* (New York, 1936), 625.

22. Ibid., 609. George Templeton Strong, characteristically, disagreed. On 1 August 1842, he wrote, "There's nothing new in town, except the Croton Water, which is full of tadpoles and animalculae, and which moreover flows through an aqueduct which I hear was used as a necessary by all the Hibernian vagabonds who worked upon it. I shall drink no Croton for some time to come. Post has drunk some of it and is in dreadful apprehensions of breeding bullfrogs inwardly" *Diary*, ed. Allan Nevins and Milton H. Thomas, 4 vols. (New York, 1952), 1:184.

23. See James D. Barnett, "The Foundations of the Distinction between Public and Private Functions in Respect to the Common-Law Tort Liability of Municipal Corporations (The Antecedents of *Bailey* v. *The City of New York*)," *Oregon Law Review* 16 (1937):250; E. M. Borchard, "Government Liability in Tort," *Yale Law Journal* 34 (1924–25):1–43, 129–43, and 36 (1926–27), 1–41, 757–807, 1039–1100, and *Columbia Law Review* 28 (1928):557–614, 734–75.

24. *Bailey* v. *The Mayor*, 3 Hill 531, 537–38.

tinued, the city was not acting in its public capacity. The power to construct the Croton waterworks had not been "conferred for the benefit of the public." It was, rather, "a special, private franchise, made as well for the private emolument and advantage of the city, as for the public good. The State, in its sovereign character, has no interest in it. It owns no part of the work. The whole investment . . . are a part of the private property of the city; as much so as the lands and houses belonging to it."[25]

The difference between public powers and private grants was "quite clear and well settled, and the process of separation practicable." Citing his opinion in *People* v. *Morris*, as well as *Dartmouth College*, Nelson argued that if a power were granted "for public purposes exclusively," it belonged to the corporation in its "public, political or municipal character." But whenever a grant offered a private advantage to the city, "though the public may derive a common benefit therefrom," the city owned it in the same way as if it were a private company.[26] The municipal corporation obtained the benefits of public status only when its actions bore no similarity to those of a private entity. Thus securing the public health by providing a public water supply was not enough to make the Croton waterworks a public activity of the corporation, at least for the purpose of assigning liability.

Once Nelson had determined that the Croton project was part of the private sphere of the corporation, it followed that the commissioners were the corporation's agents. The fact that the commissioners had been appointed by the state made no difference, for their appointment was "but one of the conditions upon which the charter [of the project] was granted." When the corporation accepted that "charter" it also accepted the commissioners as its agents. That acceptance must have been voluntary, according to Nelson, because under *Dartmouth College* the state could not have enforced a private grant against the wishes of the corporation. And in this case that legal conclusion was reinforced by the actual terms of the legislation, which permitted the city to adopt or reject the commissioners' plans, even after their appointment.[27]

Bailey is usually regarded in modern local government law as the foundation of the distinction between the public and private spheres of the municipal corporation.[28] That distinction, of course, had roots in earlier judicial analyses of the corporation of the city of New York, and Nel-

25. Ibid., 538–39.

26. Ibid., 539.

27. Ibid., 543–45. Nelson's opinion was affirmed by the Court of Errors. See *Mayor of New York* v. *Bailey*, 2 Denio 433 (1845).

28. See Borchard, "Government Liability in Tort," *Yale Law Journal* 34 (1924–25): 132–34; Dillon, *Treatise on Municipal Corporations*, 82–84. For modern reliance on the

son's opinion borrowed the vocabulary of cases such as *Brick Presbyterian Church*. Yet the field of action to which that vocabulary was applied had changed.[29] The Croton waterworks was not a part of the private holdings of the old corporation. Nor did it resemble other "private" franchises. Nelson analogized the water supply to a hypothetical legislative grant to the city of banking powers or of a railway charter. But obvious distinctions could have been drawn. The state legislature had not authorized the project as a source of municipal revenue. Whatever fees the city might ultimately secure from the distribution of Croton water were dwarfed by the monumental costs of the project. As of 1842, construction of the works had already produced a $7 million debt for the city. Taxes had to be raised to pay the interest throughout the 1840s and 1850s, for revenues never approached the size of the debt service.[30] If this was private enterprise, it was of a remarkably unsuccessful form.[31]

The effect of Nelson's holding was to transform a municipal activity assumed by city leaders as well as the legislature to be part of the corporation's public sphere into a private activity, at least for purposes of assessing liability. To Dillon, who lamented the division of municipal powers into two classes, this particular public-private dichotomy had no logical basis within the law of municipal corporations. The only explanation lay in Nelson's desire "to escape technical difficulties in order to hold such corporations liable to private actions."[32]

The technical difficulty that Dillon recognized was the doctrine of sovereign immunity. If the municipal corporation was nothing but a public entity, then it was indistinguishable from other agencies of public administration, all of which were free from the risk of civil liability. And individuals would have to look to the legislature for redress.

But the problem that municipal action presented to judges arose out of their perception that the legislature could or would not control it. In the judges' view, legislative authorization did not necessarily ensure that a public entity was acting in a properly public manner. The issue addressed by *Bailey* was how to determine when a local government was acting in

---

governmental-proprietary dichotomy, see *City of Lafayette* v. *Louisiana Power & Light Co.*, 435 U.S. 389 (1978) (particularly the concurring opinion of Chief Justice Burger).

29. See, likewise, *Britton* v. *Mayor of New York*, 21 How. Pr. Rep. 251 (N.Y. Sup. Ct., 1843).

30. See David T. Valentine, "Financial History of the City of New York," *Manual of the Corporation of the City of New York* (New York, 1859), 535; Edmund Durand, *The Finances of New York City* (New York, 1898), 54.

31. But, of course, the Croton waterworks was not usually considered as private enterprise. See the comments of Myndert Van Schaick in Valentine, *Manual of the Corporation of the City of New York* (New York 1864), 197–201.

32. Dillon, *Treatise on Municipal Corporations*, 84.

such a way as to become entitled to the privileges (or immunities) of acting under the aegis of the sovereign.

In declaring that the corporation's legislatively delegated activities divided between those that were public and those that were private, Nelson freed judicial analysis from dependence on legislative pronouncements. The standard he developed in *Bailey* was substantively incoherent. His opinion suggested that only activities that constituted traditional or customary municipal responsibilities could be characterized as part of the corporation's public sphere. New undertakings were prima facie private. But *Bailey*'s significance lay in its methodology rather than in its substantive analysis. Other judges included different activities on the public side of the line, without harming the basic bifurcated structure.[33] The point is that only judges would draw the line of demarcation. *Bailey* was a victory for judicial power rather than for doctrinal substance.

After *Bailey*, judicial analysis of municipal activities followed a predictable pattern in the New York courts. Judicial opinions would begin by suggesting the dichotomous consequences that followed from labeling an activity either public or private. If public, there would be immunity from private suit; if private, there would be liability. "The distinction between these two classes of power is obvious, and has been frequently recognized and established in our courts."[34] The only difficulty was in deciding which activities belonged in which category. And at that point the claimed deductive formalism of the public-private rhetoric would break down, leaving judges free to legislate their own values.

To take a typical example, in 1851 the corporation was sued for the negligence of its agents when a horse died after it fell into an open sewer excavation on Broome Street. The lawyers for the city argued that "where public duties are cast upon them as a municipal body, they are entitled to all the immunities incident to a public employment." And because the streets and the sewers were traditional public responsibilities of local governments everywhere, the city should not be subject to suit.[35]

According to the New York Court of Appeals, however, the corporation had a private "ministerial" duty not to leave open excavations in the streets. The court agreed with the city's lawyers that there was a difference between the public and the private powers of the corporation, a difference that was "plain and marked," although the court conceded that "as they approximate each other, it is oftentimes difficult to ascertain the exact line

33. In 1853, for example, Jeremiah Sullivan Black would hold that financing a railroad could be a "public purpose" of the municipality; see *Sharpless* v. *Mayor of Philadelphia*, 21 Penn. St. 147 (1853).

34. *Lloyd* v. *The Mayor of New York*, 5 N.Y. 369, 374 (1851).

35. Ibid., at 372.

of distinction." That line, it should be emphasized, was not drawn by the language of the legislative delegations. To the contrary, it was founded on the court's prediction of what would happen if either a public or a private label were assigned to municipal action. Thus the court held against the corporation because if the actions of the corporation were declared public, and therefore immune from liability,

> the natural and certain consequence . . . would be, innumerable applications to the common council for redress legislatively, and which would bring in their train an organized body of soliciting parties and agents, the allowance sometimes of extravagant and unjust claims, the rejection at other times of meritorious ones, in a word, all the evils attending a legislative body having control over large funds and exposed to solicitations and devices of a corps of artful and unscrupulous claimants and their hired or interested agents.
>
> Where the city now pays in accordance with just legal principles hundreds of dollars, it would probably then pay thousands, besides having in the halls of its local legislature scenes of a most forbidding character.[36]

Without ever denying that a municipal corporation was an agency of the state legislature, possessing no rights that vested against the state, Nelson's opinion in *Bailey* added two assumptions that significantly qualified the basic norm set out in *People* v. *Morris*. First, municipal powers and duties were to be interpreted in accordance with uniform judicial standards (like the public-private dichotomy) largely unconnected to actual legislative intent. And second, although a municipality was a public entity, it did not thereby gain the privileges or entitlements of sovereignty.

The significance of these doctrinal assumptions first emerged as Nelson and other New York judges developed the law respecting a municipal corporation's potential liability for neglect or negligence in the care of streets and sewers.[37] In the early nineteenth century, courts throughout America followed English precedent in holding unincorporated local governments free from liability on the grounds that they were merely instruments of legislative policy.[38] Would the same immunity be granted to the corpora-

36. Ibid., at 374–75.
37. The intensity of street growth in the 1840s and 1850s was a source of continuing amazement to New Yorkers. See Hone, *Diary*, 721–22; Strong, *Diary*, 1 : 302. Strong wrote, "How this city marches northward! The progress of 1835 and 1836 was nothing to the luxuriant rank growth of this year. Streets are springing up, whole strata of sandstone have transferred themselves from their ancient resting places to look down on bustling thoroughfares for long years to come. Wealth is rushing in upon us like a freshet" (2 : 24).
38. See Chapter 12.

tion of the city of New York, now that it too was recognized as an instrument of legislative policy?[39]

The answer Chief Justice Nelson gave in 1842 was no. But to do so meant turning the analysis inaugurated in *Bailey* on its head. The case of *Mayor* v. *Furze* arose because the building of the plaintiff, a baker, flooded when the sewers of Pearl Street overflowed. The city constructed those sewers under the authority of a statute permitting it to make public sewers and drains. In this instance, Nelson could hardly contest the "public" quality of the delegation.[40] The construction of sewers was a traditional responsibility of local government, one for which there could not be any conceivable private profit for the corporation.

Still, Nelson held that the public delegation of authority to build sewers did not carry with it any immunity from liability. He provided two alternative justifications. First, the statute, "upon well settled rules of construction," was interpreted as "imperative and peremptory upon the corporation." Even though the statute indicated only that the corporation "may" cause sewers and drains to be built, "where a public body or officer has been clothed by statute with power to do an act which concerns the public interest or the rights of third persons, the execution of the power may be insisted on as a duty." In such case, "*may . . .* is tantamount to *shall.*" And the city would be subject to liability, not because it was acting in its private capacity, but rather because of the public interest in making it pay.[41]

Alternatively, Nelson argued, even if the decision to construct sewers were regarded as within the discretionary authority of the corporation, it retained a public duty to keep them in repair, once the decision had been made to construct them. And any failure of duty that could lead to the criminal indictment of the corporation or of the officials responsible for a particular condition was sufficient to create civil municipal liability.[42]

In *Bailey*, the fact that the Croton waterworks was a "private" enterprise of the corporation provided the foundation for imposing liability. In *Furze*, by contrast, the public duty to provide and maintain sewers and drains justified imposing liability. *Furze* was decided only weeks after *Bailey*, and the apparent inconsistency warranted comment. But only at the very end of *Furze* did Nelson cite *Bailey*. *Bailey*, he claimed, explained the distinction between a municipal corporation's freedom from liability "for the improper execution of a public work by agents whom they are

39. For an affirmative answer to that question, incorporating an extensive critique of New York cases, see *Detroit* v. *Blackeby*, 21 Mich. 84 (1870).

40. *Mayor of New York* v. *Furze*, 3 Hill 612, 614 (1842).

41. Ibid., 615.

42. Ibid., 615–18.

obliged to employ" and its liability "where a duty, specifically enjoined upon the Corporation as such, has been wholly neglected by its agents," as in *Furze*.[43] One may wonder, however, how a public-private dichotomy developed in one case to differentiate immunity from liability could be simply discarded in the first succeeding case to which it appeared to apply.

Yet if the argument of this chapter is correct, the public-private dichotomy developed in *Bailey* served primarily to free judicial considerations of local government powers and duties from the strict language of legislative delegations. In *Furze* as well, Nelson managed to impose liability on the municipality by insisting on a judicial standard for interpreting legislation, without at the same time questioning the public nature of the corporation. Public duties would create municipal liability because public corporations were not themselves imbued with sovereignty.

Over the next twenty years, the judges of New York's appellate courts generally rejected the "may equals shall" standard of *Furze*. Instead, they relied on Nelson's alternative basis for liability.[44] On issues for which a municipal corporation received its power to act from the legislature, its decision to do so would not subject it to liability. If the city chose to regrade or pave streets or put in sewers that caused flooding or other harm to an individual's property, it was *damnum absque iniuria*. A lawful use of the land or of its power to make street improvements would not subject the municipal corporation to liability if consequential damages resulted. Such acts left the legal position of a city just like that of a private land developer.[45]

Although courts analogized the municipal corporation to the private landowner, the basis for a city's freedom from liability lay in the fact that those discretionary decisions constituted public "judicial" choices as opposed to private "ministerial" duties.[46] "Judicial" decisions were those expressed as legislative authorizations. The statute that made it lawful for New York City to make and maintain sewers and drains, for example,

43. Ibid., 618–19.
44. See *Wilson* v. *The Mayor of New York*, 1 Denio 595, 599 (1845); *Griffin* v. *The Mayor of New York*, 9 N.Y. 456 (1854).
45. "An unimproved lot of land in the city of Brooklyn would be worth little or nothing to the owner, unless he were allowed to dig in it for the purpose of building; and if he may not dig because it will remove the support of his neighbor's soil, he has but a nominal right to his property, which can only be made good by negotiation and compact with his neighbor. A city could never be built under such a doctrine. . . .

"The case before us seems to fall within the principle that a man may enjoy his land in the way such property is usually enjoyed, without being answerable for the indirect or consequential damages which may be sustained by an adjoining landowner" (*Radcliff's Executors* v. *The Mayor of Brooklyn*, 4 N.Y. 195, 203 [1850]).
46. *Wilson* v. *The Mayor of New York*, 1 Denio 595 (1845); *Rochester White Lead Company* v. *Rochester*, 3 N.Y. 467 (1850).

created a judicial power (and perhaps a duty) to do so. Such an authorization necessarily mandated the exercise of judgment. The statute did not
specify where or when or by whom sewers and drains should be built; in
providing authorization the statute vested the power to make those decisions in the officers of the municipality.[47] There would be no liability for
the consequences of those decisions, for those decisions were public acts of
the municipal corporation.[48]

By contrast, "ministerial" duties were public tasks that lacked an element of discretion or judgment; they were duties "absolute, certain, and
imperative."[49] To return to the example of New York's sewer statute, the
power to make choices was said to be exhausted once the municipality had
decided to act. "It is the duty of a municipal corporation to build a sewer
so that it shall not become a nuisance to the neighborhood, as much as it is
to avoid the same results, by keeping it in repair, after it has been built."[50]
There could be no immunity from liability or injuries that resulted from
the exercise of ministerial duties.[51] In those situations, the city was acting
"privately," as a trustee for the public, and would be held to the highest
"private" standard of fiduciary responsibility.[52]

Paradoxically, this new judicial-ministerial dichotomy identified a municipal corporation as a public entity for purposes of liability when it exercised judgment and discretion and characterized it as a "private" entity
whenever it was bound strictly by the dictates of legislation. As an autonomous decision maker it was public; as a dependent agency it was private.[53]
The elaboration of this dichotomy in one street liability case after another
in mid-nineteenth-century New York carries us into a realm of judicial

47. *Revised Laws of New York*, 36th sess. (Albany, 1813), sec. 175.
48. *Mills* v. *City of Brooklyn*, 32 N.Y. 489, 495 (1865); *Rochester White Lead Company* v.
City of Rochester, 3 N.Y. 463 (1850); *Martin* v. *Mayor of Brooklyn*, 1 Hill, 545 (1841); *Weaver*
v. *Davendorf*, 3 Denio, 117, 120 (1846).
49. *Mills* v. *City of Brooklyn*, 32 N.Y. 489, 497 (1865).
50. *Rochester White Lead Company* v. *City of Rochester*, 3 N.Y. 463 (1850).
51. *Barton* v. *City of Syracuse*, 36 N.Y. 54 (1867).
52. *Hutson* v. *The Mayor of New York*, 9 N.Y. 163, 168 (1853).
53. "There is a manifest distinction between the political powers of a municipal corporation, by virtue of which it exercises, in a subordinate degree, the functions of government,
and those private and civil duties of a ministerial character merely, which devolve upon it,
either as a tenure by which it holds its property, or in consequence of duties imposed upon it
by the sovereign authority. The first are partly legislative and partly executive and sometimes
even judicial in character, and it is a fundamental principle, that officers exercising these high
duties, cannot be held answerable for the mode in which they exercise them, except by im-
peachment or indictment. But with regard to the latter, there is no difference, as to liability
between a municipal corporation and individual . . . where an individual or corporation have
a fixed and certain duty assigned to them, of a merely ministerial character, and the means
placed at their disposal are sufficient for its performance, they are under obligations to perform it, at the risk of being made to answer for the consequences of their neglect" (*Hutson* v.
Mayor of New York, 5 Sandford 289 [N.Y. Sup. Ct., 1851]).

decision making open to the charge of blind conceptualism. The categories lacked substantive content, reflecting instead an obsessive tidiness, a thoroughgoing reductionism, and an unwillingness to connect analytic structures to social reality. In the pursuit of binary clarity, the developing law of municipal corporations seemed to lose contact with the subject of its contemplation.

Still, one substantive effect of this enveloping conceptual structure was to impose a much firmer distinction in judicial rhetoric between the municipal corporation and the sovereign state. A public entity the city remained, but one largely shorn of the immunities to which other public institutions and officers were entitled.

Courts in general seemed to assume that such a distinction did not deserve any justification, that there was an obvious difference between municipal corporations and other public administrators (like township trustees), at least for purposes of assessing liability. In *Hutson* v. *The Mayor*, Judge John L. Mason of the Court of Appeals suggested that because a municipal corporation owned the fee to the streets in trust for the public it could be held to a private, fiduciary standard.[54] And four years later Judge Samuel Selden of the same court argued that municipal corporations were not ordinarily entitled to immunity from liability because they were fundamentally private entities contracting with the state.

Relying for authority on a group of eighteenth-century English cases he accused Nelson of having misread in *Furze*, Selden's opinion in *Weet* v. *Brockport* is a model of legal anachronism. "It may, no doubt be said," he began, that eighteenth-century charters were unlike nineteenth-century municipal incorporations because they "not only vested in the corporations certain governmental powers and privileges, but conveyed to them valuable rights of property, and that it was solely in view of the latter that these public corporate bodies were placed upon a footing with private corporations and individuals." By contrast, municipal incorporations were "usually granted from motives of public policy, and with a view to the better government of the districts which they embrace, and not for the purpose of conferring any private benefit upon the individuals composing the corporation." And thus, Selden conceded, perhaps such a modern charter could not be regarded as "an implied contract on the part of the corporation to perform its corporate duties."[55]

But, he continued,

> it is well known that such charters are never imposed upon municipal bodies, except at their urgent request. While they may be governmental bodies in theory, they are, in fact, regarded as privileges

54. *Hutson* v. *The Mayor of New York*, 9 N.Y. 165, 168 (1853).
55. *Weet* v. *Brockport*, 16 N.Y. 161, 171 (1857).

of great value, and the franchises they confer are usually sought for
with much earnestness before they are granted. The surrender by
the government to the municipality of a portion of its sovereign
power, if accepted by the latter, may with propriety be considered as
affording ample consideration for an implied undertaking, on the
part of the corporation, to perform with fidelity the duties which the
charter imposes.[56]

Thus, according to Judge Selden, municipal corporations could be held to
the strictest standards of private liability without doing violence to the traditional immunity of government entities.

By the mid-1850s, labeling a municipal corporation private for purposes
of assessing liability did not suggest a judicial rethinking of the place
within the legal order of entities such as the corporation of the city of New
York. Selden was perhaps correct that municipal charters were not usually
imposed on municipalities, that most of their powers were eagerly sought,
that, indeed, in the case of a city like New York most state legislation affecting the city was drafted by the corporation counsel or by its "agents"
in the legislature. But for Selden such descriptive observations did not imply that he considered the municipal corporation anything but a dependent agency of state power. His argument for the "private" nature of the
municipal corporation occurred within the context of an established doctrinal law of municipal corporations that was founded on a rejection of the
autonomy of local government. *Weet* v. *Brockport* was not written as an
attack on that structure of judicial understanding. To the contrary, it was
intended to provide a more adequate explanation for one "curious" result
produced by that judicial "law."

The problem mid-nineteenth-century judges saw in the municipal corporation was its reliance on legislation, as a result of which it was "wrought
into the framework of our government."[57] Lacking a constitutional perspective that justified regular overturning of legislation, yet imbued with a
passionate moralistic concern for the ways in which local governments in-
vaded individual rights, judges struggled to develop a legal analysis that
would separate cities from their source of legislative authority. If viewed
solely as agencies of the legislature, cities were protected from judicial restraints because of the principle of separation of powers. Local powers, of
course, remained subject to legislative control. But "to the extent of the
power delegated to them in their exercise of it [legislative power], and the
immense discretion that is conferred with it, they are as exempt from judicial interference, dictation and control, as is the state government itself;

56. Ibid.
57. Dillon, *Treatise on Municipal Corporations*, 775–76.

and for the same political reasons, to keep separate and distinct the three departments of government—legislative, executive, and judicial—so that neither shall interfere with, dictate to, or control the other."[58]

Rules mandating strict construction of legislative powers provided one technique for justifying judicial intervention. But a formal expansion of the "private" sphere of municipal existence offered judges a different way of exercising that "learning and conservative wisdom," which Dillon sought "to photograph" in the pages of his treatise.[59]

Consider again New York City's control of its streets. Every commentator from Kent on analyzed the streets as the paradigm of the public responsibility of the corporation. Unlike the ferry franchise, streets were regarded as subject to the absolute and continuing control of the legislature. They were, as Judge Morris of the New York Supreme Court wrote in 1853, "a subject purely governmental . . . in the exercise of which, no judicial power had the legal right to interfere, nor any power except the legislature of the state."[60]

But Morris wrote those words in dissent. By the early 1850s, the New York courts were coming to a different understanding of the legal significance of the city's control of its streets. In the case in which Morris dissented, *Milhau* v. *Sharp*, residents of the city living on Broadway asked for a permanent injunction against the defendants, licensees of the corporation, to prevent them from constructing a railroad on the street. The central issue, according to Judge Henry P. Edwards in his opinion for the majority, was whether the corporation had the right to make the grant. But to answer that question Edwards felt obliged to recite a general statement of the "nature" of the corporation so that he could establish his right to judge it.

Relying on Kent's *Commentaries on American Law*, *People* v. *Morris*, and *Dartmouth College*, Edwards began with the conventional wisdom that the corporation was a "public municipal corporation . . . created for political purposes," whose charter was not a contract within the meaning of the federal Constitution. So long as it acted "in the exercise of its public political powers," it was vested with the "largest discretion." But such discretion did not exist when the corporation acted with regard to its private property. Such property, according to Edwards, was held in trust for the common benefit of all the corporators (whoever they were), and in its use the corporation would be held to a high, fiduciary standard of conduct.[61]

Because Edwards had already determined that the fee in the streets was vested in the corporation, the rest was easy. He did not contend, as the

---

58. *Milhau* v. *Sharp*, 15 Barb. 193, 239–40 (N.Y. Sup. Ct., 1853) (Morris, J. dissenting).
59. Dillon, *Treatise on Municipal Corporations*, 776.
60. *Milhau* v. *Sharp*, 15 Barb. 193, 242 (1853).
61. Ibid., 212–13.

plaintiffs had argued, that the use of the streets for railroads was inherently beyond the powers of the corporation as a public trustee; indeed, he held that a railroad was not a per se nuisance. But the corporation had received better offers than the one it accepted from the defendants. Therefore, if one looked at the corporation as a fiduciary, there was a clear breach of trust, justifying a permanent injunction.[62]

Why call the management and use of city streets a private obligation of the corporation, when such activities had always been part of its public responsibilities? To that question Edwards offered only the observation that because the corporation had "granted" the defendants a right to lay track on Broadway, the corporation must have been dealing with them in its private capacity. As we have seen, however, earlier New York courts explicitly denied the proposition that the city's actions were "private" whenever those who dealt with it received private rights.[63] To the contrary, in the early nineteenth century, judges consistently held that New York City always acted as a public entity whenever it could show public purposes to justify its behavior.

By the 1850s, however, such functional analysis had become a peripheral part of judicial decision making. Labeling the city's use of the streets as public or private no longer suggested a concern for the reality of city administration. The goal of legal analysis was to bolster the authority of the court to determine when individuals had been harmed by city action. And to do that courts had to separate the city as a legal entity liable to private suit from its place within a legislatively controlled political order. The point was made forcefully by Edwards's colleague, S. B. Strong, in a pointed concurrence in *Milhau*. Strong thought that there was "undoubtedly a wide difference . . . between the acts of the state legislature and a municipal corporation" with regard to their respective powers over public property. The state was sovereign and could do whatever it pleased. No power could annul a legislative grant "as improvident or destitute of any valuable or appropriate consideration." On the other hand, cities were "inferior" bodies, holding only such powers as had been expressly granted them. Because nothing in the city charter authorized it to make "improvident" grants of public property, "its disposition of such property . . . is therefore subject to the common law principles applicable to the grants made by trustees to whom the management of private property is confided." It was, thought Strong, "right on every account that it should be so."[64]

62. Ibid., 207, 218; see *Drake* v. *The Hudson River Railroad Co.*, 7 Barb. 508 (1849).
63. See the discussion of *The Mayor of New York* v. *Scott* in Chapter 8 and of the *Brick Presbyterian Church* case in Chapter 6.
64. *Milhau* v. *Sharp*, 15 Barb. 193, 231 (1853).

Students of New York City's municipal government have usually regarded the year 1857 as "the date of a great change in the legal position" of New York City.[65] The year before, in *Davis v. The Mayor*, the Court of Appeals had overruled *Milhau v. Sharp* insofar as it held that a railroad constructed on Broadway under municipal authorization alone was not a per se nuisance. The city had only such powers as the legislature directly granted it. And even a general statutory delegation of authority to manage and control the streets would be limited to those activities that a court defined as traditional or conventional. "A railroad," Chief Justice Denio declared, "has no necessary relation to or connection with a common highway or street." Thus "the establishment of such a road is not within the jurisdiction conferred upon the corporation of New York over the roads and streets in that city."[66]

In 1857 the state legislature rejected the precedents of half a century and proclaimed that it was free to intervene at will in the affairs of the city. No longer did the legislature feel obliged to respect the traditional autonomy of local administration. In the words of Frank J. Goodnow, the Republican-controlled legislature determined "to arrange certain departments of the local government of the city in such a way that the party in power in the State government might obtain a portion at least of the good things offered by the city of New York to those who filled her numerous offices." Local service agencies, traditionally manned by officers appointed by the Democratic-controlled Common Council, became metropolitan service districts, whose offices would be filled by appointments made by the governor and senate. The geographical area of these service districts encompassed both Brooklyn and the city of New York, and they can be viewed as precursors of the 1898 consolidation of the two cities. But, from the perspective of the city, the establishment of those state agencies constituted a divestment of much of the city's traditional responsibilities. Police, fire, and health were all removed from local control, as was the administration of the new Central Park (which previously had even been the property of the city).[67]

And when Fernando Wood, the Democratic mayor of the city, brought an action *quo warranto* challenging the right of the new state administrators to exercise the offices of commissioners of police, the Court of Appeals

65. Frank J. Goodnow, "The Tweed Ring in New York City," in James Bryce, *The American Commonwealth*, 4 vols. (London, 1888), 3:173; Frank J. Goodnow, *Municipal Problems* (New York, 1897), 1–20; Howard Lee McBain, *The Laws and Practice of Municipal Home Rule* (New York, 1916), 6–9, 36; Durand, *Finances of New York City*, 76–79; Leo Hershkowitz, *Tweed's New York: Another Look* (New York, 1978), 57–63.
66. *Davis v. The Mayor of New York*, 14 N.Y. 506, 515 (1856).
67. Goodnow, "Tweed Ring," 175–76.

unambiguously affirmed the power of the legislature to rearrange local affairs to suit its own purposes. According to Denio, nothing in the state constitution required local governments—let alone the city of New York —to exercise particular functions or powers. Indeed, "if we were to establish the principle that the legislature can never reduce the administrative authority of counties, cities or towns . . . we should, I think make an impracticable government." Any other decision would undercut the sovereignty of the legislature and make it difficult for the legislature to govern.[68]

In light of the events and cases narrated in the preceding pages, nothing about Denio's opinion is very surprising. To him, New York City was just another local government, just another municipal corporation, entirely lacking in any inherent or natural rights beyond legislative control.[69] The structure of legal rules developed in the years after *Dartmouth College* could hardly have suggested any other result.[70]

And so nothing happened in the year 1857 to change the legal position of the corporation of the city of New York. But the date is significant because it inaugurated a new period in the institutional history of the city. Until then, *Ordrenan* remained good law. It was still a valid presumption that legislation affecting the city was usually passed with the consent of the city's government. But when the Court of Appeals sustained legislation divesting New York City of many of its traditional public responsibilities— legislation unmistakably passed over the strong objections of the city's leadership—the dam burst. An era of state-local comity ended. From then on, "domination over the affairs of New York City went merrily and perniciously on from session to session of the legislature."[71]

68. *People ex. rel. Wood* v. *Draper*, 15 N.Y. 532, 543 (1857).

69. The lack of distinction of New York City as a legal entity did not mean that judges regarded New York City as just another place: "The city of New York is the commercial metropolis of this continent; its port is filled with shipping from every clime; its streets crowded with residents and sojourners, intent on business, pleasure and crime; and through its gates into the interior of the state, come swarming myriads of emigrants, from every kindred, tongue and people of the old world. And how have the local authorities of that great city discharged its duty of local government to its citizens and the state at large, in protecting them in their liberty, life and property? Let the statistics of crime answer, and convict that authority, either of remissness in duty, or the system of the police hitherto in force as radically defective. But let the cause be what it may, which has paralyzed the arm of criminal law, the state is bound to protect the citizen in his life and property, irrespective of locality; and if, in the judgment of its representatives, the local authorities have failed to accomplish this object, it was their duty to substitute another system more effectual in execution" (ibid., 556 [Shankland, J., concurring]). But see ibid., 557 (Brown, J., dissenting).

70. *People ex. rel. Wood* v. *Draper* was one of the first of the "ripper" cases in which the state legislature "ripped" away the traditional responsibilities of a city. For other versions, see *Coyle* v. *Grey*, 7 Houst. (Del.) 44, 30A 728 (1884).

71. McBain, *Municipal Home Rule*, 8.

The new legislative style of domination and control was, of course, fueled by party politics, patronage claims, ethnic conflicts, and a tangled history of municipal and legislative corruption. But that style rested on what by 1857 was a fixed judicial understanding of the city as an inferior public entity lacking in rights, privileges, or immunities. The principles underlying that understanding were not beyond argument or debate.[72] But after 1857 it had become impossible to articulate any alternative vision of the legal nature of the corporation of the city of New York.

72. See Cooley's concurrence in *People ex rel Le Roy* v. *Hurlburt*, 25 Mich. 44, 93 (1871); Amasa Eaton, "The Right to Local Self-Government," *Harvard Law Review* 13 (1900):441, 570, 638; 14 (1900):20, 116; Eugene McQuillen, *A Treatise on the Law of Municipal Corporations* (Chicago, 1911), chap. 1; Gerald Frug, "The City as a Legal Concept," *Harvard Law Review* 93 (1980):1057–1154.

CHAPTER 15

The Private Property of a Public Entity
Crossing Brooklyn Ferry

When mid-nineteenth-century New York judges spoke of the "private" or "proprietary" sphere of the municipal corporation, what they described bore only a remote connection to the older chartered property rights of the corporation of the city of New York. That new "private" sphere—inhabited by municipal liability, ministerial duties, and public enterprise—was one part of the reified municipal corporation for which courts were busily inventing doctrine during the middle third of the century. It had little in common with the particular properties of particular, ongoing institutions.

By the middle of the century, only a small part of the estate granted to the corporation in 1730 in the Montgomerie Charter remained under municipal control. "Common" lands had been sold; market rights divested by legislative action. And most of what the city retained was now committed to narrowly defined public purposes.[1]

But as of 1850 the corporation still had its "ancient" ferry franchise. The Montgomerie Charter granted it the sole and exclusive power to establish and maintain ferries to and from all the opposite shores from Manhattan Island and expressly confirmed the 1708 grant by Lord Cornbury of the Long Island ferry. Kent, writing in 1836, considered these provisions "an absolute grant of vested property, or an estate in fee, which could not lawfully be questioned or disturbed, except by due process of law." Such a "freehold right," even when held by a public corporation generally subject to legislative intervention, was "as much beyond the reach of a gratuitous legislative resumption, as any other franchise or property held by grant or charter." To Kent, there was nothing incongruous about the government

1. George Ashton Black, *Municipal Ownership of Land on Manhattan Island* (New York, 1891), 81.

of New York City having a private sphere, protected from public scrutiny.[2]

But in the wake of the 1846 state constitution, which implicitly reduced the status of the corporation of the city of New York to that of other local governments, how would a court regard such a franchise? In 1845, before the passage of that new constitution, the state legislature enacted a statute that granted to three centrally appointed commissioners the power to institute new ferry routes between New York City and Long Island. Litigation resulted. And in 1850, in the case of *Benson* v. *The Mayor of New York*, Judge Seward Barculo of the New York Supreme Court ruled at special term that the ferry franchise remained a vested right not to be disturbed by the state legislature. The judge's opinion could have been written by Kent. According to Barculo, the language of the charters revealed that the corporation's authority to control the ferry was not just a political trust, subject to legislative superintendence. It was a private right whose inviolability rested on the contract clause of the United States Constitution (relying on Story's opinion in *Dartmouth College*), as well as on the "sacredness of vested rights." Barculo noted that when a public entity like the corporation claimed private rights, those claims had to be strictly construed. But when, as in this case, there was no doubt or ambiguity about the intent of the grant, a city was as capable of holding rights against the state as any private individual.[3]

This opinion stands as evidence that in 1850 New York City's corporate estate remained secure. Although perhaps circumscribed by two generations of public regulations and certainly separated from the processes of government, what the corporation retained from the estate granted in its charter, it "owned."

But such a conclusion would mistake an isolated anachronistic opinion by a single judge for an ongoing political struggle in which by 1850 the corporation of the city of New York was clearly on the defensive. Barculo's holding in favor of the corporation was an episode in a political contest for control of the ferry franchise. His opinion articulated no judicial consensus about the legal status of New York City's private rights. By 1850, those who opposed the city's management of the ferries had several holdings by the Supreme Court under Roger Taney to bolster their cause.[4] On the

2. James Kent, *The Charter of the City of New York, with notes thereon. Also a Treatise on the Powers and Duties of the Mayor, Aldermen, and Assistant Aldermen, and the Journal of the City Convention* (New York, 1836), 140–41; see also Murray Hoffman, *Treatise upon the Estate and Rights of the Corporation of the City of New York, as Proprietors*, 2d rev. ed., 2 vols. (New York, 1862), 273–302.

3. *Benson* v. *The Mayor of New York*, 10 Barb. 223, 240–42 (N.Y. Sup. Ct., 1850).

4. See *Charles River Bridge* v. *Warren Bridge*, 11 Pet. 420 (1837); *East Hartford* v. *Hartford Bridge Co.*, 10 How. 511 (1848); *Martin* v. *Waddell*, 16 Pet. 367 (1842).

other side, there was little besides Kent's treatise on the charter and Story's concurrence in *Dartmouth College.*

Issues of legal right were not peripheral to this conflict. Indeed, the residents of Brooklyn who led the struggle to wrest control of the Long Island ferry from the corporation always clothed their arguments in legal garb. And the representatives of the corporation likewise rested their case on the sanctity of private property and the contract clause. But battles between the two sides were primarily staged in petitions to the legislature and in pamphlets and newspaper editorials rather than in the courts.

Between 1820 and 1860 the legitimacy of New York City's claimed right to profit from the ferries that ran between Manhattan and Long Island was the most important issue in the political life of the young city of Brooklyn. Throughout this period, Brooklyn's goals remained constant: to assure sufficient, regular, and inexpensive transportation across the East River for Brooklyn's residents. But both the legal content and the intended audience of arguments for improved ferry service changed radically after about 1830. Earlier, Brooklynites still conceded the dominion of the corporation over its holdings. Thus they directed their petitions to the New York Common Council, which was expected to use its property to serve the public interest. But, as the legal perception of the corporation of the city of New York changed, so too did the strategies of those opposed to its management of the ferries. And during the late 1820s and the 1830s, Brooklynites worked out a legal theory of the nature of public ownership of a franchise that justified legislative intervention and, when accepted by the courts, undid the vestiges of the "private" corporation of the city of New York.

To trace the evolution of argument about the Long Island ferry, we need first to sketch the peculiar place that that ferry held in the early history of Brooklyn.[5] At the end of the eighteenth century, Brooklyn was a tiny settlement huddled around the "old" Long Island ferry to lower Manhattan, surrounded by farms still heavily dependent on slave labor. Many city butchers kept slaughterhouses in the settlement to escape the corporation's regulations, and the farmers of Kings County were well off because of the dependence of New York City on their produce. But Brooklyn expe-

5. The following section is based on Ralph Foster Weld, *Brooklyn Village, 1816–1834* (New York, 1938); Jacob Judd, "The History of Brooklyn, 1834–1855: Political and Administrative Aspects" (Ph.D. dissertation, New York University, 1959); Henry R. Stiles, *A History of the City of Brooklyn, in Three Volumes* (Brooklyn, 1867, 1869, 1870); Henry R. Stiles, ed., *The Civil, Political, Professional and Ecclesiastical History and Commercial Industrial Record of the County of Kings and the City of Brooklyn, N.Y., from 1683 to 1884* (New York, 1884); and Gabriel Furman, *Notes, Geographical and Historical, Relating to the Town of Brooklyn on Long Island* (Brooklyn, 1825).

rienced little of the intensive growth that characterized New York City in the two decades after the end of British occupation.[6]

In 1816 the state legislature granted the settlement by the ferry a village charter. And at about that same time, the population of the new village began to grow at a rate exceeding that of its larger neighbor across the river. From a population of about 4,000 at the time of its incorporation, Brooklyn grew to encompass about 25,000 inhabitants by 1834, when it was chartered as a city. Then, between 1835 and 1850, its population almost quadrupled, making it the seventh largest city in the nation. In 1855 Brooklyn annexed the neighboring towns of Williamsburgh and Bushwick, and by 1860 it had grown to more than 250,000 inhabitants and was the third largest city in the United States.[7]

Brooklyn's growth was founded on its proximity to lower Manhattan. Land developers advertised their lots as healthful and attractive alternatives to uptown Manhattan for the family residences of gentlemen "whose business or profession require their daily attendance in the city." And they emphasized Brooklyn's situation as the "nearest country retreat, and easiest of access to the centre of business that now remains unoccupied."[8]

Brooklyn, therefore, stayed a suburb as it also became one of the largest cities in the country. Even those who asserted Brooklyn's "rights" against the chartered claims of the corporation of the city of New York conceded that status. By the late 1820s, some were already convinced that its destiny lay in merger with New York City. Such an event, wrote George Wood in 1828, could not take place immediately, for "the minds of men must be prepared for the measure, and the plan of union proposed, agitated, and digested." But "an identity of interest, already commenced, must be completed."[9]

Little went on in Brooklyn that was not directly connected to residential land development. Street improvements seem to have constituted the only regular form of public activity. In 1832, the village president complained that there was probably no place "where the public good, in a dense popu-

6. Ira Rosenwaike, *Population History of New York City* (Syracuse, N.Y., 1972), 29–31.
7. Ibid., 49–52.
8. Henry E. Pierrepont, *Historical Sketch of the Fulton Ferry* (Brooklyn, 1879), 27–28, quoted in Weld, *Brooklyn Village*, 28.

9. *All the Proceedings in Relation to the New South Ferry, between the City of New York and Brooklyn, from December 1825 to January 1835* (New York, 1835), 5; George Wood, *Opinion on the Subject of a New South Ferry* (New York, 1828), 2–3; see also Gideon Lee, Mayor of New York, *Communication Respecting the Application of the Village of Brooklyn to the Legislature to Become a Chartered City* (Document 30, Board of Aldermen, 14 October 1833); "Chronicles of Brooklyn, of Remarkable and Passing Events, from 1806 to 1848," in Thomas P. Teale, ed., *Municipal Register of the City of Brooklyn, and Manual of Kings County* (Brooklyn, 1848), 57–63; Weld, *Brooklyn Village*, 50–51.

lation, has been . . . so entirely subservient to individual convenience."[10] The city's economic dependence on New York City, a local historian commented, "though conducive to personal convenience does not, in ordinary cases, exert the happiest influence on the public weal. It is extremely difficult for any man, to take all that interest in the good government of a place, where he considers himself a *mere lodger*, that would be felt, if he realized, that all his interests both personal and pecuniary, were identified with the community, in which his political rights and responsibilities are involved."[11]

The exception was the ferry franchise. If Brooklyn's citizens took little interest in local public affairs generally, the ferry service between Long Island and New York City provided a subject of intense and continuing concern. And the antebellum history of Brooklyn is replete with mass public meetings, petitions and memorials to the state legislature and the New York Common Council, and reports of local agitation over the quality, price, and quantity of ferry service.[12]

Of the three, the quality of service raised the least controversy. Brooklynites complained regularly about delays, about the practice of diverting ferry boats from course to pick up goods at warehouses, and about a variety of negligent failures of care on the part of those who "farmed" the ferry.[13] But even those most bitterly critical of the conduct of the corporation of the city of New York and its lessees admitted that the comfort and speed of an ordinary passage had improved remarkably after the introduction of steamboats in 1814.[14]

10. Weld, *Brooklyn Village*, 29.

11. Nathaniel S. Prime, *A History of Long Island, from its First Settlement by Europeans, to the Year 1845; with Special Reference to its Ecclesiastical Concerns* (New York, 1845), 365–66.

12. See "Chronicles of Brooklyn," 38–96; Weld, *Brooklyn Village*, 3–53; Judd, "History of Brooklyn," 172–85.

13. Weld, *Brooklyn Village*, 23; see Petition of Robert White to the Ferry Committee (on the noncompliance of the ferry company with the laws of the state), June 1826, Ferry Committee File, 1826, Municipal Archives and Record Center, New York; and "Petition of William Gowe(?) to the Ferry Committee," 16 September 1826, ibid. The latter petition reported what happened when Gowe tried to cross on the ferry the evening of 24 June. He heard the bell ring ten minutes before the expected time of departure. He paid his fare and then walked toward the boat, "when I soon found to my astonishment that the Boat had not arrived; in consequence of the night being dark and having no lights on the float, nor even a proper Rail or guard to prevent any person of going forward, I unfortunately stepped off into the river. I immediately gave an alarm. When some persons came to my assistance one of them asked the ferryman for a Lantern with a light in it, which he refused to give. I was placed in a dangerous Situation having a plain cloak Buttoned on me and a Cage & Parrot together with an Umbrella when I fell in. The cage, parrot & umbrella I have lost and my watch very much injured."

14. "Those, who in these latter days, pass quickly and comfortably over the East River in the elegant, capacious and swift ferry boats, can scarcely imagine the discomforts, hindrances

The price charged for a ferry ride was a much more serious concern. Brooklynites never considered the price they had to pay reasonable. But their explanations for the excessiveness of the rates changed considerably between the 1820s and the 1830s. At first, responsibility for high fares was located in the greed of the lessees, who had managed in 1813 to obtain from the corporation a twenty-five-year exclusive lease. But by the late 1820s petitions and reports shifted the blame to the corporation itself, which had caused the high fares by preventing competition and by selling the lease off at public auction to whomever would pay the most for it (instead of granting leases to public-spirited citizens of Brooklyn who would run the ferry as a public utility). By the 1830s it had become a commonplace that the corporation's claimed right to profit from its chartered franchise was a "tribute" exacted from its smaller neighbor on Long Island.[15] Brooklynites, according to Nathaniel Prime, were mortified "to see their own natural boundaries encroached upon, by another corporation lying on the other side of an arm of the sea—a public highway of the nation; and still more to see it monopolizing to itself, the vast income of ferries, in which they have an equal interest, and naturally an equal claim."[16] And when in the 1840s both the Fulton and the South ferries were leased out at more than two and one-half times the previous rent, the resulting fare "was regarded by those who were interested in Brooklyn, and Long Island generally, as the payment of an unjust and onerous tax."[17]

This recurrent vision of the ferry fare as a tax on entry into the city was closely linked to New York's repeated attempts to obtain legislative authorization to tax Brooklynites who worked in the city.[18] In 1833, in fact, the New York Common Council resolved not to allow any further expansion of ferry accommodations to Brooklyn until the state tax law was altered to permit the city to tax the personal property of those who worked in the city. Brooklynites, however, regarded high ferry rates as an attempt to accomplish the goal of taxing nonresidents by other (unlawful) means—a

---

and even dangers which accompanied the ferry travel of the last century" (Stiles, *History of Brooklyn*, 3:530).

15. "Chronicles of Brooklyn," 71; Judd, "History of Brooklyn," 174.

16. Prime, *History of Long Island*, 375. As this quotation indicates, the attack on the ferry franchise was intertwined with Brooklyn's longstanding resentment of New York City's ownership of the Long Island shoreline. See Furman, *Notes*, 21–25; George Wood, *Opinion on the Extent and Character of the Title of the City of New York, to the Land Lying between High and Low Water, on the Brooklyn Side of the East River* (Brooklyn, 1843). See generally, Stuart Archibald Moore, *A History of the Foreshore and the Law Relating Thereto* (London, 1888).

17. Alfred G. Benson, Edgar J. Bartow, Charles Kelsey, and Elihu Townsend, *A Statement of the Origin and Progress of the Present Controversy between Brooklyn and New York on the Subject of Leasing the Ferries between the Two Cities* (Brooklyn, 1851), 1–3.

18. See the debate on this question in the 1846 constitutional convention, S. Crosswell

goal they considered illegitimate. According to George Wood, a leading spokesman for Brooklyn, "Such a doctrine is repugnant to all liberal views of legislation and political economy prevailing at the present day, and I should suppose no man would be found willing to avow it, and that no public body would be willing to record it as the rule of their conduct."[19] An ad hoc committee, appointed in 1833 in the wake of the Common Council's resolution, expostulated on the unfairness of such a "new fangled scheme of taxation." Brooklyn, because of its youth, already required as much tax revenue as New York. And soon, according to the committee, it would require more, for it lacked any corporate property of its own. Those who lived in Brooklyn while working in New York, moreover, were by and large active merchants, mechanics, and professionals without much capital. The very rich—the *rentiers*—resided in New York because the "families of such men will continue in a city which will supply them with the gaiety and amusements it affords." If dull and austere Brooklyn was going to have to make do without the very rich to help fatten its tax coffers, it was only fair that New York City should have to make do without the hard-earned wealth of the plain citizens of Brooklyn.[20]

But the most important criticisms of the corporation's management of the ferry franchise centered on the quantity of service provided. Whenever citizens of Brooklyn petitioned for new boats to and from newly subdivided locations along the Long Island shore, they were met by resistance from the New York Common Council. Not only did the corporation tax them on their entry into the city, but it seemed ultimately not to want them to come at all.[21]

An explanation for the city's conduct was not hard to find. Brooklyn's land developers competed directly with those who were subdividing uptown Manhattan. Those uptown land speculators controlled the city's government. And the city's actions, or more precisely its refusal to act, was meant to protect and enhance the value of Manhattan's land developments.[22]

---

and R. Sutton, reporters, *Debates and Proceedings in the New York State Convention for the Revision of the Constitution* (New York, 1846), 84–88; Judd, "History of Brooklyn," 186–88.

19. Wood, *Opinion*, 8.

20. *All the Proceedings*, 7.

21. Ibid., 4.

22. Support for this hypothesis came from residents and landholders of lower Manhattan, as well as those of Brooklyn. "When we, and all the persons who own property in the lower wards of the city, purchased the same," wrote one pamphleteer, "we then paid the value of the situation which our land possessed. When the men who now control the Common Council purchased Stuyvesant's Meadows, they took the same, subject to its disadvantages, and they paid in like proportion. By what rule of Justice can these speculators lay a tax upon the whole city, to improve their individual estates?" By making living in Brooklyn difficult or

That hurting Brooklyn was the goal of the city government's policy did not have to be inferred from its behavior. Responding to a speech in favor of granting a new ferry, Assistant Alderman Bruen stated those ends openly (one might even say brazenly) in 1834:

> I will make one remark in reply to an observation of the gentleman, in which with great earnestness he made an appeal to our liberality. In the expansiveness of his generosity he seems to have comprehended the whole human race as well as our sister city. The members of the Common Council who act with me in this matter, profess to be governed by no such expanded views. I am of the English doctrine of free trade, which is only free where it can benefit England. I am sent here to legislate for the city of New York, and not for Brooklyn, . . . and if I shall think that the establishment of this ferry will abstract from the southern extremity of New York and centre of its commerce of population which would otherwise reside upon this island, I am bound to vote against it.

He did not think it worthwhile to respond to the charge that he was "unjust, illiberal or an up-town land speculator." In fact, he assured his audience, he held land speculators "in great favor": "They have been to this city what Augustus was to Rome—they found it built of Dutch bricks, and they have left it of granite and marble. If any speculators are to be favored, they are in my judgment the speculators of New York—and not the speculators of Brooklyn, those who are within our jurisdiction and liable to our taxation." If the result of city policy was that New York City's speculators acquired a monopoly over residential land development for the metropolis, at least it was one "bought with good consideration," unlike the expectations of Brooklyn's developers, who insisted on all the services of the city while paying none of the costs.[23]

Chancellor Kent insisted that there was "no danger that the power of establishing ferries in discretion, will be abused to the prejudice of the inhabitants of the city, or of its neighbors, considering the popular foundation of the council,"[24] but that was small comfort to the citizens of Brooklyn. According to the *Brooklyn Eagle*, Brooklynites were "entirely at the mercy of the mammoth city which lies opposite to us, the narrow views and selfish interests of whose up-town land holders induce them to throw every obsta-

---

impossible for those who worked in the city, the Common Council's actions provided a windfall for uptown speculators, at a cost to the city as a whole, which might lose the benefits of an enlarged commercial community (Joshua [pseudonym], *Ferry Rights Etc.* [articles reprinted from the *New York Gazette*] [New York, 1835], 1–6).

23. *All the Proceedings*, 49–51.

24. Kent, *Charter*, 142.

cle which they can in the way of our growth."[25] And so Brooklyn's leaders resolved that their city's future depended on taking the ferry franchise away from the corporation of the city of New York.

At the heart of the ferry fight lay the question of in whose interest the ferry ought to be managed. For Kent, let alone Assistant Alderman Bruen, the answer to the question was the people of New York City. The grant made in the Montgomerie Charter was meant both to provide revenue for the city and to accommodate the public. But when Kent spoke of "the public" in his treatise on the charter, he made it very clear that he meant one defined by residence in the city: "The inhabitants in their aggregate corporate capacity, have as vested an interest in the entire grant of the old ferry [to Brooklyn] and of the right to establish others, as they have individually in any government grant of lands, tenements and hereditaments."[26]

But many disagreed.[27] When Henry Warner wrote in 1826 that "the owner of a ferry is obliged by law to provide and maintain facilities for accommodating the public, at all times, with prompt and convenient passage," the public to which he referred included the entire state. The corporation's responsibility over the ferries was "of a tenure and character materially different from those of their ordinary powers of municipal legislation. In general, their functions are employed upon subjects purely local, confined within the bounds of their proper and undoubted authority; whereas the regulation of the public ferries is of common interest to the city and country too; the whole community are concerned in it. . . . It is plainly a control that pertains of right to the government of the state, and not of the city."[28] Similarly, George Wood argued in 1828 that the ferry franchise was given to the corporation as "a delegated power, [not] to be exercised for private emolument, but for the public good and convenience. . . . They should exercise the power as the Legislature would and ought to have done." If, instead, the corporation served only the narrow interests of its immediate constituents, Wood did not "hesitate to say, that it will be a good cause of forfeiture."[29] Ferry service was vital to the entire

---

25. *Brooklyn Eagle*, 7 May 1844, quoted in Judd, "History of Brooklyn," 176.

26. Kent, *Charter*, 142.

27. Often they relied on Kent's own holdings and rulings as Chief Justice and Chancellor. See [Henry A. Warner], *The Question of a South Ferry to Long Island, Stated and Argued: in Several Papers Originally Published in the New York American. By a Freeman* (New York, 1826), 29–32. On the general legal controversy over exclusive franchises, see Morton Horwitz, *The Transformation of American Law, 1780–1860* (Cambridge, Mass., 1977), 109–39.

28. [Warner], *The Question of a South Ferry*, 29, 44.

29. Wood, *Opinion*, 5, 10.

state, and according to Brooklyn's ad hoc committee, "This great commercial emporium, of which Brooklyn is now a small part, and destined to become a more important part, is the pride and boast of this State, and the legislature will be disposed to counteract local influences conflicting with the general welfare."[30]

The constancy of Brooklynites' conviction that the ferry should be run to serve their interests as well as those of residents of New York did not necessarily mean that they challenged the corporation's title to the franchise.[31] In fact, when Brooklynites first complained about the management of the "old" ferry, they did so while explicitly recognizing New York City's ownership.

After Robert Fulton and Robert Livingston succeeded in obtaining a state monopoly on steam navigation in 1808,[32] they began negotiations with the corporation of the city of New York for an extended lease of the Brooklyn ferry. In 1813, Fulton and his brother-in-law William Cutting received a twenty-five-year exclusive lease, to run from 1814 to 1839. The conditions of the lease included an obligation on the part of the lessees to provide one steamboat on the route by May 1814 and a second one by 1819.[33]

All went well with the introduction of the first steamboat. But by 1817 Fulton and Cutting's New York and Brooklyn Steam Boat Ferry Association had concluded that it would not be able to finance a second steamboat in 1819. Instead, it offered to institute a "team boat" (with paddle wheels moved by horse power) in 1818 to run as a second boat on the old ferry line and to provide evening service. The village of Brooklyn was asked to petition the corporation in support of this modification of the lease, which it did after a stormy village meeting. And in 1818 the corporation agreed to modify the lease.

But by 1821 and 1822 Brooklyn had become convinced that it needed still more ferry service, which the ferry company was not inclined to provide. And general dissatisfaction with the company was compounded by poor service during the unusually heavy winter of 1821–22. As a result, there began "an animated struggle for relief . . . carried on in the news-

30. *All the Proceedings*, 5.

31. There was, on the other hand, a longstanding quarrel about the legitimacy of New York's original acquisition of title both to the ferry and to the Long Island shoreline. See Furman, *Notes*, 21–25; Stiles, *A History of the City of Brooklyn*, 3: 505–24.

32. See George Dangerfield, *Chancellor Robert R. Livingston of New York, 1746–1813* (New York, 1960); James Thomas Flexner, *Steamboats Come True*, rev. ed. (Boston, 1978), 333–62; Horwitz, *Transformation of American Law*, 122–24.

33. Stiles, *History of Brooklyn*, 3: 536.

papers, in pamphlets, by means of public meetings and before the corporation of New York," all to the end of convincing the corporation that it could and should dispossess the ferry company of its lease.[34]

That "struggle" failed, for the corporation was uninterested in evicting the ferry company (and perhaps uncertain of its right to do so). The vital point, though, was Brooklyn's willingness at this time to found its case on New York City's *legal right* "to oust the present occupants from the ferry." Nothing was said to challenge the legitimacy of New York's "ancient" rights. Petitions drafted at village meetings detailed how the "wealth and prosperity of Brooklyn depend upon the liberal and accommodating manner in which the public ferries are conducted between this place and the city of New York" and that the directors of the ferry company (Fulton and Cutting were both dead by 1822) "evinced an overbearing spirit, little calculated to remove real grounds of complaint, or to quiet imaginary causes of clamor." But they did not argue that New York City was under a legal obligation to use its franchise as if it was an administrative responsibility delegated by the state. Brooklynites urged the New York Common Council to consider the contract with the ferry company as broken, but they recognized the ferry franchise as New York's private property.[35]

Three years later, Charles Hoyt, a land developer subdividing property in South Brooklyn, petitioned the corporation for a new ferry to run to the Joralemon Street dock on Long Island. The exclusive lease held by the New York and Brooklyn Steam Boat Ferry Association was, of course, still in effect. But proponents of the new route argued that a ferry to this new, southerly location, in one of the fastest growing areas of the village of Brooklyn, would not violate the earlier lease. Their reasoning went as follows. When the Fulton ferry lease was signed in 1813 Brooklyn was not yet incorporated. The result, according to Chancellor Kent (whose opinion was one of several solicited by the Common Council's ferry committee), was that the corporation's lease restrained it only from granting a competing ferry to the "settlement" by the old ferry. Because the word "Brooklyn" had not been used in the lease to refer to a political jurisdiction, Kent and others recommended that the council look to the common usage and meaning of the word at the time when the lease was signed and not to the shifting boundaries of the growing community.[36]

In December 1825 the council's ferry committee reported against giving

34. Ibid., 543.

35. *The Laws, Papers, and Documents Relating to the Management of the Old, or Fulton Ferry* (Brooklyn, 1822), 45, 41.

36. *All the Proceedings*, 70–71; see also ibid., 73 (opinion of Benjamin F. Butler), "Report of the Law Committee on the Subject of a New South Ferry, September 11, 1826," 6, bound in ibid., 80–87; Warner, *The Question of a South Ferry*, 26–27.

a new "south" ferry to Brooklyn, presumably because uptown landowners objected to allowing the owners of Brooklyn's newest lots easy access to the city.[37] By 1826, however, a majority of the members of the ferry committee had changed their minds, and from then on the committee regularly recommended to the council that it grant a ferry to the Joralemon Street dock. Similarly, the law committee of the council argued forcefully in 1826 that the corporation was legally obliged to grant reasonable requests for new public accommodations. But a majority on the Common Council remained adamantly opposed to the new route. By 1833, even the ferry company had stopped objecting to the grant of a competing route. But still the council resisted, now arguing that the tax law first had to be changed so that Brooklynites working in New York City could be taxed.[38]

The 1826 report of the law committee demonstrates a strikingly new perception of the nature of the ferry franchise as corporate property. In that report the franchise was characterized as a "*delegated legislative authority*," to be used by the corporation as a surrogate for the legislature. It was, in the committee's words, "a very high public trust. . . . It is the public convenience alone, which is the great object to be attained—revenue to the city or profits to the lessee are mere incidents." And the committee considered "the interest and convenience of our neighbors on Long Island . . . equally with that of our citizens." Here, as in other aspects of its governmental life, the corporation was "bound to consider not only the existing state of things, but the probable future wants of the public. The increasing population of their own city and of Brooklyn, and of other parts of Long Island, are facts which they [council members] are not only bound to know, but to notice in their legislative capacity." If, through ignorance or greed, an "improvident" lease had been made in 1813, it was liable to be set aside by an action *quo warranto*.[39]

This analysis of the city's ferry rights was extended in a variety of ways over the next eight years. In a debate in the Common Council one assistant alderman argued (relying on Marshall's opinion in *Dartmouth College*) that "whatever property is given for public purposes is subject to the law of the state." Powers like the ferry franchise had been granted by the state to be exercised for the public good; and if that "cardinal principle" were forgotten, such powers would be taken away from the corporation, and the legislature would "make your supposed private interest yield to the public good." Benjamin F. Butler, whose opinion was solicited by the ferry committee in early 1834, insisted that "the authority to establish ferries granted

---

37. Stiles, *History of Brooklyn*, 3:555; Warner, *The Question of a South Ferry*, 1–27.
38. *All the Proceedings*, 77–92.
39. "Report of the Law Committee," 6–7, 11; see also Joshua, *Ferry Rights Etc.*, 73–74.

to the city by the charter, is a branch of the sovereign powers" rather than a property right. And he distinguished that authority from the "express grant" of the old ferry to Brooklyn settlement. He regarded the covenant in the lease to Fulton and Cutting restraining the corporation from establishing new ferries to Brooklyn as "absolutely void" because that covenant attempted to "abridge the legislative power of the Common Council."[40]

The arguments of proponents of the new ferry merged a traditional characterization of a franchise as a property right with an image of a delegated public responsibility. In 1826, in perhaps the most extended analysis of the ferry question, Henry Warner began with the claim that legally ferries were "mere instruments of public accommodation." But he then argued that the ferry franchise also constituted a particular kind of property right: "A franchise [is] . . . a liberty or immunity above common right . . .; it is a species of distinction, a pre-eminence or privilege, which the government alone has power to confer. . . . [A] franchise lies in grant alone: and this grant can only be derived from the state. In short, the genius of the law, whether here or in England, permits no man or men to hold a franchise otherwise than of the *sovereign* power, and in strict subordination to it." The fact that the franchise was founded on a royal grant made no difference. Whatever its source, the franchise made its holder into "an agent of the government, a trustee for the public, and accountable for his stewardship."[41]

According to Warner, calling the ferry a private right of the corporation could not protect it from public scrutiny and invention. If, in Warner's lexicon, it was a franchise, it was a kind of "state property," and "the Corporation of New York, in making the old ferry lease, acted not as private individuals, but as public functionaries; they granted nothing of their own; they stipulated nothing by which they could be personally affected: the subject of their grant was a state prerogative which they held in trust; and the contract they made concerning it, so far as it was lawful, must be considered as the work of a confidential agency exercised on behalf of the state government, for the benefit of the public at large." Alternatively, even if the ferry "did not sustain the character of a franchise" but was to be regarded as some more "private" form of corporate property, it remained as part of "the city public, and the corporation would be but agents, but trustees, but administrators of the affairs of their constituents, in disposing of it." Whichever way "the glass is turned," Warner concluded, "we see the immediate lessons in no other light [than] that as disinterested men, acting exclusively for the public, not at all for them-

40. *All the Proceedings*, 63, 73–74.
41. Warner, *The Question of a South Ferry*, 32, 43–44. This argument is drawn from Taney's opinion in *Charles River Bridge*.

selves," the members of the Common Council were obligated to grant the new route.[42]

Similarly, George Wood, in his 1828 *Opinion on the Subject of a New South Ferry*, relied on the *Brick Presbyterian Church* case to argue that even if the ferry constituted the private property of the corporation, still the corporation could not abridge its derivative legislative power by making an "unreasonable and improvident" contract. To Wood the situation here was stronger than in the *Brick Presbyterian Church* case. The covenant at issue in the latter case had been for the quiet enjoyment of a cemetery granted by the corporation. Such a covenant was integral to the grant and "ran with the land." The covenant with the ferry company to prevent competition, by contrast, was "collateral and independent" to the lease. Nothing that the corporation had granted to the ferry company depended on sustaining that covenant. Thus that covenant could not be relied on to excuse the city from fulfilling its public responsibilities.[43]

Although phrased as if meant to convince the Common Council of the errors of its ways, the feisty rhetoric of these arguments suggests that proponents of the new ferry no longer seriously hoped for change from the corporation. By 1834 Brooklyn's ad hoc ferry committee announced that it "deem[ed] all further applications to the Common Council for relief in the premises, useless and that the inhabitants of Brooklyn and Long Island must hereafter look to the government of the State." The committee conceded that competition between land developments in Brooklyn and Manhattan was at the heart of the ferry conflict. But that competition was one, "which, if fair play is given, will be beneficial to the public." And thus, the "general interest, the great commercial interest," would be promoted by a legislative assumption of ferry traffic. In the committee's report, the New York Common Council was characterized as acting as if the corporation were "an empire within an empire, like the pretensions of the feudal barons in the middle ages," and beyond legislative control. But, the report continued, in fact the legislature has "never hesitated to interfere and change, modify or supersede these powers and rights of a public character with which this Corporation has been vested." In this respect the corporation "stood upon the same footing with all other public bodies and inferior officers, and must bow to the supremacy of the legislative power."[44]

In 1835 a bill was submitted in the legislature that would have vested in an impartial tribunal the right of granting ferries. It passed the house without significant opposition and was sent on to the senate. The senate determined that under the 1821 Constitution such a bill required a two-thirds

42. Ibid., 56.
43. Wood, *Opinion*, 7.
44. *All the Proceedings*, 4, 11.

vote, and then the senate sat on the bill while New York mustered a counterattack.[45]

Daniel Tallmadge was sent by the city to argue its cause, and he drafted a long "opinion," which asserted that the franchise was absolute private property protected from legislative intervention. Did the fact that the corporation was "of a *public and political* character" give the state "powers of revocation, which it does not possess over similar grants to individuals, or *private* corporations?" Tallmadge's answer was obviously no. "The right and power of the Legislature do not so much depend on the *kind* of corporation, to which the grant is made, as upon the *subject matter* of the grant." This grant was private and therefore beyond the control of the legislature, even if there was evidence of misuse by the corporation. Only the courts had the right to revoke a private grant for misuse.[46]

In the end, however, the corporation saved its franchise in 1835 not through legal argument but by agreeing to establish a new south ferry. According to Henry Stiles, "This stratagem was successful in relaxing the efforts of the Brooklynites" in the legislature, and the bill was permitted to fail. But when the legislature had adjourned, the Common Council shifted the Manhattan ferry landing for the new line from Old Slip, where "all negotiations expressed, desired and expected" to locate it, to Whitehall, "the remotest southern point of the city, and a place manifestly inconvenient and unsuitable to the existing wants of the public."[47]

For ten years relative peace reigned between New York City and Brooklyn. In 1836, citizens of Brooklyn bought the entire stock of the Fulton steamboat company. And in 1839, in the wake of several years of losses, the corporation permitted the company to reorganize—merging the south and the old ferries—with a five-year lease at an annual rent of $12,000. But in 1844 the ferry company's offer of $20,000 per year for a new lease was rejected by New York City, and the Common Council advertised for bids. The winners of the resulting auction then leased the ferry for $30,500. A new cycle of public agitation in Brooklyn then began. The East River, stated a resolution drafted at a "great" public meeting on 8 May, "ought to be and is, of right, as free to all, as the air and light of heaven." But the excessive rent that the corporation had managed to exact of its new lessee meant that Brooklynites were going to have to pay much higher fares for unchanged service.[48]

There is little about the arguments raised against the ferry franchise

45. Stiles, *History of Brooklyn*, 3:556–57.

46. Daniel B. Tallmadge, *Opinion of . . . in Relation to the Constitutional Powers of the Legislature, to Take from the City of New York, the Ferry Franchise, between New York and Brooklyn. Prepared at the Request of the Mayor of the City of New York* (March 1835), 14–17. This argument was heavily dependent on Story's concurrence in *Dartmouth College.*

47. Stiles, *History of Brooklyn*, 3:557.

48. Judd, "History of Brooklyn," 173–74, 176.

in the 1840s to distinguish them from those made a decade earlier. Time had sharpened the public-private dichotomy on which those arguments rested. But in legal theory the debate of the 1840s was largely a repeat performance.

In 1845 Brooklyn's representatives submitted basically the same bill to the legislature that had almost passed a decade earlier. George Wood then wrote an argument in its support. He believed the bill raised two legal questions: Can the legislature interfere? Ought it to interfere? The answer to each question was, of course, yes. But most of his attention was devoted to answering the first. The corporation, he began, was a "PUBLIC, POLITICAL Corporation. Her charters are granted for political purposes. viz: the GOVERNMENT OF A COMMUNITY, *not* to create a *franchise of a private nature*. Grants of such a body are governed by entirely different rules from those applicable to private Corporations or individuals." Property held by a municipal corporation was held as a public trust, and the grantee had to be considered "a mere subordinate agent" of the legislature. A city, therefore, had no vested political rights against the state, and the legislature was always free to intervene.[49]

Wood also gave a number of reasons why the legislature ought to intervene in this situation. First, "The course of New York towards Brooklyn, has been both illiberal and unjust." Second, it should not be within New York City's powers, as one subordinate unit of the state, to control the growth of another delegate of state power. But most important, the East River was a natural and public highway, which ought not to be used to enrich New York City.[50]

This time the bill was passed into law. Section Ten of the new act stated: "Nothing herein contained shall be construed to annul, impeach, or in any wise impair the rights of the Mayor, Aldermen, and Commonalty of the city of New York . . . and nothing herein contained shall be construed to supersede the privileges, powers, and emoluments of a private nature, which have been granted to the Corporation of the city of New York, by charters and legislative acts." But the right to establish new ferry routes was clearly denominated a part of the public sphere of the corporation— subject to legislative repeal and alteration.[51] And the stage was set for *Benson v. The Mayor of New York*.

In *Benson*, Judge Barculo left undecided the question of the right of the corporation to establish new ferries after passage of the act of 1845 and the

---

49. [George Wood], *New-York and Long-Island Ferry Bill: A Brief Argument on Behalf of the Applicants* (Brooklyn, 1845), 3, 4, 7.

50. Ibid., 7–8; see also Benson et al., *Statement of the Origin and Progress of the Present Controversy.*

51. *Laws of New York*, 68th sess. (Albany, 1845), c. 352.

1846 state constitution. That issue was argued in 1852 at the Supreme Court's special term before Judge James J. Roosevelt, who held, in an unpublished opinion, that the rights of the corporation were absolute and vested over both present and future ferry routes. The legislature had no legal right to authorize its ferry commissioners to set up any ferries. Roosevelt granted the corporation a perpetual injunction to restrain those commissioners from granting any ferry leases in derogation of the rights of the corporation.[52]

By 1858, though, the law committee of the Brooklyn Common Council resolved to try again. According to the committee, New York City's conduct was unchanged. Ferry rates were still "kept up by the high rents demanded by that city, and Brooklyn [was] taxed hundreds of thousands of dollars to enrich New York without right, other than the right of usurpation."[53] And there was much recent legal authority to support Brooklyn's claims. In the case of *East Hartford* v. *The Hartford Bridge Company*, the United States Supreme Court had held that a franchise granted to a public corporation did not imply any contract on the part of the legislature not to reassume, modify, or discontinue that "privilege" in the future, "as the public interests should appear to require." And from Taney's opinion in *Martin* v. *Waddell*, the committee derived the conclusion that all real estate granted to the city under its charters was held solely as a public trust delegated by the state. Indeed, it seemed "idle" to waste words on the "self-evident principle" that a city like New York had no powers or privileges that could not be taken by the state:

> Could not the State make New York, Brooklyn and Williamsburgh one? Where then resides the ferry power? Could not the State divide New York into as many cities as she has wards? Where then goes the ferry power? Could not the State authorize the erection of a bridge over the East River? Where then is the ferry power? The City is absolutely dependent on the State for its power in regard to these very ferries; the City has leased them always under the laws of the State, and the lease of the Fulton and South Ferry had in it a clause providing that the lessees "shall and will in all things conduct and manage the said ferries respectively in conformity with all acts of the Legislature of the State of New York," and the Legislature of the State of New York has repeatedly passed acts controlling them, in which the city always acquiesced, excepting only the act of 1845.[54]

52. Hoffman, *Treatise*, 300.
53. *Report of the Law Committee on Ferry Rights* (Brooklyn, 1858), 3–4.
54. *East Hartford* v. *Hartford Bridge Company*, 10 How. 511, 536 (1848); *Martin* v. *Waddell*, 16 Pet. 367 (1842); *Report of the Law Committee on Ferry Rights*, 10–11.

In the resulting appeal of the prior holdings of Barculo and Roosevelt, Brooklyn's claims were finally vindicated in a court of law. Judge Henry Hogeboom's opinion made all the usual obsequies to the validity and sanctity of New York's charters. So far as those charters conferred rights of property, they were "inviolable, and they rest for their security not merely upon the constitutional provision that 'no state shall pass any law impairing the obligations of contracts,' but upon the immutable principles of justice and equity, which require the rights of private property to be respected, even when governments are overthrown." But whatever rights the corporation of the city of New York took in its charters it took subject to government regulation and control. And the only private rights involved in the grant of the ferries was the actual ownership of the old route to Brooklyn. The "powers" to control, establish, and maintain ferries found in the Montgomerie Charter were "public or governmental" rights properly belonging only "to the sovereign authority." They were "a delegation of authority for public purposes, and not for private emolument," subject to the continuing intervention of the legislature.[55]

By the amended New York City charter of 1857, ferries had to be leased by the corporation at public auction to the highest bidder. Did that new legislative charter repeal the 1845 law, which took the ferries out of the hands of the corporation? Hogeboom thought that it had. Thus his opinion ended with the paradoxical holding that the ferry franchise was, again, a part of New York City's governmental estate.[56]

But in leaving the ferry franchise in city hands at the same time that he also held that such "property" was entirely subject to legislative control, Hogeboom effected a radical shift in the nature of corporate property. The eighteenth-century corporation had regarded that property as essential to an autonomous government. The corporation of the early nineteenth century had worked to separate corporate property from dependent republican government, leaving that property in a residual sphere of private, corporate autonomy. But now the walls of that sphere of autonomy had been breached. To reactionaries like Murray Hoffman it meant the end of responsible public authority: "From the period when Corporate franchises of every nature were looked upon with favor, and guarded with jealousy, we are perhaps wandering into an opposite and dangerous extreme. The absorbing doctrine of public utility, and the arbitrary force of what is termed the eminent domain, threaten to merge respect for private rights in the magnificence of a speculation, and the sounding of a phrase."[57]

The implications that we should draw from Hogeboom's holdings are

55. *People* v. *The Mayor of New York*, 32 Barb. 102, 111, 119–120 (1860).
56. Ibid., 119–21.
57. Hoffman, *Treatise*, 296–97.

less apocalyptic but equally serious for the history of American local government law. The formal legal basis for distinguishing a city like New York from other local governments was at an end. The fact that it had received "powers" in the form of conveyances from the crown created no vested rights against central authority. The ferry grant, which Kent had regarded as the paradigm of the private property of the corporation, was now considered indistinguishable from the city's power over its streets, which Kent had regarded as the paradigm of a public grant. In legal theory, the private sphere of the corporation (as distinguished from the "proprietary" sphere of the municipal corporation) no longer existed.[58]

58. The fact that the ferry would no longer be a part of the corporation's private sphere did not mean that complaints disappeared. See *New York* v. *New England Transfer Company*, 18 Fed. Cas., 138, 140 (1877). Nor that the "monopolistic profits" of the corporations that farmed the ferry were expropriated. Of the ferry companies one journalist wrote: "Though all of them do a very profitable business, and consider their privilege, or right, better than exclusive ownership in a mine of gold. They do not say so openly; for all corporations that make large sums of money put forward the assumption of benefiting the public for a very small consideration.

"It is singular how disinterested monopolies are. Instead of confessing that they have no souls, they declare they are all soul. They are the embodiment of generosity, chivalry, self-sacrifice. Their controllers exist only for the people. They suffer to serve the masses. They shed tears of blood when the dear public is not pleased with their magnanimous labors. They sympathize with it, with full stomachs and fuller purses" (Junius Henri Browne, *The Great Metropolis: A Mirror of New York* [Hartford, Conn., 1869], 101).

The real end of controversy over the ferry was probably the construction of the Brooklyn Bridge.

Conclusion

One final step in the judicial subjugation of the corporation of the city of New York took place in 1865 in the case of *Darlington v. The Mayor*. During the Draft Riots of 1863, much private property had been destroyed. Traditionally, courts did not hold municipalities liable for the damage done by rioters. But in 1855 the New York legislature had passed a statute ordering cities to compensate those injured by mobs. *Darlington* was brought to test the reach and the relevance of that statute.

The central issue argued before the New York Court of Appeals concerned the power of the legislature to compel a municipal corporation to pay damages out of its "private" estate. Could legislation transform private property into a public fund to satisfy public obligations? The answer, according to the corporation's lawyers, was obviously no. "As respects their private property, and its disposition, the defendants [the corporation] are as free from legislative interference and control as is any private individual in the possession and enjoyment of his property."[1]

The plaintiffs' lawyers, however, denied the corporation's premise. "What, then," they asked, "is the corporation of the city of New York? Nothing but a trustee, created for a specific and defined purpose, with no powers and no rights but in the execution of its trusts. It was created for public purposes only, and in the execution, by the sovereign power, of the great trusts of government." Relying heavily on Marshall's and Washington's opinions in *Dartmouth College*, they insisted that the corporation's only right was to use the property "for the purposes of good government— those purposes for which it was originally vested in the corporation." And it was the state that would determine what constituted the needs of good government. Indeed, the statute should not be regarded as taking any private property at all, "for there is no private property vested in the city of New York."[2]

1. *Darlington* v. *The Mayor of New York*, 31 N.Y. 164, 166 (1865).
2. Ibid., 183, 184.

Chief Judge Denio's opinion for the court unambiguously confirmed the correctness of that latter claim. The corporation owned nothing subject to the just compensation clauses of the state and federal constitutions. Even property "held for purposes of income or for sale, and unconnected with any use for the purposes of municipal government" existed to serve legislative purposes. And a corporation chartered under royal grant was as much a public agency in this regard as boards of supervisors, sheriffs, and township trustees. "In cities, for reasons partly technical, and in part founded upon motives of convenience, the title [to public property] is vested in the corporate body. It is not thereby shielded from the control of the legislature as the supreme law-making power of the state."[3]

Denio's opinion shifted the rhetoric used in judicial analyses of the corporation of the city of New York. Until *Darlington*, courts had justified legislative control of corporate property by labeling that property as public (or as not property at all), while conceding that there remained a private sphere—somewhere—beyond legislative reach. Now the emptiness of that concession stood revealed in an opinion that Denio himself admitted was "dogmatic."

The chief judge, however, bolstered his argument with a review of the various relevant doctrinal authorities. Marshall's and Washington's opinions in *Dartmouth College* were shown to leave the public corporation entirely subject to legislative action. Kent's statement in the *Commentaries* to the effect that municipal property was invested with the same "security" as other private rights was "understood" to mean "only that it possesses such rights against wrongdoers, and not that it is exempted from legislative control." Nelson's opinion in *Bailey*, Denio confessed, stood in direct opposition to the merger of public and private spheres for which Denio contended. But, because the Court of Errors had affirmed Nelson's holding in *Bailey* without accepting his theory of the governmental-proprietary dichotomy, Nelson's opinion remained "but the opinion of the eminent chief justice and learned associates, and does not . . . settle any principles of law."[4]

By 1865, then, the corporation of the city of New York had become legally indistinguishable from propertyless institutions of derivative public administration. The governmental-proprietary dichotomy developed in *Bailey* did not disappear, but its use was decisively separated from any notion of municipal autonomy. And *Darlington* came to stand for the proposition that New York City was in no sense a private corporation, that even its

3. Ibid., 193.
4. Ibid., 194, 198–201. Likewise, he disagreed with Barculo's opinion in *Benson* (ibid., 203).

corporate capacity to own property existed only as a function of its representation of the interests of the state.[5]

From the 1860s on, judicial rhetoric characterized the city in ways that differed dramatically from the language used in the first years of the nineteenth century. Where once courts saw a more or less private entity that might be empowered by a state legislature to engage in useful public projects, now they saw a public entity that lacked any "real" existence. Where once courts saw enabling legislation as an imprimatur of republican virtue, now the structure of statutory authority built up by the corporation of the city of New York became the field on which judges constructed "their" law of municipal corporations. A statute was no longer a guarantee of legitimacy, the end of judicial inquiry. It was, instead, a starting point.

There are numbers of possible reasons for the mid-nineteenth-century emergence of this revised judicial understanding of New York City's government. One can point to a forceful critique of legislative sovereignty, to the willingness of business lawyers to construct a legal defense of laissez-faire, to a relatively new insistence on the autonomy of judge-made law.[6] Experience had taught judges that innovative public action did not invariably result in reciprocal benefits to the private individuals burdened with the costs of municipal improvements.[7] Much municipal action now seemed little more than a forced and arbitrary redistribution of wealth from property owners to a greedy and unrestrained public sphere.

Some have characterized the second third of the nineteenth century as a time of the breakdown of shared republican values.[8] Judges worked to develop a distinctively judicial ideology, whose notable feature was an overt defense of "vested" property rights against the depredations of public authority.[9] Their public values were not the same as those public values embodied in legislation and in the behavior of municipal officials. For them,

5. See the note in *American Decisions* 88 (1887): 270–71.

6. Louis Hartz, *Economic Policy and Democratic Thought* (Cambridge, Mass., 1948); Morton Horwitz, *The Transformation of American Law, 1780–1860* (Cambridge, Mass., 1977), 253–66; Edward S. Corwin, "The Basic Doctrine of American Constitutional Law," in Association of American Law Schools, ed., *Selected Essays on Constitutional Law*, 5 vols. (Chicago, 1938), 1: 101–28. One should also note that it is only in this period that state legislatures began to pass numbers of statutes—such as free incorporation and banking acts, the Field Code, and married women's property acts—whose effects were felt systematically throughout the society. The result may have been that courts had more to react against.

7. See Stephen Diamond, "The Rise and Fall of Benefit Taxation," *Journal of Legal Studies* (forthcoming).

8. See Oscar Handlin and Mary F. Handlin, *Commonwealth*, rev. ed. (Cambridge, Mass., 1968); and Hartz, *Economic Policy and Democratic Thought*.

9. Gerald Frug has argued that American judges were moved by a fundamentally aesthetic distaste for the merger of public and private spheres implicit in autonomous local government ("The City as a Legal Concept," *Harvard Law Review* 93 [1980]: 1057–1154).

the existence of a still-virtuous realm of "law" depended on its separation from a corrupt and degraded realm of politics.

But these labels only beg the question of what made the years after 1835 the critical period in the doctrinal history of the municipal corporation. Arguments for a more active and less deferential judicial role had been heard for years. Property owners had always contested municipal action that harmed their holdings. The forms their arguments took had changed little. Why the new success? Was the sheer volume of business the significant variable? What made a city like New York so different (in judicial eyes) in 1850 than it had been twenty-five years before? Filth, corruption, mobs, and immigrants were not mid-nineteenth-century novelties. Nor was a characteristically American distrust of the capacity of the big city to sustain the virtue of the republican citizen.[10]

A rethinking of the legal nature of the city may have been inevitable, but what determined the content of the new judicial doctrine? If there was in mid-nineteenth-century America an "emergent" legal attack on legislative sovereignty, there remained a powerful legal defense of legislative preeminence. Even the new insistence on judicial power vis-à-vis the legislature hardly fixed doctrinal content. Indeed, if all judges wanted was a stick to beat the legislature with, the "inherent right to local self-government" would have offered a more useful *grundnorm* for the new legal subject than Dillon's Rule.[11]

I believe that we can get closer to an understanding of the nature of judicial behavior if we think of it as shaped in part by the nineteenth-century middle-class movement to control and remake the American city.[12] Like their evangelical counterparts, judges distrusted the ability of public authorities (both legislators and city officials) to choose wisely. Their insistence on the autonomy of the law can be viewed as one way of distinguishing themselves from the political apparatus of the state, as, conversely, a way of identifying with the goals of moral reform. The doctrines they developed, although formally committed to legislative sovereignty, were shaped to ensure that courts would determine the legal consequences of public action.

10. See Thomas Bender, *Towards an Urban Vision* (Lexington, Ky., 1976), 3–17; Morton White and Lucia White, *The Intellectual versus the City* (New York, 1962).

11. See Thomas M. Cooley's concurring opinion in *People v. Hurlburt*, 25 Mich. 44, 93 (1871); Edwin A. Gere, "Dillon's Rule and the Cooley Doctrine: Reflections of the Political Culture," *Journal of Urban History* 8 (1982):271–98. On Cooley as a jurist whose thinking remained rooted in antebellum political values, see Alan Jones, "Thomas Cooley and 'Laissez-Faire Constitutionalism': A Reconsideration," *Journal of American History* 53 (1967): 751–71.

12. See Paul Boyer, *Urban Masses and Moral Order in America, 1820–1920* (Cambridge, Mass., 1978).

From this vantage point, Dillon's Rule becomes an appropriate moral gesture, a way of compelling the legislature to take responsibility for the actions of an errant child. The city was not to be set loose on the streets of public action and expenditure freed from the constraints of its parent. The law would compel the legislature to superintend its charge.

Just as moral reformers worked to create urban institutions that replicated agrarian values and discipline, so the makers of the law of municipal corporations worked to make cities conform to an idealized polity based on the primacy of small-town America. New York's judges knew, of course, that New York City was not a small town, knew that judicial decisions could not undo urban growth. But their decisions assumed an institutional equivalent of the egalitarianism that is the hallmark of the period. New York City was obviously different from other local governments, but it would have no more legal rights than any other local government. Before the law, all localities would be equal and held to the same standard of conduct.

Thus the mid-nineteenth-century corporation of the city of New York was a municipal corporation like other municipal corporations. The distinctive, bifurcated entity described in the *Brick Presbyterian Church* case in 1826, not to mention the private institution of the Montgomerie Charter of 1730, no longer existed in judicial rhetoric. The formal doctrinal law of municipal corporations now reigned over a unified domain of dependent local governments. Where Charles II failed in his attempt to make the metropolis into the legal equivalent of the smallest rural community, the judges of the New York appellate courts succeeded. New York City had been compelled to return its charter and its franchises to the state.

Yet that conclusion can only be stated ironically. Whatever New York City might be in legal theory, in practice it has not been powerless. There have been periods (like the 1850s) when political controversy interrupted its ability to use legislative power to serve local ends. And most cities, of course, have remained dependent on legislative enactments. But formal dependence is not the same as powerlessness. For the past century and one-half, cities like New York have usually been able to get what they wanted from state legislatures.[13] The particular problem of the American city has not been its separation from legitimate public authority so much as its continuing success in harnessing state power to serve limited local interests.[14]

13. See Donna E. Shalala and Carol Bellamy, "A State Saves a City: The New York Case," *Duke Law Journal* (1976): 1119–32; Association of the Bar of the City of New York, *Proposals to Strengthen Local Finance Laws in New York State* (New York, 1979).

14. Modern variants on this problem are often posed in terms of the legitimacy of zoning and of the power delegated to local governments through the standard zoning enabling acts.

The law of municipal corporations was less the emblem of liberal victory over archaic, "feudal" local autonomy Dillon described than a limited, rear-guard action by men witnessing a frightening and unstoppable expansion of public authority. The judicial world of the municipal corporation was a world created to reassert formal control over a political order oblivious to notions of republican restraint. The image of a dependent and powerless city, propounded by judicial doctrine as the official legal concept of American local government, was never universalized and incorporated systematically into public practice. The law of municipal corporations would be the worst possible example of the moral hegemony of the law. It stands, instead, as a wish or a dream of how the political order ought to look.

Even dreams have their effects on waking life. Local government casebooks are filled with stories about the ways that courts have managed to defeat or limit local public action. Courts are not as powerless as the lighthouses Dean Prosser once described as the acme of impotence.[15] Lighthouses, for all the noise and illumination they express, can do nothing about the fog that quickly envelopes them. Courts in local government cases have done more, at least making "their" fog mold its conduct in more formally correct ways and making it feel a good deal of discomfort for breaches of proper public standards.

Still, the successes of American municipal corporation law cannot mask the fact that today, as in 1860, the governmental and legal foundations of the American city lie less in judge-made law than in legislative power. Two centuries ago, the authority of a borough like the corporation of the city of New York lay in the law of property. But after the revolution in political theory that occurred at the end of the eighteenth century, governmental power became the public monopoly of a centralized state. Cities like New York had to learn to depend on legislative authority as the basis for local public action. Their success in so doing permitted them to become the partially autonomous, public corporate bodies, serving distinctively local interests, that common sense and political science tell us they have always remained.

See *Village of Euclid* v. *Ambler Realty Co.*, 272 U.S. 365 (1926); Charles M. Haar, John P. Sawyer, and Stephen J. Cummings, "Computer Power and Legal Reasoning: A Case Study of Judicial Decision Prediction in Zoning Amendment Cases," *American Bar Foundation Research Journal* (1977): 651–768; Frank Michelman, "Political Markets and Community Self-Determination: Competing Judicial Models of Local Government Legitimacy," *Indiana Law Journal* 53 (1977–78): 145–206; Robert C. Ellickson and A. Dan Tarlock, *Land Use Controls* (Boston, 1981).

15. "Lighthouse No Good," *Journal of Legal Education* (1948): 257.

Index

Aerison, Ann, 61n
African Zion Methodist Episcopalian
   Church, 72n
Albany, 21, 23, 145, 148, 208–9 , 216
Albany v. *State of New York*, 172n
Albion, Robert, 58n
Allen, Stephan, 72
Almshouse, 65n, 132
Angell, Joseph, and Samuel Ames, *Law of
   Private Corporations Aggregate*, 211
A Poor Citizen, *Appeal*, 162n
Appleby, Joyce Oldham, 10n, 92
Armstrong v. *Board of Commissioners*, 199n
Artisans, 92, 140–41
Ashurst, Lord, 189
Astor, John Jacob, 174
Astor v. *Hoyt*, 174n
Astor v. *Miller*, 174n

Bailey v. *New York*, 125n, 225, 227–31,
   260
Bailyn, Bernard, 66n
Baker v. *Boston*, 201
Ball, Doctor, 93
Banning, Lance, 87
Barculo, Seward, 241, 255, 257
Barron and Craig v. *Baltimore*, 201n, 222n
Barton v. *Syracuse*, 232n
Bayard, Nicholas, 41n
Bayard, Stephan, 48n
Bayley, David, 205n
Beekman, Stephan, 114n
Beekman's Slip, 118
Beekman Street, 170
Bellamy, Carol, 263n
Bender, Thomas, 167n
Benjamin, Walter, 167n
Benson v. *New York*, 241, 255
Berger, Peter, 8, 144n
Bergh, Dirrick Van Den, 61n

Berlin v. *Gorham*, 211n
Bigelow, Melville M., 199n
Black, George E., 105
Black, Jeremiah Sullivan, 228n
Black's Law Dictionary, 14
Blackstone, Sir William, 196; *Commen-
   taries*, 19, 22–23, 33, 190; on corpora-
   tions, 22–23; on municipal law, 190
Blunt, Edward M., 94n, 162
Bogart, Henry, 50n, 52
Bolander v. *Stevens*, 215n
Bonomi, Patricia U., 13n, 22n, 65
Boorstin, Daniel, 10n, 46n
Borson, Henry Van, 51n
Boston, 35, 91, 200
Bouvier, John, 190, 221n
Bow v. *Allentown*, 211n
Boyer, Paul, 207n, 222n
Bradford v. *Cary*, 187
Brewerton, Jacob, 41
Brick Presbyterian Church v. *New York*, 74,
   77–80, 181, 201, 227, 236n, 253, 263
Bridenbaugh, Carl, 45n, 54n
Bridges, William, 94, 160
Bristol, England, 62
Britton v. *New York*, 227n
Bronson, Greene C., 213, 214
Brooklyn, 153–54, 205, 237; waterfront
   granted New York City in Montgomerie
   Charter, 16; ferry to New York City, 25–
   27, 240–58; charters, 145–46n. *See also*
   Ferry franchise
Broome Street, 228
Browne, Junius Henry, 258n
Bruen, assistant alderman, 247–48
Bryce, James, 5n, 126n
Bureaucracy: absence of prior to revolution,
   64–68; growth of, 130–35, 142, 143
Burr, Aaron, 149
Burrill, Alexander M., 221n